The Plays
of Frances Sheridan

Mrs Frances Sheridan.

Author of Sydney Biddulp, Nourjahad, The Discovery &c.

Mother of the late Rt. Hon. Richard Brinsley Sheridan.

Published by G. & W. Whitaker, March, 1814

Courtesy of the National Gallery of Ireland

The Plays
of Frances Sheridan

Edited by
ROBERT HOGAN
and
JERRY C. BEASLEY

Newark: University of Delaware Press
London and Toronto: Associated University Presses

© 1984 by Associated University Presses, Inc.

Associated University Presses
440 Forsgate Drive
Cranbury, NJ 08512

Associated University Presses
25 Sicilian Avenue
London WC1A 2QH, England

Associated University Presses
2133 Royal Windsor Drive
Unit 1
Mississauga, Ontario
Canada L5J 1K5

Library of Congress Cataloging in Publication Data

Sheridan, Frances Chamberlaine, 1724–1766.
  The plays of Frances Sheridan.

  Includes bibliographical references.
  Contents: Introduction—The discovery—The dupe
—[etc.]
  I. Hogan, Robert Goode, 1930–   . II. Beasley,
Jerry C.   III. Title.
PR3679.S5A19   1984   822'.6   82-49304
ISBN 0-87413-243-6

Printed in the United States of America

Contents

Acknowledgments

We would like to thank the many librarians who have given so generously of their time and energy in helping us to gather the materials for this edition. Their expertise has been invaluable to us, but we have been just as grateful for their patient and courteous handling of a voluminous correspondence, which, to them, must have often seemed trivial. We mention with special gratitude the librarians and staff members at the Bodleian Library, the Huntington Library and Art Gallery, the William Andrews Clark Memorial Library, the Yale University Libraries, the Folger Shakespeare Library, the British Library, the National Library of Ireland, the Library of Trinity College, Dublin, and the University of Delaware Library.

The following libraries have kindly allowed us to use materials in their holdings. We should like to thank them all.

The Bodleian Library, for permission to transcribe the manuscript copies of James Boswell's two prologues to *The Discovery* (MS Douce 193, fols. 54rv and 55r), and for permission to make use of the Bodleian copy of the first London edition of *The Discovery*.

The British Library, for permission to use the manuscript of *A Journey to Bath* (BM. Add. Ms. 25,975) as our copy-text.

The Huntington Library and Art Gallery for permission to photocopy the manuscripts of *The Discovery* and *The Dupe* (the Licenser's copies), both in the Larpent collection (LA 219 and LA 228); and for allowing us to use the Huntington copy of the second London edition of *The Discovery* as our copy-text.

The National Library of Ireland for permission to photocopy and use the London and Dublin editions of *The Dupe*.

The Library of Trinity College, Dublin, for permission to consult the London, Dublin, and Edinburgh editions of *The Discovery*.

The Public Record Office in Dublin, for cooperation in allowing us to consult and use materials relating to the Sheridan family.

Professor Arthur H. Scouten read our work with great care during the final stages of its preparation, and he saved us from several embarrassing errors of fact and judgment. We appreciate his interest and are most thankful for his expert advice. We must also gratefully mention the University of Delaware for its award of a small grant-in-aid that helped us to defray some of the costs of getting this edition ready for the press. And finally, we wish to offer special thanks to Lori Henderson for her cheerful helpfulness at the typewriter and the photocopying machine, and to Rita Beasley, who prepared the final typescript with amazing speed and meticulous attention to detail.

The Plays
of Frances Sheridan

Introduction

I. Frances Sheridan, Her Family and Career

Frances Chamberlaine Sheridan is scarcely known at all today, and then mainly as the mother of the playwright Richard Brinsley Sheridan. But in her own time she and her work were admired by Dr. Johnson, Samuel Richardson, and James Boswell. One of her novels was a genuine best-seller, and David Garrick regarded her first play, *The Discovery,* as the best comedy of the age. In another of her plays, her son Richard found the inspiration for his most famous character, Mrs. Malaprop, and also the embryonic versions of Mrs. Malaprop's funniest lines. Less considerable novelists and dramatists than Frances Sheridan have been better remembered than she.

Frances Sheridan was born in Dublin in 1724, and much of what we know of her life derives from the single, full-length biography published exactly one hundred years later by her granddaughter Alicia Le Fanu.[1] Alicia, a prolific poet and novelist like many of the Sheridans and their connections, never knew her grandmother. Much of her information came from her aunt and mother, Frances' daughters. Le Fanu's aunt, Alicia or Lissy Sheridan, was Frances' older daughter and had married Joseph Le Fanu of Dublin; her mother, Betsy Sheridan, had married Joseph Le Fanu's younger brother, Henry. Lissy Sheridan wrote two plays, one adapted from Frances, and was the grandmother of the popular novelist Joseph Sheridan Le Fanu. Betsy Sheridan wrote a novel and also kept a fascinating journal that has only been published in our own time. From these two intelligent sisters, Alicia Le Fanu gleaned many anecdotes of her grandmother which have the ring of utter authenticity.

Still, not all of the information contained in Le Fanu's biography is entirely correct. For instance, she wrongly names Sir Oliver Chamberlaine, an English baronet, as Frances Sheridan's grandfather. This allegation seems convincingly refuted by T. P. Le Fanu, who demonstrates in his *Memoir of the Le Fanu Family*[2] that Frances' grandfather was actually Walter Chamberlaine, a proctor of the Ecclesiastical Courts in Dublin. Indisputably, though, Frances' father was Philip Chamberlaine, or Chamberlain, a well-known cleric of his day who held the several titles of Prebend of Rathmichael in the Diocese of Dublin, Archdeacon of Glendalough, and Rector of St. Nicholas Without in Dublin. The Reverend Philip married an English woman, a Miss Whyte, and they had five children: Walter, who went into the church and died unmarried; Richard, who became a surgeon on a man-of-war and inherited a considerable estate in County Longford; William, who became a lawyer and died a judge in Jamaica; Anne, who married the Rev. John Fish, M.A., a clergyman in County Kildare; and, lastly, Frances.

Frances' education was somewhat eccentric. Alicia Le Fanu writes in her biography that

> Dr. Chamberlaine was an admired preacher, and strict in the performance of all his clerical duties. He was, at the same time, a great humourist, the strongest proof of which is that he was with difficulty prevailed on to allow his daughter to learn to read; and to write, he affirmed to be perfectly superfluous in the education of a female. The Doctor considered the possession of this art, as tending to nothing but the multiplication of love letters. (p. 4)

Nevertheless, Miss Fanny—as Frances seems then to have been called—was surreptitiously taught to read by her brother William, who also taught her some Latin, while her brother Richard taught her a little botany. Miss Fanny must have been a clever pupil, for in her first novel, *Memoirs of Miss Sidney Bidulph,* she refers to the acquisition of Latin by a girl as an elementary accomplishment. There was also a family tradition that Frances had, as a young girl, written a couple of sermons. However, she most showed her precocity by writing, when she was about fifteen, a two-volume novel called *Eugenia and Adelaide.*[3] She composed it, according to Alicia Le Fanu, on paper that was supposed to have been used for the housekeeping accounts. This early work was accomplished enough for Samuel Richardson some years later to persuade Frances to undertake another novel, her very successful *Sidney Bidulph.*

Frances was certainly not conventionally attractive. "Her figure," Alicia Le Fanu observes,

> would have been good, but for an accident that happened when she was an infant, by which she contracted a lameness that prevented her from going to any distance without support. This, by taking pains, she could disguise in walking a short way; but if she attempted more, it was perceptible. (p. 204)

The one contemporary portrait of Frances is conventionally bland, but she must have been distinctly plain, as even the partisan Alicia all but admits: "Mrs. Sheridan, though not strictly handsome, had a countenance extremely interesting. Her eyes were remarkably fine and very dark, corresponding with the colour of her hair, which was black" (p. 204). Eyes and hair, of course, are those female beauties that may be praised when there is little else to admire. In 1762, James Boswell, whose "amorous propensities" surely qualified him as a connoisseur of women, remarked in his journal: "I was introduced to Mrs. Sheridan, a woman of very homely looks, but very sensible and clever. . . . I let myself appear by degrees, and I found that I was agreeable to her, which flattered me a good deal."[4]

Philip Chamberlaine died in the early 1740s following an apparent descent into imbecility. In some ways, the death of her repressive father made life more pleasant for Miss Fanny. For one thing, she was now able to attend the theater with her brothers. The dominant theatrical personality in Dublin during those years was young Thomas Sheridan. He was born in 1719, and his father had been for many years the boon companion and collaborator of Jonathan Swift. Swift esteemed his friend as a superb schoolmaster and a considerable wit, but all of the older Sheridan's friends knew that he was a most feckless manager of his own affairs and perpetually plagued by bad judgment and bad luck. Young Thomas Sheridan was also a constant victim of bad luck, though he was a man of considerable talents and an indefatigable worker and projector. By 1743, he had already made a name for himself as an actor in Dublin; and, when he appeared in London in 1744, he was hailed as the first rival of Garrick. Like Garrick, Sheridan went into theatrical management; and his tenure at the Theatre Royal, Smock Alley, Dublin, was distinguished by useful theatrical reforms. It was also marred by public uproar, violent disruptions, and a culminating riot that destroyed the interior of the theater and drove Sheridan to more congenial pursuits.

According to Alicia Le Fanu, Frances much sympathized with the plight of the young manager during the celebrated Kelly riot of 1747, and published an anonymous poem called "The Owls" in his defense. The difficulty with this statement is that Alicia Le Fanu quotes the poem from *Faulkner's Journal* of 1746, a year before the Kelly riot. Further, as Esther K. Sheldon has established, Le Fanu omitted one of the ten stanzas of "The Owls," and that stanza refers clearly to an earlier brouhaha, the *Cato* affair of 1743. Indeed, the entire poem has been discovered by Sheldon in the 1743 pamphlet, *Cibber and Sheridan.*[5] The first meeting between the future Mr. and Mrs. Sheridan was doubtless occasioned by the appearance of "The Owls," but it very likely occurred much earlier than Alicia Le Fanu's account supposes. Thomas Sheridan's youngest sister Anne had married John Sheen of Dublin; and, as the Sheens were acquainted with the Chamberlaines, Sheridan contrived to meet the author of "The Owls" at Sheen's house, probably before the end of the year 1743. According to family tradition, Thomas and Frances were married by Walter Chamberlaine in 1747.

The Sheridans had six children: Thomas, who was born in 1747 and died in 1750; Charles Francis, who was born in June 1750 and became a minor diplomat, public servant, occasional political pamphleteer, and—so his sisters thought—the inspiration for the unctuously hypocritical Joseph Surface of *The School for Scandal;* Richard Brinsley, who was born in late September 1751, and became celebrated as a dramatist, theatrical manager, and Whig politician; Alicia, who was born in January 1753; Sackville, who was born in 1754 and died of convulsions as an infant; and finally Anne Elizabeth, called Betsy, who was born in London in 1758. Their father built a substantial Georgian house at No. 12 Dorset Street, Dublin. This was rather far from his theater across the Liffey in Smock Alley, but Frances was strongly attached to her uncle, Solomon Whyte, who lived in Dorset Street and who was anxious that his niece live close by him. The Sheridan house still stands, although in a considerably dilapidated state.

Thomas Sheridan had also inherited a small property of about seventy acres, called Quilca, in County Cavan. His father had prized the house and acreage as a country retreat, and Swift and Stella had visited there. It is an Irish characteristic to esteem land and family, and the Sheridans perhaps overvalued the modest Quilca as a symbol of times past when, according to Thomas Sheridan the Jacobite, the family had owned a castle and large tracts of land. Swift's view of Quilca was somewhat more sardonic:

> Let me my Properties explain.
> A rotten Cabbin, dropping Rain;
> Chimnies with Scorn rejecting Smoak;
> Stools, Tables, Chairs, and Bed-steds broke. . . . [6]

At any rate, both Swift's friend Thomas and Swift's godson Thomas spent money on the place and delighted to entertain there. Alicia Le Fanu tells a family story of how Thomas the younger entertained some friends who were, even in those pre-Gaelic revival days, enthusiastic about native customs. Consequently, Thomas served them an authentic old-Irish dinner, the main course being a traditional dish called swilled mutton. This consisted of a sheep roasted whole and stuffed with a lamb that was in turn stuffed with a hare and rabbits. The dish proved highly disagreeable, but the guests bravely downed it with a show of pleasure. Only then did Thomas bring out the real meal of well-prepared conventional dishes.[7]

Under Thomas Sheridan, the popularity of theatergoing in Dublin greatly increased. He instituted many reforms at Smock-Alley, both backstage and in the front of the house, and he drew about him a strong company that included at various times Charles Macklin, Spranger Barry, West Digges, George Anne Bellamy, and the celebrated Peg Woffington. According to some Dublin gossip, Sheridan and Peg Woffington were more than merely friendly, but such a liaison seems out of character for Sheridan. And, indeed, Alicia Le Fanu reports that Frances was quite satisfied with her husband's behavior. Mrs. Sheridan was certainly somewhat straitlaced, and Thomas never did present his raffish leading lady to his wife, although he did value Peg's companionship enough to introduce her into the all-male Beefsteak Club.

After the disruptions of the Kelly riot in 1747, the fortunes of the theater continued serenely enough until March 1754, when Thomas Sheridan offered the play *Mahomet,* adapted from Voltaire. Partly because of a falling-out with his leading actor, West Digges, but mainly because of the inflammatory political situation, the house was quickly in an uproar. Frances was not at the theater, but at home in Dorset Street with her cousin Sam Whyte. Years later, in Whyte's *Miscellanea Nova,* the scene was described in connection with an explication of Frances' "Ode to Patience."

> In the last stanza but one . . . she alludes to the fatal riot that took place at the Theatre, on the second representation of Mahomet, the 2d of March, 1754, which eventually proved the ruin of her husband, and in a moment totally eclipsed the flattering prospects of better days. That evening she was peaceably sitting at home, in conversation with a friend, the person to whom these Letters are addressed; when a Man, horrour in his counte-

nance, breathless and pale, without ceremony rushed into the parlour. . . . Oh, Madam! Smock-alley is in flames! . . . In flames?! . . . Yes, all in a blaze, Madam. . . . She rose, and looking wistfully at the door, advanced a step or two towards it; but a little recovering herself in a half-smothered, under voice, she scarcely articulated, Where is your Master? . . . At the house; all is uproar and distraction, and I just got away with my life.

The alarm was sudden; it was too much:
Yet not a tear dropt, not a sigh escaped her. . . .
With eyes uprais'd, she, for the worst prepar'd,
With pious resignation sits her down,
And her smooth cheek upon her white arm leaning,
Pensive and calm, awaits the dread event.

But she remained not long in this disconsolate posture; the carriage stopped at the door, and Mr. Sheridan came in, unhurt. The servant, early in the disturbance, anticipating the consequence, in a panic ran home and was premature in his account; but she overlooked his rash precipitance, and never revealed it to his Master.[8]

However, according to Alicia Le Fanu, the shock to Frances was so great that the child she was carrying at the time, Sackville, was affected and died in convulsions three months after his birth.

At the theater, everything was in an uproar, and the riot lasted from eight o'clock until two the next morning. The furnishings of the auditorium were destroyed, the curtain and scenery were slashed, and a fire started. On March 9, Sheridan announced in the *Dublin Journal* that he had "entirely quitted the Stage, and will no more be concerned in the Direction of it." According to Esther Sheldon, Sheridan let the theater to the players and retired for the summer to Quilca, while in the press and in pamphlets his actions were hotly debated. On September 15, he left for England and was presently followed by Frances and their oldest child, Charles.[9]

Sheldon's account, however, may not be quite accurate. In the Public Record Office of Ireland is a copy of a mortgage, dated May 30, 1754, and registered on August 15, 1754, in which "Thomas Sheridan for £2000 Grants unto Benjamin Victor Two Theatres Situate in Aungier Street and Smock Alley. . . ." Also in the Public Record Office are extracts from an Exchequer Bill filed against Thomas Sheridan by William Sheridan, "late of Shercock, County Cavan, now of Quilca, Same County," which throw further light on the Sheridans' movements. William Sheridan was a Cavan relative whom Thomas had asked in 1750 to manage Quilca, and in this bill William summed up his various complaints against and indebtednesses from Thomas.[10] William noted with some rancor that "in 1754 Thomas Sheridan went for London and that his wife resided at Quilca from his departure till 22nd November 1754 and that Suppliant had frequent conversations with her about her husband's affairs and found them to be in a bad state. . . ." The many details in the Exchequer Bill make it clear that Thomas Sheridan was much pressed for money, and that he treated William badly.

In London, the Sheridans took lodgings "next door to the Cross Keys, in Henrietta Street, Covent Garden."[11] For most of the rest of his life, Thomas Sheridan was constantly struggling with debts and ceaselessly looking for means of some relief from them. The month of October 1754 found him acting on shares at Covent Garden. Despite his eminence, he was received coolly, his detractors sometimes describing him as "Old Bubble and Squeak," and his last performance was on April 7, 1755. In December of this same year, Thomas published a 536-page book entitled *British Education,* and Esther Sheldon surmises that the writing of this long volume occupied him during the intervening months.[12]

Among the friends the Sheridans made during this time were Dr. Johnson and Samuel Richardson. Thomas was growing ever less interested in the stage and ever more interested in theories of education, elocution, and language. He and Johnson shared much in common, and initially valued each other highly, although there was certainly more admiration on Sheridan's part than on Johnson's. For instance, in a letter to Bennet Langton on October 18, 1760, Johnson waxed critical about Sheridan's acting at Drury Lane, but concluded, "However I wish him well, among other reasons because I like his wife."[13] In any event, Johnson often visited the Sheridans. On several occasions, Frances' young kinsman Sam Whyte met him there, and later in his *Miscellanea Nova,* Whyte recounted some amusing anecdotes of the great man.

Frances in particular seems to have become quite friendly with Samuel Richardson and his family, and she showed Richardson the manuscript of her early novel *Eugenia and Adelaide.* A letter from Frances, dated February 5, 1756, and printed in Richardson's *Correspondence,* would seem to refer to *Eugenia and Adelaide,* and even to suggest that Richardson liked it enough to contemplate publishing it. For some reason, he did not publish it, and Frances herself referred to it in her letter as "the efforts of a very young girl."[14] When this two-volume work was finally printed some years after the author's death, it proved to be a quite readable romance. It is most conventional, but yet a polished and certainly precocious production for a girl of fifteen. The complicated dual plot is set in Italy and Spain, and involves clever intrigues and disguises and an elaborate series of attempted seductions and kidnappings. The writing is terse and lucid, and the whole production indicates that the young Frances was a voracious reader who had thoroughly assimilated—indeed, mastered—her sources. However, the real importance of *Eugenia and Adelaide* is that its qualities prompted Richardson to encourage Frances to return to writing.

In early 1756, Thomas Sheridan attempted to organize a series of subscription lectures on elocution, but this project fell through. He was always a dreamer full of plans, even a grandiose one for an academy in Ireland. However, his plans usually did not materialize, and he was constantly drawn back to the stage to make his living. The theater in Dublin was not prospering, and Sheridan went over from London for several months during the summer of 1756 to discuss resuming command of Smock-Alley. He was gone from April to early August, and left Frances and Charles behind him in England. By late August he was with his wife and son again, but in the interim he had happily made satisfactory arrangements for the upcoming theatrical season and had also accepted the office of "Deputy Master of Revels and Masques" in Ireland. In October, he and Frances returned to

Dublin in style on the viceregal yacht, the *Dorset.* The voyage was a brief moment of triumph for the distinguished actor and manager.

Esther Sheldon suggests that the Sheridan family did not return to Dorset Street, but lived for a short while in Sheridan's apartments on Blind Quay, adjoining the theater.[15] If these apartments were the same as those described in the mortgage to Benjamin Victor of May 30, 1754, as "one room and the passage leading thereto," they must have been cramped quarters indeed. Late in November, the Sheridans seem to have moved north across the river and out to Glasnevin, where they took larger and more comfortable lodgings.[16] Thomas, meanwhile, was plagued by the threat of Spranger Barry returning to Dublin to erect a rival house, and his own present audiences at Smock-Alley were much diminished by the harshness of the weather, the severest of any winter since, as Frances put it (in a letter to Richardson written February 8, 1757), "the remarkable frost, in the year 1739. . . ."[17]

The theatrical seasons of 1756–57 and 1757–58 at Smock-Alley were not particularly successful, but they were frantically busy. In addition to managing the theater, acting, and attempting to protect Smock-Alley from the imminent new house of Barry in Crowe Street, Thomas Sheridan was trying to extricate himself altogether from the difficulties of theatrical life by promoting a Hibernian Academy. He was simultaneously preparing courses of lectures on elocution, writing an English grammar and an instructional treatise on reading the liturgy, and participating in the education of his sons. During the summer of 1758, accompanied by Frances (who was pregnant with their last child, Betsy) and their oldest boy, Charles, Thomas traveled to London to recruit performers for the upcoming season.

There the Sheridans stayed, leaving their son Dick and daughter Lissy enrolled for the time being in Sam Whyte's newly opened academy in Grafton Street, Dublin. The unexpected decision to remain in England seems to have been a relatively easy one. Thomas, though he would for a short while remain nominally the manager of Smock-Alley, was discouraged by Barry's successful application for a patent in Crowe Street and quite ready to turn over his own theater to other management. He was pressed by Irish creditors, whom he wished to escape; and, perhaps most important, he was excited by the success of his lectures on elocution, which he had begun delivering in London and at the universities in Oxford and Cambridge. Frances, meanwhile, was glad to be away from Dublin and established in the land she had come to regard as home. "I long to return to England," she had written to Richardson during the preceding summer (July 24, 1757). "I call it returning; that expression, I think, gives me an idea of a sort of home, and such I must consider it, endeared as it is to me by the friendship of some who hold the warmest place in my breast."[18]

In the early fall of 1759, Thomas Sheridan removed his family and their three servants to Windsor. Dick and Lissy were sent for from Dublin, their old nurse brought them over, and on September 12 Frances sent a letter to Sam Whyte saying that they had arrived "safe and well."[19] In subsequent letters, Frances wrote to Whyte of her husband's constant labors and many projects (including acting on shares at Drury Lane, under Garrick), of her own indifferent health, of the unsociableness of Windsor, of her assisting the boys in their studies, and, as usual, of the continuing impossibility of paying off old debts. However, in a long letter of February 26, 1761, she added this short paragraph:

> As for myself you will see how my solitary hours were employed last winter at Windsor, if you have time enough to bestow the reading on the Memoirs of Miss Sidney Bidulph, which will soon be published by G. Faulkner. (p. 102)

According to Alicia Le Fanu, Thomas knew that Frances was writing something, but did not know what. The *Memoirs of Miss Sidney Bidulph* was published anonymously, although it was an open secret who had written it. Frances dedicated her book to Richardson, and it entirely justified his faith in it, for it immediately became a most considerable success.

Sidney Bidulph is unabashedly sentimental, and surely gained popularity in part because it tells an engrossing story in generally lean, uncluttered prose. The innocent and inexperienced heroine, Sidney, is about to be married to a personable youth named Falkland. Just before the wedding, she learns that Falkland had committed an earlier indiscretion with a young woman who had borne his child. The match is broken off, and Sidney, languishing and reluctant, is at length persuaded by her mother to marry a presentable young man whom she does not love. In time she dutifully learns to esteem her husband, but he gradually changes in character as he comes increasingly under the sway of a cunning adventuress and at last brutally drives his wife and children away. Sidney is extricated from some of her difficulties by Falkland, who lures her husband's mistress to France and marries the woman off to one of his own servants. But Sidney is soon left a penniless widow by the death of her profligate mate, and when Falkland proposes marriage to her after a decent interval has passed, she self-sacrificingly persuades him to marry instead the supposedly innocent young woman whose child he had fathered earlier. Then, to add to her mounting miseries, Sidney's mother dies and her brother casts her off, leaving her destitute. The complications of the plot multiply from this point forward, for some 950 occasionally tedious pages. An eccentric, wealthy Jamaican cousin eventually rescues the heroine from her financial distresses. Falkland kills (or thinks he kills) his treacherous, scheming wife and her lover when he discovers them together—it turns out that she was only an evil predator who had seduced him so as to trick him into marriage. Wronged and miserable, Falkland flees from prosecution, and after much pleading prevails upon Sidney to marry him. He dies almost immediately following the ceremony, apparently before their union can be consummated.

Sidney Bidulph is for the most part a very conventional sentimental novel, though it studiously avoids a happy ending and the easy option of virtue rewarded. It is difficult to know whether Mrs. Sheridan meant the reader to believe that Sidney is denied fulfillment because she made the wrong decision at last and married Falkland, the reformed libertine and apparent murderer, or because she ruined both their lives by being too scrupulously pious and conventional and by delaying the right decision for too long. Possibly the ambiguity was deliberate, for the author certainly proved herself capable of real subtleties of character and situation in her other works. At any rate, *Sidney Bidulph,* though overly long and too often strained, is a genuinely moving work, something after the tragic manner of Richardson's *Clarissa.* Dr. Johnson spoke feelingly of its power when he said to Mrs. Sheridan, "I know not, Madam, that you have a right, upon moral principles, to make your readers suffer so much."[20] It should also be said that Frances' story is on the whole more tough-minded and honest in its representation of human emotions than that most celebrated of eighteenth-century tales of sensibility, Henry Mackenzie's *The Man of Feeling,* published ten years after Frances Sheridan's work first appeared. Less estimable novels than *Sidney Bidulph* have been considered minor classics.

Sidney Bidulph remains a work extremely good for its own day. If it does not seem quite worth resuscitating for ours, it nevertheless had one important influence, and that was upon the achievement of the author's most notable son. The book does have its comic as well as its pathetic touches, and Richard Brinsley Sheridan seems to have used suggestions from it in both *The Rivals* (the characters of Faulkland and Julia Melville, for example) and *The School for Scandal* (Lady Teazle, Sir Oliver, and the two Surface brothers, Joseph the hypocrite and Charles the good-natured ne'er-do-well). *Sidney Bidulph* was the most conspicuous literary achievement yet produced by a Sheridan, and it heralded the long series of noteworthy works by which members of this remarkable family would distinguish themselves during the next several generations.

Following Frances' burst of success with her novel, she spent the summer of 1762 at Windsor with her husband and their children. During these months she worked on her first play, *The Discovery,* and in a letter written from London to Sam Whyte on November 29 she conveyed the following interesting information:

The truth is, since my return to town from Windsor, I have been much employed though often interrupted by intervals of bad health, which of late have frequently returned on me. I have however mustered up spirits enough to write. . . . what do you think? Why, a Comedy! which is now in rehearsal at Drury-lane. I had formed my plan, and nearly finished the scenes last summer at Windsor (the place of my inspiration,) when I came to town, and shewed it to a few people, what was said to me on the occasion encouraged me to take some pains in the finishing of it. Mr. Garrick was pressing to see it, and accordingly I read it to him myself. What his opinion of it is, you may judge by his immediately requesting it to be put into his hands, and undertaking to play the *second* character, a comic, and very original one. Mr. Sheridan is to play the first, one of a graver cast, and a great deal of variety, and which requires a considerable actor to perform. My first theatrical essay has so far met with an almost unprecedented success; most of *us,* poor authors, find a difficulty in getting our pieces on the stage, and perhaps are obliged to dangle after Managers a season or two: I on the contrary was solicited to give mine as soon as it was seen. It is to come out early in January (the best part of the winter) and as it is admirably well cast, I have tolerable expectations of its succeeding.[21]

On December 31, James Boswell went to the Sheridans to drink tea and to hear them read *The Discovery*. "He and she read alternately," Boswell wrote in his journal entry for the day. "I liked it much and was well entertained."[22] Possibly it was on this night that Frances finally asked Boswell to write a prologue for the play, as he had hoped she would do. The invitation, when it came, touched Boswell's vanity. As he explained later in his journal entry for January 18, Mrs. Sheridan remarked that there were "few good poets in this age; and she said that if they had been in good terms with Johnson, she would have asked him. Her applying to me after this no doubt flattered me a good deal."[23] Boswell actually wrote two prologues. The first, rejected by Frances as too general, was followed by a long effort upon which the author pinned some rather high hopes. "The thing now pleased me exceedingly," he wrote in the same entry for January 18. "I thought it fine to have my lines spoken by Mr. Garrick and resounding through Drury Lane." But Boswell was to be disappointed. Thomas Sheridan ridiculed his verses, and Frances assented to her husband's judgment, explaining that she intended to write a prologue herself. Boswell was a "good deal mortified" by the entire episode, and at first decided to conceive an "aversion to Sheridan," who had indeed treated him very roughly. He recanted this hasty decision, perhaps realizing that his two attempts at prologue writing were at best indifferent.[24] Incidentally, he nowhere mentions that Frances' prologue borrows his ideas and repeats a couple of his lines. Boswell is, in this instance, more charitable to the Sheridans than they were to him and his feelings.[25]

On opening night at Drury Lane (February 3, 1763), according to Boswell, *The Discovery* "acted heavily," though it boasted Garrick in the comic role of Sir Anthony Branville and Thomas Sheridan perfectly cast in the part of the stuffy, feckless Lord Medway. It was "allowed to jog through" without interruption, but Oliver Goldsmith, who sat behind Boswell, said "many smart acrimonious things" about it.[26] Others took a less sour view of the performance. The young playwright John O'Keeffe was on hand and, as he wrote years later, found the evening much to his liking:

> I saw Mrs. Frances Sheridan's Comedy of *The Discovery* at Drury Lane Theatre the first night of its presentation. Garrick performed Sir Anthony Branville; his great laugh-exciting point was speaking the most impassioned speeches with a calm voice and placid face. Thomas Sheridan played Lord Medway and was dressed in a full suit of crimson velvet. Garrick's dress was very fantastical; his acting made such an impression on my mind, that I can now figure his first coming on, at the near entrance at the right hand, as you look towards the stage. The Comedy gave great delight, and the success was perfect.[27]

The play had a good run of seventeen nights. Though it was never so enormously popular as the comedies of Goldsmith or Richard Brinsley Sheridan, it enjoyed repeated revivals throughout the later years of the eighteenth century—most conspicuously by Garrick, who staged it for six nights during the season of 1775–76. *The Discovery* appeared in published form several times during these years and into the nineteenth century, in separate editions put out in London, Dublin, and Edinburgh, and in some important theatrical anthologies. It has been revised or adapted a half-dozen times, most recently in a rather phlegmatic version by Aldous Huxley (1924), who attempted unsuccessfully to rewrite the play for the modern stage. Since then Mrs. Sheridan's comedy has had no discoverable editions or productions, and it appears in none of the modern anthologies of eighteenth-century drama. This is a pity because it is better than a number of plays that do get reprinted, among them some tedious things by Addison, Steele, Lillo, Cibber, Kelly, and Cumberland.

The Discovery is a multiplotted piece concerning happy marriage and the question of what-boy-gets-what-girl. There are three, or possibly four, such plot strands, all intricately connected with each other. By far the best of these is the one involving Sir Harry Flutter and his wife, an attractive and naive young married couple who constantly quarrel over trivialities. Their early dialogues are as charmingly amusing as anything to be found in eighteenth-century comedy, and this brilliant beginning is the main interest of the first half of the play. Unfortunately, the Flutters have nothing significant to do in the second half, and the play suffers somewhat.

Another plot line concerns the curmudgeonish father, Lord Medway, who wants to marry his children well as a means of redeeming his own wasted fortunes. He offers his beautiful daughter Louisa, whose character bears hints of the Lydia Languish of *The Rivals,* to the pedantic-romantic old fool Sir Anthony Branville, although she loves this buffoon's young and presentable offstage nephew. Lord Medway meanwhile persuades his son to wed the clever and wealthy widow Mrs. Knightly, the former object of Sir Anthony's ridiculous addresses, instead of her lovely sister Miss Richly, to whom the youth has pledged his eternal adoration. Mrs. Sheridan imparts real freshness to her development of this hackneyed domestic conflict through several effective comic scenes, the most successful of which center on Sir Anthony and Mrs. Knightly. Sir Anthony is hardly a comic creation of the first rank, but he was good enough for Garrick to sense and exploit his possibilities. The greatest actor of the age must have enjoyed playing this verbal and social bungler, whose eccentricities of language and manner almost always delight while they display impressive skill and ingenuity on the part of the author. Mrs. Knightly is interesting, but troublesome. She is not one but three separate characters, and this multischizophrenia is not the result of any insight by Frances into abnormal psychology but simply an answer to the necessities of her many-stranded plot. For one plot, Mrs. Knightly is a witty woman-of-the-worldish Millamant, and these scenes are carried off with some panache. For another plot, she is one of Cinderella's nasty-tempered older sisters. Although this complex of contradictions is acceptable enough, Mrs. Knightly's incarnation as the crushed and reformed devious female is not, for it dulls the brightness of her character and is finally just unconvincing.

Whatever coherence there may be among the various plot strands of the play is imparted by making Lord Medway in each instance the villain. For four acts, Frances paints him effectively as wastrel and middle-aged late-Restoration rake. A mere twisting of circumstances radically changes him in the end—it is, like Mrs. Knightly's reformation, a purely theatrical device;

and the Lord Medway of Act V is a creature of the theater rather than of reality. The "discovery" that provides the twist and leads to the comic ending of the play is the revelation that Mrs. Knightly is Lord Medway's daughter. Naturally, she cannot marry Medway's son, her own brother. In a gesture of goodwill, then, she persuades Sir Anthony to renew his court to her. Both Medway children are released from the bondage of their chastened father's wishes, and there is the promise of happiness for all. This elaborate contrivance, of course, is a hoary stock device, but in this play it even remains undramatized, for the discovery occurs between Acts IV and V.

Despite such a trite and awkwardly handled resolution, and despite large dollops of eighteenth-century sentiment, *The Discovery* is nowhere so maudlin as parts of plays by Steele and Lillo, and it has nothing quite so stilted as portions of Julia's dialogue in *The Rivals*. In fact, a saving grace of the play is that it is written with uncommon fluency, so that even the more tedious parts of the plot and the more lachrymose revelations of feeling flow smoothly by. A chief glory of Richard Brinsley Sheridan's three great comic plays is a consciousness of language that is comic by its divergence from a civilized norm. Among dramatists of the time, perhaps only Fielding and Goldsmith approached Dick Sheridan in the consummate use of quirky, mangled language. But much more than a hint of this same gift was there in the comedies of his mother. Lord Medway's first-act injunction to Sir Harry about how to control his wife really comes down to what kind of language Sir Harry should use. And the language of spleen and anger, with all of its inadequate silliness, is scarcely less brilliantly employed in Sir Anthony and Jack Absolute than it is in Sir Harry and Lady Flutter. In sum, the finest parts of Frances Sheridan's play, mostly contained in the first half, are as good as anything in all but the best of eighteenth-century comic drama. And two of the greatest comedies of the period, *The Rivals* and *The School for Scandal,* owe more than a little to *The Discovery*.

Emboldened by the success of her first play, Frances completed a second, called *The Dupe,* during the middle months of 1763. This new work was staged at Drury Lane by George Colman (Garrick being away in France) toward the end of the year, beginning on December 10. This time, however, the play failed, receiving only three performances, and it seems never to have been revived. Sam Whyte and Alicia Le Fanu both attribute the failure to "the theatrical cabals of a popular actress."[28] The reason, however, may partly reside in the work itself. Certain scenes seem written more for psychology than for theater, and the manner is sometimes talky and novelistic. Still, there are definite theatrical qualities of both characterization and language. Frances' most theatrical character is Mrs. Friendly, a sympathetic and pleasant middle-aged woman who is hopelessly given to brainless, aimless talk full of inconsequential and maddeningly boring detail. Whenever Mrs. Friendly has something of import to say, it is so burdened with superfluous facts that her hearers are reduced to exasperation. This engaging featherhead, in both her character and her speech, seems taken directly from life. She has been limned with little theatrical broadening, but she is a theatrical delight.

Some other characters are nearly as fine. The rakish, middle-aged curmudgeon Sir John Woodall, his unscrupulous mistress Mrs. Etherdown, her disreputable accomplice Sharply, and the quick-tongued servant Rose—all are products of Mrs. Sheridan's genuine wit and real sensititivity to manners and language. The play's flabby verbosity, however, comes close to undermining the strengths of its several crisp characterizations, some good theatrical scenes, and a plot that is tighter and less awkwardly contrived than that of *The Discovery*. This prosiness, together with the author's generally unsentimental treatment of love and marriage and her avoidance of conventional morality, may have cost *The Dupe* any chance of a long run on the stage.[29] As closet drama it enjoyed somewhat greater success. The London and Dublin editions (both 1764) seem to have sold briskly, and Mrs. Sheridan's London publisher, the exemplary Andrew Millar, made such profits that he was able to send her £100 beyond the copyright money—surely this remittance from the honest Millar was prompted in part by his compassion for the disappointment he knew Frances must have been feeling over the failure of her play upon the stage.[30] Millar believed, rightly, that *The Dupe* deserved better than the rejection it had endured at Drury Lane, and indeed it is worthy of better than the utter neglect it has suffered in our own day.

Thomas Sheridan had been playing in Dublin when *The Dupe* was produced, but he returned in the spring of 1764. He and Frances then went to Bristol and Bath where he lectured on oratory, and in Bath they met the musical Linley family who were to figure so importantly in the life of their younger son. Following some summer weeks spent in London, Frances accompanied her husband to Scotland where he played two or three nights at the Edinburgh Theatre. Even his many Herculean efforts did not enable Thomas to stave off his increasing debts, which had become so pressing by September that he found it necessary to escape to France. He took his wife and three children with him, leaving behind only Richard, who was in school at Harrow. The Sheridans set up housekeeping in a cottage at Blois; there they all commenced learning the native language while Thomas worked on several literary projects, chief of which was a new dictionary of English. Frances struggled along with her French, and in the meantime she took music lessons from (according to Alicia Le Fanu) a Jesuit master, wrote a two-volume sequel to the *Memoirs of Miss Sidney Bidulph* (published posthumously, in 1767), and completed her third comedy, *A Journey to Bath*.

The new play was submitted to Drury Lane apparently through Benjamin Victor, Thomas' old deputy manager at Smock-Alley who was now Garrick's treasurer. Garrick did not like it; and, when Mrs. Victor communicated his reasons to Frances, she wrote back at once, obviously as irked as she was polite. Frances devoted the latter part of the letter to a refutation of Garrick's objections, one by one, and these pages constitute her fullest extant discussion of any of her works:

> There are four heavy accusations laid against it: any one of which being sufficient to weigh the stripling down. I think it a maternal duty to exculpate my child, as far as it is in my power, from so many complicated faults, more especially as these vices have not been acquired by evil communications, but were born with it, and consequently take their rise originally from myself.

Imprimis, the play is without fable; secondly, all the scenes are detached; thirdly, there is nothing to interest the audience; and lastly, it has no humour. Tell Garrick I have thrown my gauntlet down, and am going to defend myself.

To the first charge, I plead not guilty, and will maintain that the fable is fully sufficient to build a series of events upon,—that there is as much as most of our comedies have, and more than in many which have been well received.

For the second, I cannot pretend to say (contrary to the opinion of so good a master of his art) whether the scenes are laid with that rigorous exactness that theatrical architecture may require, but this much I will venture to assert, that their succession is regular and natural, and that they all tend to the main purpose of the drama, which is comprised in the two or three last lines of the play.

For the third objection, perhaps, I may be singular in my opinion; but I own, I do not think it absolutely necessary to interest the passions in a comedy; in a tragedy it is indispensable; but if the Comic Muse can excite curiosity enough to keep up the attention of the audience, she has, in my mind, acquitted herself of her duty; and I think this seems to be the general style of some of our most entertaining comedies, and the one in question, I should hope, is not entirely void of this merit; as the fate of an unworthy project against two innocent young people, artfully carried on, on one side, by a designing pair, and ridiculously supported, on the other, by an absurd pair, is not decided till the very last scene. As to the fourth charge, I shall leave it as I found it; for unless I were to use Bayes's expressions, I should be at a loss for words to defend it—I promised you but pleasantry, and if I have utterly failed in that, I am more unfortunate than I expected to be. Just give me leave to add, what I think will not be denied me, that there is a good moral, and some character in this piece. The latter of these two articles seems to be growing fast out of fashion; the late writers treating the taste of the times as physicians do the stomachs of their sick patients, which, finding two [sic] weak for substantial food, they supply with slops. But the reason of this is obvious: our present race of poets not abounding with invention of their own, have taken stories they found ready to their hand, which never having been intended for representation, the authors did not think themselves tied down to rules with which the stage ought not to dispense; yet I thought that Mr. Garrick, who himself knows so well how to support this grand requisite of dramatic works, would willingly have encouraged every effort which had the least pretensions to merit of this kind.[31]

A large anthology could probably be made of such letters from disappointed dramatists, and it is to Frances' credit that she, for the most part, avoids taking a strident tone. However, such letters, no matter how mild or how ferocious, are practically always futile—as, indeed, Mrs. Sheridan's was. Garrick's response, addressed to Mrs. Victor, is courteous, even friendly, but unmistakably firm. It is worth repeating in its entirety partly because it displays the courtly Garrick at his critical best, and partly because it shows so clearly just what kind of arbitrary power aspiring and even established playwrights were up against at the hands of theatrical managers.

Dear Madam.

I am got into a Scrape—to have a gauntlet thrown down to me by a Lady! & one who can Use her weapons with such skill too! I wish myself a good deliverance!—let what will be the Consequence, I must not turn my back upon a female Challenger.

As I have not the Comedy, I must be very short and general in my answer; & give an account only of the particular Effect it had upon Me—that there were Characters in the play I allow'd but I thought they were not well employ'd: I felt the scenes languid for want of an interesting fable, & that Spirit of dialogue of Vis comica, which was to be found in many Scenes of the Discovery:

Mr. Smith's criticism in the Rehearsal, that the *Plot stands still,* might I think be apply'd in some measure to the play in question, but I am sure, that Mrs. Sheridan (who is so unlike Bayes in Every thing else) will never agree with Him in this—that *a Plot is only good to bring in fine things*[32]— How could Mrs. Sheridan imagine that I wanted the passions to be interested? I should as soon expect to have my laughter rais'd in a tragedy—I said indeed that the Comedy wanted interest, but not of ye *Passions*—I meant a Comic interest, resulting from ye humours of the Characters thrown into spirited action & brought into interesting Situations, naturally arising from a well-constructed fable or Plot—This, with a good moral, deduc'd from ye whole, is all I wish or look for in a *Comedy.*

Mrs. Sheridan hints, (if I mistake not, for I read her letter but once) that I judge of these matters by some peculiar (I am afraid she means confin'd) notions of my own—perhaps I may—I can only judge with those materials for judging which I have—but if I am not entertain'd & interested in reading a play, I judge, and I think naturally enough, that it will not have the desir'd Effect upon an Audience, & I might say for Myself that hitherto I have been tolerably lucky in my guesses—it was my opinion that the *Discovery* would have success, and that the *Dupe* wd fail of it, upon the Stage—

When You write to Mrs. Sheridan, I beg that You would present my best Compts to her & assure her, that there is no Manager more sincerely encourages Comedy in general than I do, or is more desirous of Shewing his regard to her's in particular than

Dr Madm Yr & c.
D. Garrick

PS. My Gout has almost left me—I hope that ye great hurry I have had lately with my Acting & Management, the illness I have had & the pain I now suffer will be an Apology to Mrs Sh: for this very hasty & insufficient answr to her most ingenious letter.[33]

No copy of *A Journey to Bath* in its entirety exists, but from the three-act fragment that survives we can glean enough evidence to make some assessment of the merits of Frances' and Garrick's divergent opinions. Frances seems wrong on one point and Garrick on another, but both were really in agreement that comedy should be laughing, not weeping, and that the play had well-developed characters. Indeed, one must go further and say that *A Journey to Bath* contains the freshest, most diversified collection of characters that Frances had yet created. Even her young hero and heroine have individualizing, humanizing traits not always found in such roles. The villains, Lord Stewkly and Lady Filmot, are no monsters but are urbanely plausible. And the character roles include a supercilious snob, a vulgar parvenu, a pompous politician, a sycophantic landlady, and, in Mrs. Tryfort, a widow with such absurd pretensions to polite learning that she became the pattern for Dick Sheridan's immortal Mrs. Malaprop.

To the character roles, Frances attached peculiarities of language that are both neatly apt and finely comic. Mrs. Surface, the lodginghouse keeper who tries to keep in with everybody, has a droll scene based on the confusions arising from hypocrisies of language. The language of Sir Jeremy Bull is beautifully contrasted with that of his brother, Sir Jonathan. Sir Jeremy is a family-proud egotist who has served in Parliament, and his remarks are like pronouncements—orotund, obscure, pretentious, and long-winded. Sir Jonathan is a sweet, straightforward, credulous man whose conversation is garrulously friendly and sunnily simple. In Lady Bell Aircastle, we have the language of snobbery, and in Mrs. Tryfort such an ingenious misapplication of words that Dick Sheridan later simply appropriated her best *mal mots* and burnished them a bit. Garrick went quite astray in thinking that Frances' dialogue was uncomic, for *A Journey to Bath* is the most cunningly written of all her plays.

Insofar as we can tell, however, from the extant three acts, Garrick was on much surer ground when he charged that "the scenes were languid for want of an interesting fable." Several scenes are in themselves comically effective, but the main intrigue is built up in so leisurely a manner, and with such a want of thrust, that the play ambles. Even the big scene at the end of Act III, to which all of the action has been tending, is treated somewhat lifelessly. Dick's *The Rivals* is, by contrast, composed of one bold-relief comic situation after another. Whether Frances actually managed to rise to a strongly done, climactic comic situation in her last acts, we cannot say. But even with her paleness of plot, we can say that *A Journey to Bath* contains better characterization and better writing than her previous plays, and that its pattern was developed by her son into one of the great comedies of the English stage. *A Journey to Bath* itself was unfortunately never produced, and only the surviving manuscript fragment has ever been published—most importantly in a transcription by W. Fraser Rae included in his edition of Richard Brinsley Sheridan's plays.[34]

On August 1, 1766, Thomas Sheridan wrote from Blois to Sam Whyte, saying that he was reduced to his last louis and begging Whyte to raise him £100 so that he might return to Dublin and set his affairs in order. Thomas planned to leave Frances and the children for the time being in France, and he gave an interesting account of what the family had been doing:

I have long since finished the Dictionary, and have got together the greatest part of the materials for the Grammar, which only want being reduced into order. I have likewise almost finished a volume of Dialogues in the English Language, to serve as a preparative for the other work. . . . I have finished a Grammar too in English and French, for the use of all foreigners who understand French, that are desirous of attaining a knowledge of the English tongue by an easy and short method. I have also drawn up a

Grammar in English to facilitate the attainment of the French tongue to all who speak English; a work much wanted, and which I began at first for the use of my children, upon finding the great imperfection of all hitherto published with that view. Mrs. Sheridan has writ a comedy called A Trip to Bath, in which some good judges in England find a great deal of merit. She has also made two additional volumes to the Memoirs of Sidney, and has begun a Tragedy in prose upon part of the story contained in this latter part.[35] Thus you see, that, together with the time employed in the instruction of the children, we have not been idle since our arrival here. Our coming to Blois has been attended with the happy circumstance of restoring Mrs. Sheridan to a perfect good state of health, a blessing which she had not known for ten years before; and this alone would make me think it a fortunate event which drove us hither.[36]

Poor, sanguine, busy, unlucky Thomas Sheridan, for it was not two months later—according to some accounts on September 26—that Frances died. When she died, her husband's sister Elizabeth maintained that the Sheridan Banshee had been heard wailing beneath the windows of Quilca. However, as Alicia Le Fanu tartly noted, "A niece of Miss Sheridan's made her very angry by observing that, as Mrs. Frances Sheridan was by birth a Chamberlaine, a family of English extraction, she had no right to the guardianship of an Irish fairy, and that therefore the Banshi must have made a mistake!"[37]

About a month after Frances died, Thomas wrote the following letter to Whyte:

Paris, October 13th, 1766

Often have I sat down to write to you an account of the most fatal event that could befall me in this life, and as often have thrown aside the pen. Oh, my dear SAM! the most excellent of Women is no more. Her apparent malady was an intermitting fever, attended with no one bad symptom 'till the day before her death, when she was suddenly deprived of her senses, and all the fatal prognostics of a speedy dissolution appeared. She died the death of the righteous, without one pang. Without a groan. The extraordinary circumstances attending her case made me resolve to have her opened; when it was found that the whole art of medicine could not have prolonged her days, as all the noble parts were attacked, and any one of four internal maladies must have proved mortal. If the news of this event has not yet reached Dublin, break it to my Sister as gently as you can. I set out from this in a few days for St. Quintin, a town about half way between this and Calais, where I purpose to leave my Children, in the hands of Protestants, to whom they are strongly recommended. As soon as I have settled them, I shall set out for London, and thence proceed to Dublin as speedily as possible. I thank you for your last letter and the remittance, without which I should not have been able to have made this arrangement—SAM! You have lost a Friend who valued you much. I have lost what the world cannot repair, a bosom Friend, another self. My children have lost—Oh their Loss is neither to be expressed nor repaired. But the will of God be done.[38]

Alicia Le Fanu gives some further details. A few days before Sheridan was to depart for Dublin, Frances was seized with fainting fits and took to her bed. She had been all her life subject to such seizures, but this was a particularly long one. Quickly she grew worse, and her husband put off his trip. Her illness lasted about a fortnight, and the day before her death she lost consciousness. She was buried in the cemetery of a French Protestant family, that of one Colonel de Maupas, six or seven miles distant from Blois. She was forty-two years old.[39]

Over the years, several of Frances' works have appeared posthumously—the juvenile *Eugenia and Adelaide,* the sequel to *Sidney Bidulph,* and *The History of Nourjahad.* The *Sidney* sequel is not so long as the original, but is nonetheless a substantial 125,000 words. In it, the heroine has retired to the country and raised her two daughters as well as Orlando Falkland, the son of her old lover. Told again in the form of letters, the story is basically that of the children, and Sidney only takes the center of the stage at the end of the novel, with her death. The plot concerns a love triangle, a minor seduction, a major seduction, an interesting study of near madness, and a narrowly averted marriage. The structure is tighter, more exciting, and rather more melodramatic than that of the first part. The characterization of the three young principals is rather stiff, but some of the conniving minor figures are excellent. The style is predictably fluent and supple, but the moral tone seems to have hardened into conventionality. For instance, after a minor character, Theodora Williams, has been seduced through little fault of her own other than naiveté, Frances draws this conclusion:

> There was nothing now to be done but to remove her from the scene of her misfortune, and accordingly we yesterday sent her down to the country to the house of the lady whom she is to serve; where the poor creature may pine away the rest of her life in sorrow. . . .

At the end, after most of the characters (particularly the women) have suffered and suffered and suffered, Sidney dies, the pattern of a heroic and impeccably virtuous woman. In this continuation of her first published novel, Frances Sheridan's technique has improved, especially in the staging of dramatic scenes, but her moral view has become a good deal less interesting. The sequel was published in 1770.

The History of Nourjahad appeared a year after Frances' death. It was written as the first in a projected series of moral tales exploiting the current interest in Oriental exotica, and so it is longer than a story and shorter than a novel. *Nourjahad* features a childlike arbitrariness of values, of situations, and of lucid expression that draws it closer to a fable than to a conventional work of fiction. Some quite familiar qualities of conventional novelistic fiction, however, it does possess. Its plot is developed, complicated, and so successfully surprising in its denouement that a critic must not divulge it. Its main personage, Nourjahad, is simple but well defined, and his character is made plausibly to change and grow. But overall the story is more abstract than circumstantial. The generalized rather than realistic Persian setting helps to create this effect, as does the fairy-tale device that impels the plot. And both qualities, of course, contribute to the prime excellence of the work, namely its charm.

Briefly, the narrative tells of how a pleasure-loving young man is granted

his wishes for immortality, youth, and riches, and of how he comes to realize
that other matters besides personal gratification are important. Admirers of
Johnson's *Rasselas* (1759) will recognize certain echoes of her old friend's
work in Frances Sheridan's tale, while those who have read *Vathek* (1786)
may be surprised by how close William Beckford came to repeating the
outlines of the plot of *Nourjahad*. But Frances' last book can stand on its
own without benefit of reference to these more familiar props of literary
history. Its story is so good, its details so inventive, and its telling so uncluttered that *Nourjahad* really deserves the kind of attention usually lavished
upon a minor classic. If Frances had been able to write a number of companion pieces, as she proposed, her place in English literature would have been
secured long ago. In modern times, *Nourjahad* has been once rediscovered
and reprinted, and might well be again. The style of the work could be
slightly less cluttered with eighteenth-century mannerisms, but on the whole
Mrs. Sheridan's prose is as clear and clean as Swift's and would provide no
barrier to the pleasure of a child or intelligent adult today. *Nourjahad* is not a
great lost masterpiece, but it is a worthy conclusion to the all too brief career
of a very talented lady.

II. A Note on Productions, Previous Editions, and the Present Text

The Discovery

Frances Sheridan's first play was more than modestly successful in the
theaters of London during the latter years of the eighteenth century. It
opened at Drury Lane on February 3, 1763, and ran for seventeen nights, as
follows: February 3, 4, 5, 7, 8, 9, 10, 11, 12, 14, 15, 19, 22, 26; March 3, 12;
April 26. A two-act adaptation called *The Young Couple,* by the actress Jane
Pope, was staged at the same theatre on April 21, 1767, and Mrs. Sheridan's
original was later revived there by David Garrick in January of 1776, for six
performances: January 20, 22, 24, 26, 29; February 7. There were additional
productions at Drury Lane in 1779 (February 3, 5, 27; March 8; April 9;
November 9) and in 1780 (March 7; October 28), all given while Thomas
Sheridan was assisting his son Richard with the management of the theater.
Covent Garden featured the play for three nights during the season of 1782–
83 (November 29; December 4; January 10). The original cast of the 1763
Drury Lane production included Thomas Sheridan as Lord Medway and
Garrick (who spoke the Prologue) in the comic role of Sir Anthony Bran-
ville.

The two major Dublin theaters of the day, Crowe-Street and Smock-Alley,
contended for the honor of being the first to present *The Discovery* in the
author's native city. According to some accounts Smock-Alley won out by a
few days, and the play opened on or about February 10, 1763. On Monday,
February 14, George Faulkner announced in his *Dublin Journal* that he was
ready to publish *The Discovery* as it is "performed at the Theatres-Royal in
Drury Lane and Crowe-Street," but probably the second Irish production
was delayed until March 4. The *Dublin Journal* advertised performances at
Crowe-Street for March 4, 10, and 16, but none earlier. At Smock-Alley the
celebrated Robert Baddeley acted the part of Sir Anthony to considerable

acclaim, while at Crowe-Street the manager Spranger Barry was enthusiastic enough about the play to have new scenery painted for it. Two
adaptations were presented subsequently at Smock-Alley. One, called *Sir
Anthony in Love,* was staged at a benefit for the manager, Henry Mossop, on
March 14, 1763. The other, offered as an afterpiece on June 23 of the same
year, was by the actor O'Brien; called *Matrimonial Douceurs, or, What We
May All Come to,* this version retained only the scenes with Lord Medway
and the Flutters. Since the eighteenth century *The Discovery* has only very
rarely been presented in any theater, and, so far as is known, only once
during the present century, when Aldous Huxley's revision of the play was
given a short-lived London production in 1924.[40]

The Discovery was first printed for Thomas Davies of Russell Street,
Covent Garden, in February 1763, just days after the play opened at Drury
Lane on February 3. Davies was joined by a consortium of other booksellers
who sold copies from their own stalls at other locations in London. On
Monday, February 14, George Faulkner's *Dublin Journal* announced publication of the play in Ireland. Faulkner had copies made up from the London
edition, as sent to him "by the author" and "to NO OTHER Person in this
Kingdom," and these could be had at the shops of W. Smith, H. Saunders,
and other prominent booksellers in the Irish capital. An Edinburgh edition
printed for R. Fleming, who likewise copied from the London edition, came
out almost simultaneously, so that by midway into the year 1763 the first
printed version of Frances Sheridan's popular comedy was available all over
the British Isles.

A second London edition was published before the year was out. This
version contains numerous corrections of printer's errors, it restores some
manuscript material not included in the first edition and incorporates several
other substantive changes, and it marks passages omitted in theatrical production. Undoubtedly this text of the play evolved during its rehearsal and
run; probably a good many of the substantive changes were made at the
suggestion of Garrick and Thomas Sheridan—who were surely responsible
as well, in part or whole, for the excisions made in the acting version.
Presumably Frances Sheridan had a hand in all these alterations. At any rate
we may say, though with some caution, that the revisions introduced into the
text of the second edition reflected her own best standards of judgment and
taste.

No other edition of *The Discovery* appeared prior to the author's death in
1766. The history of its publication in following years may be summarized
briefly. Mrs. Sheridan's play, at the time of its revival at Drury Lane during
the season of 1775–76, was included by John Bell in volume 5 of *Bell's
British Theatre: Consisting of the Most Esteemed English Plays* (20 vols.,
1776–78); it was later reissued (in 1792 and 1797) as part of volume 23 in a
revised version of the same collection, where it was "Adapted for Theatrical
Representation." It appeared again more than a decade later in a miscellane-
ous gathering of plays called *English Comedy* (London, 1810). In 1824 the
London booksellers G. and W. Whitaker reissued the second London edition
of 1763, bound together with the London edition of *The Dupe,* 1764, and a
1786 edition of the *Memoirs of Miss Sidney Bidulph.* Two adaptations of *The
Discovery* were issued in later years. The first was by Richard Brinsley

Peake, who joined scenes from Mrs. Sheridan's play with selections from Sir Richard Steele's *The Tender Husband* (1705) to produce a piece called *Court and City: A Comedy in Five Acts.* This adaptation was staged at Covent Garden and simultaneously published by John Cumberland in *Cumberland's British Theatre* (1830); it was reprinted in *Dick's Standard Plays,* 1885. More recently, the revision of *The Discovery* by Aldous Huxley, who mangled Mrs. Sheridan's comedy by rewriting its sentimental passages and providing a new ending, was published from the London house of Chatto and Windus in 1924.

The present edition represents the first reprinting of *The Discovery,* in any form, for some sixty years. We have sought in this new edition to supply a text that accurately reflects what appear to have been Frances Sheridan's final intentions regarding her play as a literary production *and* as a dramatic comedy to be acted. The text is based on that of the second London edition of 1763, the last to be prepared under the author's supervision, or at least with her approval. After collation with the manuscript (the Licenser's copy, submitted for approval on January 24, 1763) and the first London edition, the text of the second edition has been emended in some minor ways. Obvious printer's errors have been corrected, and in a very few cases where the manuscript version of a sentence or phrase seemed clearer or more sensible than the printed version it has been silently restored. No attempt has been made to modernize or in any way to regularize punctuation, capitalization, or spelling. It should perhaps be added that the original published versions of the play represent a considerable editing of the manuscript; some of the changes were doubtless carried out by the printers, enforcing house policy. Mrs. Sheridan's manuscript is very rough and extremely erratic, even to the point of confusion, in punctuation, capitalization, and spelling. Furthermore, the manuscript is occasionally so flabby and prosy as to need just the kind of pruning of scenes and speeches it was given before the play was acted and printed. Quite apart from the important issue of final authorial intention, the very crudeness of the manuscript makes it unsuitable as the text for an edition like the present one.

The second London edition introduces a further kind of editing by indicating those passages in the printed text that were left out of the acting version. Certain richnesses of style and nuances of character are lost in the cuts made for stage production, but the work's effectiveness as a dramatic vehicle is increased. The excisions shorten the play considerably, making for an acting script that is tighter and quicker in its movements. It is a bit of good fortune that the most authoritative contemporary edition preserves intact both the literary and the stage versions of Mrs. Sheridan's play. In this new edition we have repeated this interesting practice; the passages omitted from the actors' text appear in **bold bookface type.**

An appendix contains transcriptions of the two rejected prologues to *The Discovery* written by James Boswell.

The Dupe

Frances Sheridan's second comedy was produced to very little acclaim at Drury Lane Theatre on December 10, 12, 13, 1763.[41] There is no evidence that it has ever been performed since. The London bookseller Andrew Millar admired the play, despite its failure on the stage, and he printed it with considerable success in 1764. Another edition, apparently issued almost simultaneously, was published in Dublin by G. and A. Ewing and a group of other booksellers. The Dublin edition seems by both timing and internal evidence to have been taken not from the text of the play as it was printed in London, but directly from another copy of the manuscript. Its occasional awkwardness of phrasing and its often extremely erratic use of accidentals make it resemble the unpolished manuscript of the play sent to the Licenser in London on November 22, 1763. Thomas Sheridan was acting in Dublin during the season of 1763–64, and may himself have conveyed a manuscript copy of *The Dupe* to the printer. His wife was in London all this while, and so the more carefully prepared edition of the play published there is the one most likely to have received her imprimatur.

The Dupe was not reprinted during the lifetime of its author. The London edition of 1764 was reissued in 1824 by G. and W. Whitaker, who included it in a single volume (already described) along with earlier editions of *The Discovery* and the *Memoirs of Miss Sidney Bidulph*. There has been no other publication of the play since that time.

We have based our text on that of the original London edition, after collation with the manuscript (the Licenser's copy), which is, like the manuscript version of *The Discovery* (and for some of the same reasons of style and clarity), unsuitable for use as a copy-text. Andrew Millar, when readying Frances Sheridan's rough work for publication, introduced numerous mechanical corrections, but only very minor substantive changes—the omission or addition of a few lines here and there. For a few sentences or phrases, the manuscript offers clearer or more effective wording than either published text; in such instances the manuscript material has been restored without comment. Collation of the London and Dublin editions reveals no major substantive discrepancies. There are many trivial variants, however, particularly in capitalization, spelling, and punctuation. In capitalization and spelling, we have generally opted for the more regular and modern style of the London text, but we have taken the clearer punctuation from either text. In some few instances where the Dublin edition contains important matter not found in the London, we have included it in our text in square brackets, using **bold bookface type.** Occasionally, the Dublin edition varies slightly in its wording, and we have indicated any moderately significant differences in footnotes, each marked by an asterisk, or by a dagger if two notes fall on the same page.

A Journey to Bath

This play was written in Blois near the end of the author's life, and submitted to David Garrick for production at Drury Lane. At the time, it probably bore the title "A Trip to Bath."[42] Garrick rejected the new comedy, and there have been no recorded performances of it. Nor has any complete text of the work survived. A holograph manuscript of the first three acts was presented to the British Museum in November 1864 by Coventry Patmore;[43]

it is possible that this holograph represents an incomplete revision of the original play, and the hand may be that of Richard Brinsley Sheridan.[44] The manuscript fragment has been twice transcribed and published, most obscurely the first time by some anonymous person in 1890, and more conspicuously by W. Fraser Rae in his 1902 collection of *Sheridan's Plays*.[45] There have been no other appearances of the play in print.

We have used the manuscript as our text, but have collated it with Rae's transcription. This seemed a necessary check, as the holograph is at times quite illegible and very difficult to read. In his generally faithful transcription, Rae inadvertently introduced a number of significant errors, and we have tried to avoid similar lapses. Rae did not attempt to regularize punctuation or spelling, both of which are generally inconsistent in the manuscript. We have on the whole followed a similar policy. But as the original punctuation often gives rise to ambiguities of interpretation we have, much more freely than in our handling of the other two plays, silently introduced on occasion a necessary comma or semicolon or stop. We have usually avoided modernizing the spelling, for meaning is almost always clear despite the author's erratic orthographic habits. For some few words, such as *would, could, should, don't,* and *won't,* which are written in various ways in the manuscript, we have always chosen the modern spelling.

Frances Sheridan and her printers were most inconsistent in their manner of presenting stage directions, indicating asides, and making transitions from scene to scene. To avoid the confusion that occasionally results from such inconsistency, we have regularized all of these matters of form.

The texts are annotated sparingly throughout. Mrs. Sheridan is an editor's delight. She avoids pedantry in her works, she favors language as simple as it is crisp and clear, and she is among the least allusive of eighteenth-century playwrights. Obscure words and obsolete usages are explained in the annotations, as are the occasional literary references and quotations with which the characters indulge themselves.

THE PLAYS

The Discovery

A Comedy

PROLOGUE[1]

A Female culprit at your bar appears,
   Not destitute of hope, nor free from fears.
Her utmost crime she's ready to confess,
A simple trespass—neither more nor less;
For, truant-like, she rambled out of bounds,
And dar'd to venture on poetic grounds.
   The fault is deem'd high-treason by the men,
Those lordly tyrants who usurp the pen!
Then try the vile monopoly to hide
With flattering arts, 'You, ladies, have beside
'So many ways to conquer—sure 'tis fit
'You leave to us that dangerous weapon wit!'
For women, like state criminals, they think
Should be debarr'd the use of pen and ink.
   Our author, who disclaims such partial laws,
To her own sex appeals to judge her cause.
She pleads old magna charta on her side,
That British subjects by their peers be try'd.
   Ladies, to you she dedicates her lays,
Assert your right to censure or to praise;
Nor doubt a sentence by such lips decreed,
Firm as the laws of Persian or of Mede:
Boldly your will in open court declare,
And let the men dispute it if they dare.
   Our humble scenes no charms of art can boast,
But simple nature, and plain sense at most:
Perhaps some character—a moral too—
And what is stranger still—the story's new:
No borrow'd thoughts throughout the piece are shewn,
But what our author writes is all her own.
   By no sly hint, or incident she tries
To bid on modest cheeks the blush arise:
The loosest thoughts our decent scenes suggest,
Virtue herself might harbour in her breast;
And where our harmless satire vents its spleen,
The soberest prude may laugh, without a skreen.
But not to mirth alone we claim your ear,
Some tender scenes demand the melting tear;
The comic dame, her different powers to prove,
Gives you the dear variety you love;
Sometimes assumes her graver sister's art,
Borrows her form, and tries to touch the heart.

But fancy's pictures float upon the brain,
And short-liv'd o'er the heart is passion's reign,
Till judgement stamp her sanction on the whole,
And sink th'impression deep into the soul.—

PERSONS OF THE PLAY.²

MEN.

Lord Medway,	Mr. Sheridan.
Sir Anthony Branville,	Mr. Garrick.
Sir Harry Flutter,	Mr. Obrien.
Colonel Medway, Son to Lord Medway,	Mr. Holland.

WOMEN.

Lady Medway,	Mrs. Pritchard.
Lady Flutter, Niece to Sir Anthony,	Miss Pope.
Mrs. Knightly, a young Widow,	Mrs. Yates.
Miss Richly, her Sister,	Mrs. Palmer.
Louisa, Daughter to Lord Medway,	Miss Bride.

ACT I

Scene i. A Library.
Lord Medway reading at a Table. Enter Lady Medway.

LORD MEDWAY: How's this, madam? pursue me into my study! my sanctuary! I thought this place, at least, was to be considered by your Ladyship as inviolable.

LADY MEDWAY: I hope I don't interrupt you, my dear.

LORD MEDWAY: I should be glad, lady Medway, that we remember'd our respective bounds; I never intrude at your tea-table or toilet; and I desire my hours of retirement may be held as sacred by you.

LADY MEDWAY: I beg your pardon, my Lord, but indeed you have made me so exceedingly unhappy by this sudden resolution you have taken, in regard to marrying your daughter, that I can find rest no where.

LORD MEDWAY: And so you are come, like the evil spirit, to take possession of me, in order to make me as restless as yourself. I am really extremely obliged to your Ladyship; but you must know, Ma'am, I am of so strange a disposi-

tion, that I have an absolute dislike to the being made uneasy; and therefore shall take it as a favour, if you will either, at once, chearfully acquiesce in what I have determined, or else go, and display your plaintive eloquence to some one better disposed to sympathize with you than I am.

LADY MEDWAY: My Lord, you know your will has ever been a law to me; but I beg of you to consider the cruelty of forcing young people to marry against their inclinations.

LORD MEDWAY: Madam, I did not *expect* this idle opposition from you, especially when you know my motives to this marriage.

LADY MEDWAY: My Lord, you have not yet explained them to me; I can only guess at large.

LORD MEDWAY: You know I am harrassed with debts, and I now tell you, I don't know where to raise five hundred pounds more, if it would save me from perdition; and pray, let me ask your Ladyship, do you know any one besides Sir Anthony Branville, who will take your daughter without a fortune? for I neither am, nor probably ever shall be, able to give her one.

LADY MEDWAY: But Louisa is very young, my Lord; why need we be so precipitate? Besides, if this match between Mrs. Knightly and your son should take place, it will then be in your power to provide for your daughter.

LORD MEDWAY: Right *woman!*—a hint is but just started, and you pursue, run it down, and seize it at once. I have not yet proposed the thing to my son. Perhaps he may not like the lady when I do; and I presume you will think *his* inclinations as proper to be consulted, as those of the young lady his sister.

LADY MEDWAY: Certainly, my Lord.

LORD MEDWAY: O no doubt on't; love-matches against the world! **All you ladies, in this particular, are very ready to adhere to that christian precept, of doing as you would be done by:** and so I suppose, you, out of your maternal fondness, would recommend it to me to let Miss please herself in the choice of a husband, as her mama did before her.

LADY MEDWAY: That reproach from *you,* my Lord, is not kind—but I do not desire you to let her please herself in chusing one she likes, only do not force her to take one she hates.

LORD MEDWAY: Has she told you that she hates Sir Anthony?

LADY MEDWAY: Not in express words; but the repugnance she shews—

LORD MEDWAY: Perhaps she loves some one else.—

LADY MEDWAY: To tell you the truth, my Lord, I believe she does.

LORD MEDWAY: And she has made you the confidant of her tender passion.

LADY MEDWAY: I extorted something like a confession of this sort from her.

LORD MEDWAY: And pray who may be the happy man?

LADY MEDWAY: Young Branville, Sir Anthony's nephew, who is now on his travels, and is expected every day home.

LORD MEDWAY: A forward little gipsey—**This is the curse of marrying early, to have our children tugging at our purse-strings, at a time when we have as quick a relish for the joys of life as they have, and ten times a better capacity for pursuing them.**—Look'ee, Madam, I cannot give her a shilling; Sir Anthony is ready to take her as she is; and if they should have a family, is able to provide liberally for them all. On the contrary, if she follows her own soft inclinations, in marrying Mr. Branville, I suppose, in three or four years, I should have the pleasure of seeing myself a grand papa to two or three pretty little beggars, who, between their mother's vanity, and their father's poverty, may happen to continue so all their lives.

LADY MEDWAY: But, my Lord, as Sir Anthony has sent his nephew abroad at his own expence, it looks as if he meant to do something handsome for him: besides, he is his uncle's heir, in case he should die without children by marriage.

LORD MEDWAY: And so you think you can keep him in a state of celibacy, by refusing him your daughter—Oh fy, Lady Medway, I never heard you argue so weakly. Sir Anthony is not yet past the prime of life; besides, he has owned to me that it was his being discarded by Mrs. Knightly, which made him resolve, at once in a sort of pique, to marry the first girl that fell in his way; birth and reputation being all the fortune he desired with her. A man thus circumstanced is very little likely to continue a batchelor—No, no, I'll take him in the humour, and secure him while I may.

LADY MEDWAY: Before it be too late, my Lord, let me once more beseech you to reflect on the misery of a married life, where on either side love or esteem is wanting. Have we not a glaring instance of this in the house with us, in Sir Harry Flutter and his wife? are they not as wretched a pair as ever met in wedlock, perpetually quarrelling! I own, I almost repent my invitation to them, and wish them fairly back again in the country.

LORD MEDWAY [*Aside.*]: That must not be.—You have made a very unlucky choice in your example, Ma'am; a foolish boy, and a giddy girl, that know not either of them what they would be at. He married the wife his mother chose for him, to get rid of his tutor; and she took the husband her wise father provided for her, to escape from a boarding-school. What can be expected from two such simpletons? He, proud of the authority of a husband, exercises it from the same principle, and with pretty much the same capacity, that children show with regard to poor little animals that are in their power, in teazing and controlling them; and this he thinks makes him look manly.

LADY MEDWAY: So I imagine, for I have heard him say, he does no more than other husbands.

LORD MEDWAY: She, on the other hand, fancies the prerogatives of a wife consist in contradicting and opposing him; and this, I presume, she thinks is doing like other wives: but my life for it, when they know a little more of the world, they will be very happy.

LADY MEDWAY: Never in each other, I am afraid, my Lord.

LORD MEDWAY: And pray, Ma'am, let me ask you, what mighty felicity have you enjoyed, in being married to the man of your choice?

LADY MEDWAY: That is a strange question, my Lord! I never complained of my lot; but if I have not been completely happy, it is not owing to any fault of mine.

LORD MEDWAY: It may be mine for aught I know—but I only mention it, to shew you that *love* is not such an almighty deity, as to confer happiness without certain ingredients besides, that I could name.

LADY MEDWAY: **My Lord, where it is reciprocal, there wants not much besides.**

LORD MEDWAY: **Be sure you preach that wise doctrine to your daughter; it will become your prudence, and no doubt will be extremely agreeable to her pretty romantic notions**—But pr'ythee let us have done with the subject at once. One circumstance more, however, I shall acquaint you with; if the marriage between Medway and this Lady should be accomplished, I have other purposes to appropriate her fortune to, than buying a husband for your daughter—But this is only in speculation—the thing may never happen—for nothing but the last extremity should compel me to urge my son against his inclination. In regard to Louisa, in two words, I *will* be obeyed: do me the favour to tell her as much. I shall see her presently, and expect such an answer from her, as her duty shall dictate.

LADY MEDWAY: My Lord, it is an unpleasing task you have assign'd me, but I will obey you.

[*Exit Lady Medway.*]

LORD MEDWAY [*Looking after her.*]: *That* you have always done, so much praise I will allow you—but I am out of humour with every thing. If this boy should dislike the match, I am undone at once; and I fear, from some hints I have lately received, I shall find an obstacle in the way which will not easily be removed—**'Sdeath! what a thing it is to have poverty staring a man in the face, and no way to keep the horrid spectre from laying hold on you!**—No way but one; it all depends on Medway's filial duty—A thousand vexations crowd upon me together—'Tis a pretty time for a man to think of intriguing! and yet the blooming beauty of that little madcap, with all her childishness about her, has caught such hold on me, that I must have her—Oh with what alacrity now could I pursue the chace, if my thoughts were a little more disengaged!—She has been complaining to my wife of her husband's ill usage of her; and he, I suppose, will come to me presently, to take a lesson, as he calls it, to enable him to use her worse—he shan't want my assistance—and here he comes to receive it.

Scene ii.
Enter Sir Harry Flutter.

SIR HARRY: Oh my dear Lord!

LORD MEDWAY: Why you seem out of breath, Sir Harry; what is the matter?

SIR HARRY: Upon my soul, my Lord, I have been so stunn'd this morning, with the din of conjugal interrogatories, that I am quite bated—do, let me lounge a little on this couch of yours.

LORD MEDWAY: What, I suppose you were playing the rogue last night.

SIR HARRY: No faith, only at the tavern. I was at home before three o'clock, and yet my wife was such an unreasonable little devil, as to ask me forty questions about my staying out so late.

LORD MEDWAY: It's the way of them all—but I hope you are too well acquainted with your own prerogative, to give her any satisfaction on those accounts.

SIR HARRY: Satisfaction! ho catch me at that, and gibbet me—no, no—But pray now, my Lord, how would you behave on such an occasion? for I should be very glad to find that my conduct squared with yours.

LORD MEDWAY: Why—not roughly—you know that is not my way—it is not manly; besides, it would at once provoke, and justify your wife in her resentment.—But there is a sort of sneering, ironical treatment, that I never knew fail of nettling a woman to the quick; and the best of it is, the thing won't *bear* repetition; for let *them* deliver your very words, without the tone and air accompanying them, and there shall not appear the least harm in them.

SIR HARRY: Ay that, that's the secret I want to come at; that's the true art of tormenting, and what of all the talents your Lordship possesses, I envy you for the most—Heavens, how I have seen my Lady swell, and tears start into her eyes, when, devil take me if I thought you were not in perfect good humour all the while—Now I am rather petulant, flash, flash, flash, as quick as lightning, till I put my *self* into a confounded passion, when I only meant to vex *her*—Though I think I was rather temperate too, this morning.

LORD MEDWAY: How was it, let's hear?

SIR HARRY: Why, I came home at three o'clock, as I told you, a little tipsey too, by the by; but what was that to her, you know; for I am always good humoured in my cups? To bed I crept, as softly as a mouse, for I had no more thought of quarrelling with her then, than I have now with your Lordship—La, says she, with a great heavy sigh, it is a sad thing that one must be disturbed in this manner; and on she went, mutter, mutter, mutter, for a quarter of an hour; I all the while lying as quiet as a lamb, without making her a word of answer; at last, quite tired of her perpetual *buzzing* in my ear, Pr'ythee be quiet, Mrs. Wasp, says I, and let me sleep (I was not thoroughly awake when I spoke). Do so, Mr. *Drone,* grumbled she, and gave a great flounce. I said no more, for in two minutes I was as fast as a top. Just now, when I came down to breakfast, she was seated at the tea-table all alone, and looked so neat, and so cool, and so pretty, that e'gad, not thinking of what had passed, I was going to give her a kiss; when up she toss'd her demure little face, You were a pretty fellow last night, Sir Harry, says she. So I am every night, I hope, Ma'am, says I, making her a low bow. Was not that something in your manner, my Lord?

LORD MEDWAY: Oh very well, very well—

SIR HARRY: Pray where were you till that unconscionable hour, says she? At the tavern drinking, says I, very civilly. And who was with you, Sir? Oh, thought I, I'll match you for your enquiries; I nam'd your Lordship, and half a dozen more wild fellows (whom, by the way I had not so much as seen), and two or three girls of the town, added I, whistling, and looking another way—

LORD MEDWAY: That was rather a little, though but a little, too much.

SIR HARRY: Down she slap'd her cup and saucer; If this be the case, Sir Harry, (half sobbing) I shall desire a separate bed. That's as *I* please, Madam, sticking my hand in my side, and looking her full in the face. No, it shall be as *I* please, Sir—it *shan't,* Madam; it *shall,* Sir; and it shan't and it shall, and it shall and it shan't, was bandied backwards and forwards till we were both out of breath with passion. At last she said something to provoke me, I don't know what it was, but I answered her a little tartly. You would not have said it, I believe—I'd give the world for your command of temper—but it slip'd out, faith—

LORD MEDWAY: What was it?

SIR HARRY: Why, I said (for she vexed me cursedly) I said—faith, I think I— as good as told her she ly'd.

LORD MEDWAY: Oh fy!

SIR HARRY: She burst out a crying, I kick'd down the tea-table, and away I scamper'd up to your Lordship, to receive advice and consolation.

LORD MEDWAY: Why really, Sir Harry, I pity you; to be ty'd to such a little termagant is the devil; but 'tis the fortune of wedlock. One thing I have always observed; the more a husband submits, the more a wife tyrannizes. 'Twas my own case at first; but I was soon obliged to alter my course, and by exerting myself a little, I brought Lady Medway to be as well-behaved, I think, as any woman of quality in town.

SIR HARRY: So she is, upon my word, my Lord; I'd change with you with all my heart, if my Lady were a little younger. Duce take me but I wish we were like the Spartans; I assure you, if their laws were in force here, my wife should be at your service, and I dare say I should be as welcome to yours.

LORD MEDWAY: Oh undoubtedly, Sir Harry!

SIR HARRY: The women would like it vastly—your wife and mine I mean.

LORD MEDWAY: How do you know that?

SIR HARRY: Why I know mine doesn't care sixpence for me, and I suppose it may be pretty much the same with yours, and with all of them for that matter.

LORD MEDWAY: That doesn't follow—but how do you intend to act with regard to Lady Flutter? I suppose this little breach will be made up like all the rest.

SIR HARRY: Not by me, I assure you, my Lord; I don't intend to speak to her to-day; and when I do, she shall ask my pardon before I forgive her.

LORD MEDWAY: Poh, that's children's play, fall out, and then pray, pray, kiss and be friends. No, Sir Harry, if you would shew yourself a man, and a husband, let her see that you despise her little girlish petulance, by taking no farther notice of it. Now, were I in your case, I'd behave just as if nothing at all had happened. If she pouts, smile; and ask her how she likes your new sword-knot, or the point in your ruffles, or any other idle question. You know she must give you an answer. If it be a peevish one, laugh in her face, take up your hat, and wish her a good morning; if, on the contrary, she speaks with good humour, seem not to hear her, but walk about the room, repeating verses. Then, as if you had not observed her before, Did you speak to me, Lady Flutter? but without waiting for her reply, slide out of the room, humming a tune—Now all this, you see, were she to relate it, will not have the appearance of ill treatment; and yet, my life for yours, it humbles her more than all the blustering airs you could put on.

SIR HARRY: I am sure you are right, my Lord. The case is plain; but the difficulty is in executing the thing properly, I am so warm in my temper. Oh what would I give for your glorious cool sneer of contempt!—I'll try for it positively; and 'egad I'll now go to her and make the experiment; and so, my Lord, adieu for the present, and thanks for this lesson.

LORD MEDWAY: Sir Harry! do you dine at home to-day?

SIR HARRY: I don't know how that may be till I have reconnoitred; your Lordship, I know, does not—and I hate to dine alone with the women.

LORD MEDWAY: Oh, I shall certainly be at home soon after dinner, for I shall long to know on what terms you and my Lady may be by that time.

SIR HARRY: Oh heaven knows—we may be at cuffs by that time, perhaps; but I shall be in the way.

[*Exit Sir Harry.*]

LORD MEDWAY: If he follows my advice, I think she must hate him heartily—and then I step in as her comforter—But I have other business to mind at present—so many projects on foot without a certainty of accomplishing one of them—Z—ns, if I had not the firmness of a Stoic, I should beat my own brains out.

[*Exit.*]

Scene iii.　Changes to a Chamber.
Lady Medway and Louisa.

LADY MEDWAY: My dear, it afflicts me as much as it does you; but you know your papa is absolute: I wish, therefore, you would endeavour to reconcile yourself to Sir Anthony.

LOUISA: Indeed, Madam, it is impossible! If my heart were ever so much at liberty, it never could endure that forbidding man.

LADY MEDWAY: But, child, you are too much governed by fancy;—tho' he is not quite in the bloom of youth, yet he is far from being disagreeable. What is it you so much dislike in him?

LOUISA: Dear Madam! sure the pomp and strange turn of his phrases, and the solemnity of his manner, is almost ridiculous.

LADY MEDWAY: He is rather formal, I allow you.

LOUISA: And then his notions of love so extravagant, his address so romantic, nothing but flames and rapture in his mouth, and, according to my brother's account of him, he has no more real warmth than a marble statue.

LADY MEDWAY: You find he lov'd Mrs. Knightly.

LOUISA: His peculiarities diverted her, Madam, and she indulged him in them—I am told he used to sigh at her feet for half a day, and if he committed the smallest fault, she would impose a pennance on him, which Sir Anthony always received as a mark of favour.

LADY MEDWAY: I am sorry, my dear, it is not more agreeable to you; for I am commissioned to tell you, positively, you *must* accept of him for a husband.

LOUISA: But, Madam, he has never spoken a word to me on the subject—I have seen him but a few times, and—in short, I can't bear him.

LADY MEDWAY: Shall I tell your papa what you say? he, no doubt, will be perfectly satisfied with this determination.

LOUISA: Dear Madam! sure you will not. Save me from my papa's anger, you know I dare not open my heart to him. You (except in your maternal tenderness) are more like a companion to me than a parent. The authority of the mother is melted down in the kindness of the friend; my papa's severity had else been insupportable.

LADY MEDWAY: Louisa, you are not to give so harsh a name to your father's solicitude for your happiness. He is not to be shaken in his resolution. I have already exerted my utmost influence over him, and that I am sorry to say is less, much less, than it ought to be.—Hist!—I hear your father's voice below; he is coming up to you. I beg, my dear, you will let him see by your obedience, that my interposition has had its proper effect. I'll give you the opportunity to talk to him alone.

LOUISA: Dear madam, don't leave me—my papa is so stern.

LADY MEDWAY: I go to avoid ungrateful appeals from him. Consent with a good grace, Louisa, for 'tis certain you have no choice left.
[*Exit Lady Medway.*]

LOUISA: Heavens, what will become of me! [*She stands musing.*]

Scene iv.
Lord Medway enters, stops at the door, and looks at her,
she not observing him.

LORD MEDWAY [*Repeating affectedly.*]:

> On every hill, in every grove,
> Along the margin of each stream,
> Dear conscious scenes of former love—
> I mourn, and Damon is my theme.[3]

What is your pretty tender heart ruminating upon? your Damon, I suppose—were not you thinking of Mr. Branville?

LOUISA: No, my Lord.

LORD MEDWAY: I believe you don't tell truth, my Lady—look up, girl—Ah Louisa, Louisa, that conscious blush! but 'tis well you have the grace to be ashamed.

LOUISA: My Lord, if I do blush, I am not conscious of any cause, unless the fear of offending you.

LORD MEDWAY: Pretty innocent!—all obedience too, I warrant—I hate hypocrisy from my very soul; you know that you are a rebel in the bottom of your heart. Speak honestly now, would not you run away with Branville this very night, if it were in your power?

LOUISA: My Lord, I—I—

LORD MEDWAY: My Lord, I—I—, speak out, mistress.

LOUISA: If I had your permission, my Lord, I own I should be—inclined to prefer him to—any other.

LORD MEDWAY: Thou prevaricating monkey—dissemblers too from the very egg. And *without* my permission, miss; what answer does your modesty and filial piety suggest to that?

LOUISA: That without it, I will never marry any one.

LORD MEDWAY: I don't believe one syllable of that; but I take you at your word; and now I tell you that you never shall have it to marry *him*—How does your love-sick heart relish that?

LOUISA: My Lord, I am resign'd to your pleasure.

[*She curtsies and offers to go, he bows and lets her walk to the door.*]

LORD MEDWAY: Now Ma'am—walk back if you please—for I have not done with you yet. [*She comes back.*]—**Whither were you swimming with that sweet languishing air, like an Arcadian princess?**

LOUISA: I was going to my chamber, my Lord, if you had not forbid it.

LORD MEDWAY: Forbid! fy, what an ungenteel word to use towards a heroine in romance! There are some surly fathers, indeed, who take those liberties with their children, but I, who know breeding better, only intreat; and therefore, ma'am, beg the favour of your company a little longer; if a mind dignified by the noble passion of love, can condescend to the admonitions of a parent— What does the fool hang her head for? Sit down there—What, you are going to faint, I hope—Oh I d—y—e! I ex-*pire*—Branville take my last adieu—Here, Betty, some hartshorn for the despairing nymph, quickly— your lady is dying for love.—So, so, so, the sluice is let out at last.—

So lillies look surcharg'd with morning dew![4]

You really look very pretty when you cry, Louisa, I had a mind to see how it would become you.

LOUISA: Indeed, my Lord, you are too hard upon me.

LORD MEDWAY: How now, mistress! how dare you speak thus? What do you call a hardship? Love makes some timorous animals bold, they say; it makes women so with a vengeance.

LOUISA: My Lord, I beg your permission to withdraw.

LORD MEDWAY: Stay where you are, madam.—When I condescend to talk with you, methinks you ought to know, 'tis your duty to attend to what I have to say. You know my mind already in regard to young Branville.— **Ay, sigh on—fy, fy, do those glowing aspirations become a young lady educated as you have been? Your mother, I am sure, has always set you a good example. I was no pattern for you to follow.**—But observe what I say; I forbid you to think, but even to think, of Branville. That is the first, and perhaps the hardest part of my command. The next is, that you resolve immediately to accept of Sir Anthony for your husband. And now, miss, you may, if you please, retire to your chamber, and, in plaintive strains, either in verse or prose, bemoan your hard fate; and be sure you complain to your waiting-woman what a tyrant you have to your father.—Go, get you gone. [*Exit Louisa.*]

This is the plague of having daughters; no sooner out of their leading-strings than in love, forsooth.

Scene v.
Enter Colonel Medway.

LORD MEDWAY: Oh George, I am glad you are come; that foolish girl has ruffled me so, I want relief from my own thoughts.

COLONEL MEDWAY: I met my sister in tears—I hope, my Lord, she has done nothing to disoblige you.

LORD MEDWAY: Oh a mere trifle—only confessed a passion for a fellow not worth sixpence but what depends on the caprice of a relation, and, like a prudent as well as dutiful child, has shewn a thorough dislike of her father's choice.

COLONEL MEDWAY: My Lord, she will consider better of it; I am sure my sister would willingly obey you in every thing.

LORD MEDWAY: To what purpose is a father's sollicitude for the welfare of his children, if a perverse silly girl will counter-act all his projects?—You, Medway, have ever shewn yourself an affectionate, as well as an obedient son, to a parent who confesses himself, with regard to you, not one of the most provident—I wish I could make you amends.

COLONEL MEDWAY: My Lord, the tenderness you have always shewn me, deserved every return I could make you.—I wish for no other amends but to see you easy in your mind and in your circumstances.

LORD MEDWAY: That's well said! but I expected as much from you. Suppose, now, that it were in your power to make me easy in both, and at the same time effectually to serve yourself.

COLONEL MEDWAY: I wish it were, my Lord, you should see my readiness to embrace the opportunity—But I am afraid there is nothing now in my power.

LORD MEDWAY: Oh you are mistaken, there are ways and means to retrieve all; and it was on this subject I wanted to talk with you—There is a certain lady of fortune, son—What! droop at the very mention of her? that's an ill omen.

COLONEL MEDWAY: My Lord, I doubt my fortune never *can* be mended by those means.

LORD MEDWAY: No! Suppose the widow Knightly, with a real estate of three thousand a year, and a personal one of fifty thousand pounds, should have taken a fancy to you, would not that be a means?—You blush; perhaps you are already acquainted with the lady's passion.

COLONEL MEDWAY: My Lord, I am glad to see you so pleasant.

LORD MEDWAY: I am serious, I assure you—Why is there any thing so extraordinary in a woman's falling in love with a handsome young fellow?

COLONEL MEDWAY: My Lord, if the Lady has really done me that honour, 'tis more than I deserve; for I never made the least advances.

LORD MEDWAY: Well; but how do you like her?

COLONEL MEDWAY: She is genteel, I think—I really never examined her features.

LORD MEDWAY: That's strange! Why you visit her sometimes I find.

COLONEL MEDWAY: I go to her house, my Lord; but 'tis her younger sister whom I visit.

LORD MEDWAY: Humph—What sort of a damsel is she?

COLONEL MEDWAY: A most angelic creature.

LORD MEDWAY: Ay! then it seems you *have* examined *her* features?

COLONEL MEDWAY: My Lord, I have known her long. Miss Richly, who as well as her sister was born abroad, was sent hither some years since for her education, and *I* became acquainted with her in the house of a friend of mine with whom she lived. Mrs. Knightly, who had married an English merchant, was then settled at Lisbon, and knew but little of her sister, till lately; when, having lost her husband, she came to England, and took the young Lady under her own care.

LORD MEDWAY: So! I perceive you know their history.

COLONEL MEDWAY: I do, my Lord. Poor Miss Richly's part of it is a melancholy one; for her father was so partial to his eldest daughter, that he left her by much the greatest portion of his estate; and what the youngest had to her share, she had the misfortune to lose, by the breaking of a merchant, in whose hands her money lay.

LORD MEDWAY: You are better informed than I am, I find—Well, but what do you think of Mrs. Knightly?

COLONEL MEDWAY: Think, my Lord! I really don't know what to think. The Lady is very deserving, but—

LORD MEDWAY: But! oh those damned *Buts!* Am I to be *butted* by you all, one after the other? There's your mother first, to be sure she is very ready to acquiesce in every thing that I approve, *but* she thinks it hard a young creature should have any force put on her inclinations, though it be for her own good—Then Miss Louisa—she is all obedience and submission—*but, alas! she* has given away her heart already—And you, *you* too are perfectly disposed to oblige me; *but* you will chuse for yourself, I presume, notwithstanding.

COLONEL MEDWAY: My Lord, you really distress me, by entertaining the least doubt of that reverence I ever have borne towards you, and ever will bear; but in a case like this (pardon me, my Lord,) I cannot at once give up all that I have now left, or can claim a right in the disposal of, my honour and my love—I own I love Miss Richly, have loved her long; and if virtue, beauty, and unaffected innocence, deserve a heart, my Lord, she has a claim to mine, and is, I confess, intire mistress of it; yet I wish the evil (since it is one) had stopped there—but—

LORD MEDWAY: But what?

COLONEL MEDWAY: My Lord, she loves me too.

LORD MEDWAY: I am sorry for it—Oh, son, son, a pretty face will not redeem our acres.

COLONEL MEDWAY: I never till now lamented her want of fortune, which I knew indeed from the beginning; but still hoped that I might one day be in a condition to support her, as her own merit, and my rank required. I even flattered myself that I should obtain your consent.

LORD MEDWAY: What! to marry a beggar, Medway?

COLONEL MEDWAY: I beg, my Lord, you will not use so harsh a word. She is worthy of higher, much higher dignity, than ever I could raise her to— What is a title, my Lord, stripped as I am of every thing besides?

LORD MEDWAY: That reproach is ungenerous, Medway; but I have deserved it.

COLONEL MEDWAY: Forgive me, my Lord, I meant it not as such.

LORD MEDWAY: If you *had,* I could forgive it—but we will say no more on the subject. I will not urge you on so tender a point.

COLONEL MEDWAY: My Lord, I thank you.

LORD MEDWAY: Answer me but one question: Are you under a promise to marry Miss Richly?

COLONEL MEDWAY: No, my Lord, her generosity would not suffer her to let me bind myself by any other tie than that of inclination, as I insisted on *her* being free.

LORD MEDWAY: That's well—Then I do not see how your *honour* is so much concerned; as for your love, when I was of your age, Medway, I had so many *loves,* that it was hard to tell which of them had the best claim.

COLONEL MEDWAY: My Lord, you were so kind as to promise you would insist no farther on the subject.

LORD MEDWAY: Well, well, I have done—I'll detain you no longer. Some business calls me out at present; I shall see you in the evening.

COLONEL MEDWAY: My Lord, I'll attend you. [*Colonel bows and exit.*]

LORD MEDWAY: The firmness of this young man's virtue awes me. I know in point of interest with regard to himself at least, it will be impossible to prevail on him to think of this marriage—and the obligations he has already laid me under, will not suffer me to make, on my *own* account, so severe a trial of the tenderness and generosity of his heart—Let it go; I'll think no more of it. [*Exit.*]

END OF ACT I

ACT II

Scene i. A Dressing-room.
Sir Harry Flutter, as just dressed, a servant attending.

SIR HARRY: Is your Lady come in, can you tell?

SERVANT: My Lady did not go out at all, Sir.

SIR HARRY: Not at all! Why I understood she dined abroad.

SERVANT: No, Sir, I believe she only ordered Mrs. Betty to say so for an excuse, because she had no mind to come down to dinner.

SIR HARRY: Was that all?—Then do you step to her, and tell her I desire to speak with her—On very particular business tell her. [*Exit Servant.*] Now to put my lesson in practice—If I can but hit on the manner—I'll pretend not to see her at first—But if she should not come now—'egad, that would disconcert the whole plan—Yes, faith, here she is; her curiosity, nothing else I am sure, has brought her.

[*Enter Lady Flutter, with knotting in her hand.*]

LADY FLUTTER [*Sullenly.*]: What do you want with me, Sir Harry?

SIR HARRY: *I* want with you, Lady Flutter! I never wanted any thing with you in my life, that I know of.

LADY FLUTTER: Why didn't you send for me this minute, and say you had particular business? I should not have been so ready to come else, I assure you.

SIR HARRY [*Aside.*]: 'Egad, I believe I am wrong at setting out; it should have all been done as if by chance. What shall I say to her now!—How do you like this suit of cloaths, my dear? Don't you think it very elegant?

LADY FLUTTER: Was that all the business you had with me?

[*She offers to go.*]

SIR HARRY: Ma'am, I insist on your not going till you answer my question; just how you please now, civilly or uncivilly; I am prepared for either, I can tell you.

LADY FLUTTER: And so, Sir Harry, I suppose you think, with those airs, to carry off your behaviour to me this morning, do you?

SIR HARRY:

Ye gods, ye gave to me a wife,
Out of your grace and favour—[5]
[*He walks about.*]

LADY FLUTTER: But I can tell you, Sir, I won't bear such treatment, to be drawn off and on like your glove.

SIR HARRY: Are you speaking to me, Ma'am?

LADY FLUTTER: To whom else should I speak?

SIR HARRY: I protest I did not know you were in the room, child.

LADY FLUTTER: Oh ridiculous affectation—Child! I'll assure you.

SIR HARRY [*Aside.*]: Oh now it begins to work, if I can but keep cool.—

But if your providence divine
For greater bliss design her,
To obey your will, at any time
I am ready to resign her.[6]

LADY FLUTTER: Absurd!

SIR HARRY [*Going up close to her.*]: To resign her, to resign her.

LADY FLUTTER [*Pushing him from her.*]: Stupid!

SIR HARRY: Ay, Madam!

LADY FLUTTER: Ay, indeed, Sir.

SIR HARRY: Retire to your chamber, Madam, directly, instantly; and let me inform you, once for all, that you are not to take the liberty of coming into my dressing-room—A man's serious hours are not to be broke in upon by female impertinence.

LADY FLUTTER: A man's? Ha, ha, ha—

SIR HARRY: Those flippant airs don't become you in the least, Ma'am; but I don't think a silly girl worth my serious resentment—Retire with your trumpery work—I chuse to be alone.

LADY FLUTTER: Then I'll stay to vex you.

SIR HARRY: Then, Ma'am, I must teach you the obedience that is due to the commands of a husband.

LADY FLUTTER: A husband! Oh gracious, defend me from such a husband—A battledore and shittlecock[7] would be fitter for you than a wife, I fancy.

SIR HARRY: And let me tell your pertness, a doll would be properer for you than a husband—there's for you, Miss.

LADY FLUTTER: You'll be a boy all your life, Sir Harry.

SIR HARRY: And you'll be a fool all your life, Lady Snap.[8]

LADY FLUTTER: I shall be the fitter company for you then.

SIR HARRY: Tchou, tchou, tchou. [*Jeering her.*]

LADY FLUTTER: You are vastly polite, Sir—Did you ever see Lord Medway behave thus to his Lady?

SIR HARRY: And did you ever see Lady Medway behave thus to her Lord, if you go to that? Rat me but a man had better be a galley-slave, than married to a simpleton that ought to be sewing her sampler.

LADY FLUTTER: And I'll swear a woman had better be a ballad-singer, than joined to a Jack-a-dandy,[9] that ought to have a satchel at his back.

SIR HARRY: Devil take me but I have a good mind to break every bit of the china you bought this morning.

LADY FLUTTER: Do, do, do, and make taws[10] of them to play with.

SIR HARRY: A provoking, impertinent little—

LADY FLUTTER: How dare you call me names, Sir? I won't be called names, I'll tell my papa of this, so I will.

SIR HARRY: Pretty baby, laugh and cry—

[*Enter Lord Medway.*]

[*Sir Harry aside to Lady Flutter.*] For shame, wipe your eyes, don't let him see you thus.

LADY FLUTTER: I don't care who sees me; I'll bear it no longer. I'll write to my papa to send for me—I'll go to my uncle Branville's this very night.

LORD MEDWAY: Lady Flutter! I am sorry to see you in tears, Madam, I did not know you had been at home—Sir Harry, I ask your pardon, perhaps I intrude—no afflicting news, I hope.

SIR HARRY: News! no no, there is nothing *new* in the case, I assure you, my Lord.

LORD MEDWAY: Then, Sir Harry, I am afraid you are in fault here.

LADY FLUTTER [*Sobbing.*]: Indeed, my Lord, he is always in fault.

SIR HARRY: If your Lordship will take *her* word for it.

LORD MEDWAY: I should be glad to mediate between you, but I really don't know how, unless I were informed of your cause of quarrel.

SIR HARRY: I'll tell you, my Lord—

LADY FLUTTER: No, I'll tell him, Sir—

SIR HARRY: Lookye there now.

LADY FLUTTER: He sent for me, my Lord—

SIR HARRY: Not I, indeed, my Lord.

LADY FLUTTER: I say you did, Sir Harry, in purpose to teize me, and talk nonsense to me—

LORD MEDWAY: Oh fy, Sir Harry, could you find no better entertainment for your Lady, than talking nonsense?—[*Aside to him.*] This is a sad account.

SIR HARRY: Faith, my Lord, a man must unbend sometimes, and indulge in a little foolery—Life would be tedious else.

LADY FLUTTER: And there he went on, repeating silly verses, to shew he wanted to get rid of me.

SIR HARRY: Mere raillery, my Lord; but *she* does not understand it.

LADY FLUTTER: I should not have minded that so much neither, for I could be even with him in his gibing airs, if he had not at last call'd me names, downright abusive names, my Lord: But I'll put an end to it at once. [*She goes to the glass drying her eyes.*]

LORD MEDWAY [*Aside to Sir Harry.*]: All wrong—all wrong—was this the advice I gave you?

SIR HARRY: My Lord, you can't imagine how provoking she was.

LADY FLUTTER: I dare say, my papa will be very ready to take me home again.

LORD MEDWAY [*Aside to Sir Harry.*]: This must not be; yet don't *you* condescend to desire her to stay, *I*'ll try to persuade her.

SIR HARRY: Ough she's a vixen!

[*Lady Flutter rings a bell.*]

LORD MEDWAY [*Aside to Sir Harry.*]: I'll establish your empire, I'll engage, if you will give me the opportunity of talking with her.

SIR HARRY [*Aside to Lord Medway.*]: Faith I wish you would, for I am almost tired of the struggle.

[*Enter a Servant.*]

LADY FLUTTER: Are my chairmen in the way?

SERVANT: I'll see, Madam.

LADY FLUTTER: If they are, order them to get ready.

[*Exit Servant.*]

LORD MEDWAY: Going a visiting so soon, Lady Flutter?

LADY FLUTTER: Only to my uncle Branville's, my Lord; it is proper to acquaint him with my design.

LORD MEDWAY [*Aside to Sir Harry.*]: Make some excuse quickly to leave us, or all will be over.

SIR HARRY: I will—you shall see—Bless me! Well, I am sure-*ly* the most thoughtless fellow breathing. [*Sir Harry takes out his pocket-book, and turns over the leaves.*] My Lord, can you forgive my rudeness now, if I run away from you? I must shew you the nature of my engagement tho', and that, I hope, will be some apology—Wednesday, half an hour after five— you see—it's almost that already—

LORD MEDWAY: Humph!

SIR HARRY: Perhaps I mayn't stay long—I am very sorry to leave your Lordship alone tho'; but you'll forgive me.

[*Exit Sir Harry without looking at Lady Flutter.*]

LORD MEDWAY [*Half aside.*]: Leave me alone! 'Twere well if you were going to half as good company as that in which you leave me.

LADY FLUTTER [*Turning about.*]: What does your Lordship say?

LORD MEDWAY: Nothing, Ma'am, but that I can excuse Sir Harry's going, as he leaves me in such good company.

LADY FLUTTER: Oh, my Lord, *I* am no-body in Sir Harry's opinion; but indeed, at present, I should be but a very dull companion to any one; so I am sure your Lordship will excuse me if I take my leave.

LORD MEDWAY: A quarter of an hour, I hope, Ma'am, will not break in too much upon your time.

[*Enter a Servant.*]

SERVANT: My master is gone out in your chair, Madam; he said you might take the chariot; will your Ladyship please to have it ordered?

LADY FLUTTER: Gone out in my chair! See there my Lord! did you ever know the like? I won't have the chariot—call me a hackney chair. [*Exit Servant.*] Pray, my Lord, where is he gone? I saw he shewed you his memorandum.

LORD MEDWAY: Gone! on business, I think, of some kind.

LADY FLUTTER: Business! I don't know of any business that he has; I am sure it is some other engagement.

LORD MEDWAY: Oh—what am I thinking of? 'tis to the play.

LADY FLUTTER: The play! he could not have been in such a hurry for that, 'tis too early.

LORD MEDWAY: He was to go with a party, and to call on some people by the way; that was the case.

LADY FLUTTER: I don't much care; but I am sure that was not the thing neither; for I heard you say, it were well if he were going to half as good company, as that in which he left you.

LORD MEDWAY: And that I should certainly say, Ma'am, let him be going to whom he would. But Sir Harry has a depraved taste.

LADY FLUTTER: I don't doubt but he is going to some of his tavern-ladies. With all my heart; I don't love him well enough to be jealous of him.

LORD MEDWAY [*Aside.*]: I wish you did, for that would help on my work.— Why, indeed, my dear Lady Flutter, I can't say that Sir Harry is *quite* so deserving of you, as I could wish he were. But he is a mere boy, and can't be supposed to be so sensible of your merit, as those are, who have had a little more experience in the sex.

LADY FLUTTER: I shan't be long with him, that's one comfort.

LORD MEDWAY: But, my dear ma'am, consider how that will appear in the eyes of the world. Here you are but a little while married, what must people think of a separation? Your good understanding is unquestioned, your personal accomplishments admired by all who know you; the blame then must all fall on poor Sir Harry.

LADY FLUTTER: And so let it for me.

LORD MEDWAY: He deserves it, I confess; but, ma'am, give me leave to reason with you a little now; for I know you are a woman of sense, and capable of reasoning. Don't you think a *leetle* stroke of censure may possibly glance on you, for not endeavouring to bear, for a while longer at least, with his indiscretion; for every-body knows that your prudence is much superior to his, and therefore more will be expected from you.

LADY FLUTTER: My Lord, you compliment now.

LORD MEDWAY: Upon my life I don't. I am sure I have said it a thousand times, that I don't know a woman of fashion in town (a handsome one I mean, you are to take that into the account too) with half your talents.

LADY FLUTTER: Oh, my Lord!

LORD MEDWAY: Upon my word I am serious; and between ourselves, Sir Harry is thought to be but of very moderate parts, and that it was almost a sacrifice to marry you to him—But I would not say this for the world to any one but you.

LADY FLUTTER: That is very good of you, my Lord.

LORD MEDWAY: Your discretion, I am sure, will make a proper use of the hint. There are great allowances to be made for a raw young fellow, who, like some vain and ignorant virtuoso, is possessed of a rarity, of which he neither understands the nature, nor knows the value. Oh, Lady Flutter, a beautiful and accomplished woman is a gem fit only for the cabinet of a man of sense and taste.

[*Enter a Servant.*]

SERVANT: Madam, the chair is ready.

LADY FLUTTER: Let it wait awhile.

LORD MEDWAY [*Aside.*]: Another sip of that sweet cordial flattery, and all the rougher passions will subside.

LADY FLUTTER: What were you saying, my Lord?

LORD MEDWAY: I believe I was saying, or at least I was thinking, that you are—

LADY FLUTTER: What, now?

LORD MEDWAY: A charming woman—taking you all together—

LADY FLUTTER: Poh! fiddle, faddle—

LORD MEDWAY: Indeed you are!

LADY FLUTTER: Well, that is nothing to the purpose—What would you advise me to do with this foolish boy; for I would not have my discretion called in question neither? I am sure if he had but the sense to talk to me as you have done, he might do just what he pleased with me.

LORD MEDWAY: Amiable creature!—Well, what-ever you do, don't think of parting from him, for that would only be making mirth for all the spiteful old maids in town; who have already prophesied, that miss and master would quarrel before a month was at an end, and each run home crying to their several mama's.

LADY FLUTTER: Do the malicious creatures say so! Well, I'll disappoint them in that—But what can I do, my lord, he is so intolerably conceited and pert.

LORD MEDWAY: Oh don't mind him, and it will wear off by degrees! But, my dear Lady Flutter, are there not other pleasures with which a fine woman could make herself amends, for the ill humour of her husband?

LADY FLUTTER: Not that I know of, my Lord—[*Sighs.*]

LORD MEDWAY: I could name you some, if you would give me leave—

LADY FLUTTER: You have my leave, indeed, my Lord—My stars, what a charming thing good sense and good nature is! Your conversation has, I don't know how, soothed me so, that, tho' I am not happy, yet I don't find myself so much out of temper as I was a while ago.

LORD MEDWAY: Oh that Sir Harry and I could change situations, then would the loveliest woman in England be the happiest. [*He kisses her hand.*]

LADY FLUTTER: Lard! my Lord, what's that for?

[*Enter a Servant.*]

SERVANT: Sir Anthony Branville, Madam, comes to wait on your Ladyship.

LADY FLUTTER: Oh I am glad of that—shew him up. .

LORD MEDWAY [*Aside.*]: So am not I.

LADY FLUTTER: You know, my Lord, it will save me the trouble of going to his house this evening.

LORD MEDWAY: Let me beg of you, my dear Lady Flutter, not to mention to

your uncle any thing that has passed between you and Sir Harry. I'll give
you many good reasons for it another time. Have I so much influence over
you?

LADY FLUTTER: Well, my Lord, to oblige you, I won't.

LORD MEDWAY: Sweet condescending creature!

LADY FLUTTER: But you must tell me what you promised.

LORD MEDWAY: Not now, my dear ma'am—Some other opportunity I will
tell you *such* things—

[*Enter Sir Anthony Branville. He bows very low to both, without speaking.*]

LADY FLUTTER: Uncle, your servant.

LORD MEDWAY: Sir Anthony, your most obedient.

SIR ANTHONY: My Lord (without a compliment) I esteem myself extremely
happy, in the agreeable hope, that I now see your Lordship in perfect
health.

LORD MEDWAY: I thank you, good Sir Anthony, pretty well. [*Aside.*]
Heavens! what a circumlocution, to ask a man how he does!

SIR ANTHONY: And you, niece, I assure you, have a very proper proportion
(as undoubtedly your merit claims) of my unfeigned esteem and good
wishes; as likewise hath my worthy nephew, Sir Harry; whom I should
have been proud to have found in this good company, and deem both
myself and him unfortunate in his being absent from it.

LADY FLUTTER [*Half aside.*]: Sir Harry does'nt think so, I believe.

LORD MEDWAY [*Aside to her.*]: Hush—hush.

SIR ANTHONY: What does my niece Flutter say?

LADY FLUTTER: Nothing, uncle.

SIR ANTHONY: Pardon me; I apprehended you had utter*ed* something. Well,
my Lord, I am next to enquire (tho', to say the truth, I ought, in point of
good breeding, to have done it first); I am next, I say, to enquire how your
excellent Lady does, and the fair young Lady your daughter.

LORD MEDWAY: Both at your service, Sir Anthony.

SIR ANTHONY: May I presume to ask the christian name of the *young* Lady.

LORD MEDWAY: I would not have Lady Medway hear you make so *emphat-
ical* a distinction, Sir Anthony; ladies you know are always young—

SIR ANTHONY: 'Tis a privilege I know they claim, my Lord, and I hope you
don't think me capable of such barbarism as to dispute it with them; but at
the same time I imagine 'tis not possible in nature, but that the mother
must be rather older than her daughter—You'll excuse my pleasantry.

LORD MEDWAY: Oh surely, as the ladies are n't by—But why do you enquire
my daughter's name, Sir Anthony?

SIR ANTHONY: Why, my Lord, there is a pretty fa-miliar tenderness in
sometimes using the chris-*ti*-an name, that is truly delightful to a lover; for
such, my Lord, with all due deference to the Lady's high deserts, I wish
myself to be considered.

LADY FLUTTER [*Aside.*]: Oh Lord, Oh Lord, my uncle Miss Medway's
lover! I shall burst if I stay—

LORD MEDWAY: Louisa, Sir Anthony, is her christian's name, which you are
at liberty to use with as much familiar tenderness as you please.

SIR ANTHONY: My Lord, I have a most lively sense of the very great honour your Lordship does me; and I can assure you my heart, [*Sighs.*] if I can with certainty venture to pronounce about any thing which is in its own nature so uncertain—

LADY FLUTTER [*Aside.*]: Oh now he has got into his parenthesis—

SIR ANTHONY: My heart, I say, is endeavouring to reassume that liberty, of which it has so long been deprived, for no other purpose, than that of offering itself a willing captive again to the fair Louisa's charms.

LADY FLUTTER: *Very* well, uncle; I see this visit was not *all* intended for me; I find you have something to say to my Lord, so I won't interrupt you.

SIR ANTHONY: No, no, no, niece Flutter; upon my reputation, this visit was meant wholly for you, as I could not possibly divine that I should have found his Lordship with you; to whom I intended to have paid my respects separately and apart.

LORD MEDWAY: Lady Flutter! I ask a thousand pardons—We turn you out of your apartment—Sir Anthony, will you do me the favour to step into my study?

LADY FLUTTER: No, no, indeed you shan't stir; I'll go and see what the ladies are doing; I fancy they think I am lost. [*Exit Lady Flutter.*]

LORD MEDWAY: Sir Anthony, I assure you I should think myself very happy in an alliance with a gentleman of your worth.

SIR ANTHONY: My Lord, you do me honour.

LORD MEDWAY: I have mentioned you to my daughter—

SIR ANTHONY: Mentioned *me,* my Lord!

LORD MEDWAY: Wou'dn't you have had it so, Sir Anthony?

SIR ANTHONY: My Lord, the profound respect I have for your Lordship makes me unwilling to animadvert on such proceedings, as you in your wisdom (which I take to be very great) have thought expedient; but I am a man, my Lord, who love method.

LORD MEDWAY: Sir Anthony, I imagined it would have been agreeable to you, or it should have been very far—

SIR ANTHONY: Conceive me right, Lord Medway; 'tis perfectly agreeable to me, and consonant to my wishes, to be looked on with a favourable eye by the virtuous young Lady your daughter; but, my Lord, to tell you sincerely (and sincerity, my Lord, I hold to be a virtue) my heart is at present in a fluctuating state.

LORD MEDWAY: I am sorry then, Sir, that the thing has been mentioned at all. I understood you were determined. [*Aside.*] What can the blockhead mean?

SIR ANTHONY: Good my Lord, your patience: I *am* determined! that is to say, my *will* is determined; but the will and the heart, your Lordship knows, are two very different things.

LORD MEDWAY: Sir Anthony, I should be glad we understood each other at once. I apprehended Mrs. Knightly's ill usage of you had made you give up all thoughts of her; and as you seemed determined to marry, and declared yourself an admirer of my daughter, who I must say (the article of fortune excepted) is, I think, as unobjectionable a wife as you could chuse—

SIR ANTHONY: Undoubtedly, my Lord—

LORD MEDWAY: I was willing to give my consent, and thought you appeared as ready to embrace it.

SIR ANTHONY: True, my Lord; and so I do still, most cordially.

LORD MEDWAY: Why then, Sir, what is your determination? For a young woman of family and reputation must not be trifled with.

SIR ANTHONY: My Lord, I believe *trifling* is a fault which was never yet attributed to Sir Anthony Branville—My Lord, I am above the imputation—and your Lordship would do well to remember that I have the misfortune to be of a warm, not to say of an impetuous disposition.

LORD MEDWAY: Sir, I don't mean to provoke your wrath.

SIR ANTHONY: You are the father of my mistress, my Lord—that thought restrains my fury—But this woman (Mrs. Knightly I mean, for a *woman* I find she is, though I once thought her an angel); she, I say, has not yet dismissed me in form; and till that is done, I think myself bound in honour, not to make a tender of my heart, or hand, to any Lady whatsoever.

LORD MEDWAY: Oh, Sir Anthony, I find you have still a hankering after the widow, and only want an opportunity to endeavour at getting into her good graces again—You would fain see her.

SIR ANTHONY: By no means, my Lord; not for the world! for, as I told your Lordship, I would not trust my heart with such an interview—No, no, I know the witchcraft of her beauty too well.

LORD MEDWAY: How do you mean to disengage yourself then?

SIR ANTHONY: My design is to indite an epistle to her, and to request that she will under her hand, in full and explicit terms, give me an absolute and final release from all the vows I have made her.

LORD MEDWAY: I think you are perfectly right, Sir Anthony, and act agreeably to the dictates of true honour—[*Aside.*] I won't lose the fool if I can help it.

SIR ANTHONY: I would fain do so, my Lord.

LORD MEDWAY: I dare say you will get a full and free discharge from your sovereign Lady and Mistress.

SIR ANTHONY: 'Tis to be so presum-*ed,* my Lord—but as for seeing her, 'twere safer, my Lord, to encounter a basilisk, I assure you.

[*Mrs. Knightly rushes in, a Servant attending her to the door. Sir Anthony starts, and draws back.*]

MRS. KNIGHTLY: My Lord, I beg your pardon; your servant told me Lady Flutter was here.

LORD MEDWAY: I am glad he made the mistake, Madam, as it has given *me* the honour of seeing you. Go tell your Lady—She was here but this minute—[*Aside.*] This is unlucky.

MRS. KNIGHTLY: I am quite ashamed of this, my Lord; I just came to prattle half an hour with Lady Flutter, and to try if I could tempt her to the opera, and here I have broken in upon you so unawares—Bless me, Sir Anthony! is it you? I declare I did not see you. Why, you barbarian, where have you been for this month past? My Lord, do you know that Sir Anthony is a lover of mine.

[*Sir Anthony advances, bowing gravely.*]

SIR ANTHONY: That Sir Anthony *was* a lover of yours, Madam, he has but too fatally experienced.

MRS. KNIGHTLY: And a'n't you so still, you inconstant toad?

LORD MEDWAY [*Aside to Sir Anthony.*]: Take my advice, and make your retreat as fast as you can.

SIR ANTHONY [*Aside to Lord Medway.*]: Impossible, my Lord; the magic of her eyes renders me immoveable—but I'll try.

MRS. KNIGHTLY: What, I suppose my Lord is your confidant; you see I have made him mine too.

[*Enter Servant.*]

SERVANT: The ladies are all gone out together, my Lord.

LORD MEDWAY: Did your lady leave word what time she would be at home?

SERVANT: No, my Lord.

LORD MEDWAY: Oh once they are on the wing, there is no knowing when they will return—[*Aside.*] I wish she would go.—Will you allow me the honour of gallanting you to the opera, ma'am? I dare say Sir Anthony, on such an occasion, will excuse my leaving him—'Tis almost the time I believe.

MRS. KNIGHTLY: Oh dear, my Lord! too soon by [*Looking at her watch.*] an age—I am such an impatient creature, I can't endure to wait a minute for any thing, and therefore never go to any public entertainment till after it begins. Is not that the right way, Sir Anthony? But I should not ask you, who are so phlegmatic, you could wait till dooms-day for any thing.

LORD MEDWAY: Come, ma'am, you are too severe on my friend Sir Anthony.

SIR ANTHONY: My Lord, this is but an inconsiderable specimen, a trifle, to what I could produce, of the severity I have received from this ungrateful fair-one.

[*Enter a Servant.*]

SERVANT: There is a gentleman below desires to speak with your Lordship on business.

LORD MEDWAY: I'll come to him—[*Aside to Mrs. Knightly.*] For Heaven's sake, ma'am, don't keep this poor lover any longer in expectation, but dismiss him fairly at once, for your own honour as well as in pity to him.—Sir Anthony, you'll excuse me for a few minutes.

[*Exit Lord Medway.*]

SIR ANTHONY: My Lord, I shall beg leave to wish your Lordship a good evening—I was just going away.

MRS. KNIGHTLY: Why sure you would not be such a clown as to leave me by myself, Sir Anthony! *I* can't go; for thinking that Lady Flutter was at home, I sent my chair to pay two or three visits—Now prithee sit down, and say some sprightly thing to me.

SIR ANTHONY: Ah, Madam, my sprightly sallies were for happier days—

When Flavia listened to my sighs,
And fann'd the amorous blaze,

That love which revell'd in my eyes
Grew wanton in her praise—[11]

MRS. KNIGHTLY: I protest I did not know you were so good a poet.

SIR ANTHONY: The muses, Madam, are not such niggards of their favours. I have been indulged with some rapturous intercourses with those ladies, I can assure you.

MRS. KNIGHTLY: Oh fy, Sir Anthony. What—tell tales?

SIR ANTHONY: No aspersions, Madam—'tis very well known they are all virgins.

MRS. KNIGHTLY: Well, but now let's hear what you can say to me in prose.

SIR ANTHONY: Truly, Madam, this unexpected (I may say unhoped for) encounter, has so disconcerted me, that though I have much to say, I am utterly at a loss where to begin.

MRS. KNIGHTLY: Why then don't begin at all, Sir Anthony; for I think you are generally more at a loss how to make an end.

SIR ANTHONY: **Madam, I must beg the favour of being allowed a hearing; a patient one, Madam; for such the nature of my case requires.**

MRS. KNIGHTLY: **Is it a physical one, or a case of conscience, Sir Anthony?**

SIR ANTHONY: **Neither, Madam. I did propose to unfold my mind to you in a letter—**

MRS. KNIGHTLY: **But then if I should not unfold your letter, Sir Anthony, which is a thing *might* happen, in that case I should never know your mind, you know.**

SIR ANTHONY: If you won't hear me, Madam—

MRS. KNIGHTLY: Well, well, I will hear you; but squeeze what you have to say into as small a compass as you can, my dear Sir Anthony.

SIR ANTHONY: The occasion, Madam, of my giving you this trouble (if as such you are pleased to consider it) is as follows. I have courted you, Madam, that is made honourable addresses to you, for the space of six months, during which time you gave me all the encouragement—

MRS. KNIGHTLY [*Screams.*]: Encouragement! Oh, all you powers of chastity defend me!—Encouragement, Sir Anthony! Of what nature, pray?

SIR ANTHONY: Your pardon, Madam—Consistently with modesty I mean; or such as became a virtuous Lady to bestow on a passionate admirer; for such I pronounce myself to have been.

MRS. KNIGHTLY: Oh I understand you now—Well, Sir?

SIR ANTHONY: For a time I was favoured with your smiles, and had reason to believe that my faithful passion would have been crowned with success. When all of a sudden, to my unutterable astonishment, the sun-shine of my hopes vanished.

MRS. KNIGHTLY: I only stepp'd behind a cloud, Sir Anthony, to play at bo-peep with you.

SIR ANTHONY: Oh, Madam, a total eclipse, I do assure you.—My visits were repulsed, my letters unanswered, and finally your doors shut against me.

MRS. KNIGHTLY: Did I do all this to poor Sir Anthony?

SIR ANTHONY: You did, Madam—Tyrant, you know you did. And now, Madam, I would fain learn your reasons for such usage.

MRS. KNIGHTLY: Reasons—I never gave a reason for any thing I did since I was born.

SIR ANTHONY: That is rather extra-*or*-dinary, Madam; but if you will not condescend to give me any reasons for your cruelty, all I have left to desire, or rather to demand, (pardon me the expression, Madam) is now, from your own lips, to receive my final doom.

MRS. KNIGHTLY: Why, I shan't marry these ten years, Sir Anthony.

SIR ANTHONY: That, Madam, is an indeterminate answer. I humbly request the favour of a final one.

MRS. KNIGHTLY: Why, what are you in such a hurry for? I protest, Sir Anthony, I begin to grow jealous.

SIR ANTHONY: A final answer, Madam.

MRS. KNIGHTLY: I'll be hanged if I have not got a rival! Oh faithless man! that have sworn I don't know how many time over, to be true to me till death—and *I*, like the rest of my easy sex, to believe you?

SIR ANTHONY: Madam, let me most humbly beseech you—

MRS. KNIGHTLY: Begone, dissembler—but what could I expect from such *levity* as yours—

SIR ANTHONY: Levity, Madam! levity! I absolutely disavow the charge—pray, Madam—let me implore you, for the last time (pray observe that, Madam, for the last time) to grant me the favour—[*He advances, bowing low, she flirts from him, and he catches hold of her sleeve.*]

MRS. KNIGHTLY: Bless me! Why sure, Sir Anthony, you would not offer to kiss me!

SIR ANTHONY: Oh heavens, madam, kiss you! Madam, let me take the liberty to inform you, that since I could distinguish between virtue and vice, I never took so unwarrantable a freedom with any lady upon the face of the earth.

[*Enter Lady Flutter.*]

LADY FLUTTER: My goodness! what's all this about? Mrs. Knightly, my dear, what's the matter?

MRS. KNIGHTLY: I protest, my dear, your uncle is so very amorous, that it is not safe to stay alone with him.

SIR ANTHONY: Madam, madam, I blush for you; humbly asking your pardon for being so free as to say so.

MRS. KNIGHTLY: Blush for yourself, Sir Anthony, you have most cause.

LADY FLUTTER: What, in the name of wonder, is all this about?

MRS. KNIGHTLY: Oh, Lady Flutter, I am ashamed to tell you his behaviour!

LADY FLUTTER: My uncle's behaviour, Madam!

SIR ANTHONY: Madam, I hope my niece Flutter has too good an opinion of the propriety of my conduct upon all occasions, to be prejudiced by your uncharitable insinuations. And now, Madam, I demand, in the presence of my niece aforesaid, that you will give me a full and formal acquital of all my vows and promises to you.

MRS. KNIGHTLY: I must take time to consider of that, Sir Anthony; vows are serious things; I suppose all yours are registered in Cupid's books.

SIR ANTHONY: I insist on my release, Madam.

MRS. KNIGHTLY: I don't know whether it be safe to give you one, Sir Anthony; I must consult a lawyer first.

SIR ANTHONY: Madam, I am sorry to say, that you depart extremely from that punctilious honour, as well as generosity of sentiment, which is such an ornament to the fair part of the creation—I only ask for the favour of being discharged—a favour I was never refused by any lady before, I assure you, niece.

LADY FLUTTER [*Aside.*]: **That I dare say.**—Well, I can't for my life understand all this.

MRS. KNIGHTLY: Oh he's a rebel in his heart, that's plain, and only wants a pretence to forfeit his allegience; but I won't give him that satisfaction.

SIR ANTHONY: Then, Madam, since you urge me to it, in one word, I here cancel all my vows—

MRS. KNIGHTLY: It is not in your power.

SIR ANTHONY: Renounce your empire, Madam—

MRS. KNIGHTLY: I defy you.

SIR ANTHONY: And utterly disclaim your favour.

MRS. KNIGHTLY: Stubborn traitor!

SIR ANTHONY: And now, Madam, I will withdraw my person and my heart—

MRS. KNIGHTLY: Not your *heart,* Sir Anthony!

SIR ANTHONY: Both, both, Madam, I do aver it to you; and will make an offering of them where they will be more honourably, and more gratefully entertained. And so, Madam, I am, with proper respect, your most obedient (though rejected) humble servant. Niece Flutter, I have the pleasure of wishing you a very good evening.

[*Exit Sir Anthony, bowing, both ladies burst out a-laughing.*]

MRS. KNIGHTLY [*Imitating his manner, looking after him, and curtsying very low.*]: And I return you my very unfeigned acknowlegements for ridding me of your most insipid solemnity, my dear Sir Anthony. Ha, ha, ha, poor soul! to whom is he going to offer his Platonic adorations, do you know, my dear?

LADY FLUTTER: Why, by what I gather'd just now from the conversation between my Lord and him (for it was a secret to me before) I find Miss Medway is likely to supplant you.

MRS. KNIGHTLY: Supplant me, my dear creature! why, sure you can't suppose I had ever any serious thoughts of the poor man; humbly begging your pardon, as he says, for taking such a liberty with your uncle.

LADY FLUTTER: I should wonder if you had, I own; I am sure nothing but his fortune could have made my Lord think of him for a son-in-law.

MRS. KNIGHTLY: Does Miss Medway approve of the thing? She is a sober sort of a girl, I think.

LADY FLUTTER: Oh intolerably so; I hardly ever converse with her, though under the same roof. She is for ever poring over a book or a needle—Yet I don't suppose she likes him either; I have heard it whispered that she loves my cousin Branville, who, I hear, is expected home every hour.

MRS. KNIGHTLY: If I thought so, I would keep Sir Anthony dangling this twelvemonth, out of mere compassion to the poor girl. For, notwithstanding his threats, I know he is still devoted to me.

LADY FLUTTER: But how would that square with your views in regard to Colonel Medway?

MRS. KNIGHTLY: Oh my sweet friend, that question has made me serious all at once. I can laugh at Sir Anthony no more; indeed I have not lately had spirits enough to be diverted with him, and, for that reason, tried to shake him off. I don't know what to think of the Colonel. I came here this evening on purpose to consult you. My Lord, who, I perceive, is a man of the world, and full of design, dropped some hints to me about his son, by which I find the thing would at least be very agreeable to *him;* yet the Colonel has not been near me since. I wish I knew his sentiments.

LADY FLUTTER: I am sure I can't inform you. There is none of the family very communicative, but my Lord; he is the best of them, that is certain.
[*Enter Sir Harry Flutter.*]

SIR HARRY: Ha, Mrs. Knightly! my adorable! I kiss your hands.

MRS. KNIGHTLY: Oh, Sir Harry, you have missed such an entertainment! Here has been Sir Anthony—

SIR HARRY: Well, and what did uncle Parenthesis say to you?

MRS. KNIGHTLY: Oh he has abandoned me—I am doomed to wear the willow garland.[12]

SIR HARRY: Oh, you cruel devil you, 'tis you who have abandoned him, I dare say—What, Lady Flutter! I am amazed to find *you* here; I thought you had *abandoned* me, as Mrs. Knightly says, and that by this time you had taken post for Oxfordshire, in order to tell papa, that Sir Harry was such a naughty boy, he would not give it its say in every thing. Mrs. Knightly, when I went out this evening, she was going to elope, absolutely bent upon running away from her husband.

LADY FLUTTER: And you see, ma'am, the return he makes me for my good nature in not doing so. I think, Sir Harry, after the provocation I received from you, if I changed my mind, you ought to be very much obliged to me.

SIR HARRY: My dear, if the changing your mind be an obligation, I own my obligations to you on that score are innumerable.

LADY FLUTTER: I suppose you think that witty, now.

MRS. KNIGHTLY: Pray, pray, good people, am I to be left out of the conversation?

SIR HARRY: Oh, ma'am, my Lady Flutter is so extremely quick in her repartees, that you will find it very hard to put in a word, I assure you.

LADY FLUTTER: And Sir Harry is so immoderately fond of hearing himself talk, that he does not desire either of us to give him any interruption, *I* assure you.

SIR HARRY: Not your Ladyship, I acknowlege.

MRS. KNIGHTLY: Well, I vow, Sir Harry, if you were my husband, I should hate you, for all you are such a handsome toad.

SIR HARRY: Indeed you would not.

MRS. KNIGHTLY: Indeed I should.

SIR HARRY: Go, you little hypocrite—

MRS. KNIGHTLY: Get you gone, you rattlepate, I don't mind what you say— Come, Lady Flutter, will you go with me to the opera, my dear?

LADY FLUTTER: With all my heart. Any-where rather than stay at home.

SIR HARRY: You see, ma'am, what a happy man I am in domestic felicity! But here, Lady Flutter, you must give me leave to interpose a little of my lawful authority; and therefore I desire, if it be not too great an honour, that you will oblige me with your company at home this evening.

LADY FLUTTER: Indeed I shan't, Sir Harry.

SIR HARRY: Then, ma'am, I say, indeed you shall.

MRS. KNIGHTLY: Bless me, Sir Harry, you an't serious, sure! I am vastly sorry I proposed the thing at all. I won't go to the opera for my part—I'll stay and chat with you, if you will give me leave—or—suppose we had a pool at piquett.

SIR HARRY: By no means, ma'am. Why should you deprive yourself of your entertainment for *her* childishness? I'll attend you to the opera myself.

MRS. KNIGHTLY: Indeed you shan't, for I won't go.

SIR HARRY: Indeed you shall, and I'll go with you.

MRS. KNIGHTLY: I vow you shall neither of you go, and so good-by to you. [*Runs out.*]

LADY FLUTTER: So, Sir Harry, you have exposed yourself prettily!

SIR HARRY: Not in the least, my dear; I have only shewn you to advantage.

LADY FLUTTER: It is well *one* of us has a little discretion.

SIR HARRY: Meaning your wise self, I presume; but, to shew you that I have a small share too, I will enter into no farther disputes with you; but leaving you to your agreeable contemplations, follow my charming Mrs. Knightly to the opera, who, I fancy, will prefer my company to your Ladyship's. [*Exit.*]

LADY FLUTTER: Very well, Sir!—if I am not even with you for this!— [*Enter Lord Medway, at another Door.*]

LORD MEDWAY: Alone, ma'am! (I have been detained longer than I expected.) What is become of Mrs. Knightly and Sir Anthony?

LADY FLUTTER: Both gone, my Lord—My uncle broke away in resentment, never, I think, to see her more.

LORD MEDWAY: So, so—What have you done with Lady Medway and my daughter?

LADY FLUTTER: They are at their evening meditations, I suppose, my Lord. They both came in with me, after we had made a short visit, but, according to custom, retired to my Lady's dressing-room.

LORD MEDWAY: Oh, they read together every evening!—But you seem ruffled, my dear Lady Flutter; what is the matter?

LADY FLUTTER: Sir Harry—

LORD MEDWAY: What of him?

LADY FLUTTER: He has been here since; but so intolerably rude and provoking, positively there's no enduring him any longer. I should be sorry to leave your Lordship's house so soon, where I have been so kindly received; but I am determined not to continue under the same roof with Sir Harry.

LORD MEDWAY: If your departure were to be a punishment only to Sir Harry, I should not oppose it; for I must allow, that he deserves all your resentment. But, my dear Lady Flutter, I could name another, whom you would make infinitely more unhappy by your absence.

LADY FLUTTER: Who can that be, my Lord?

LORD MEDWAY: Suppose I were to name myself.

LADY FLUTTER: You are very obliging, my Lord, I have not the least doubt of your friendship.

LORD MEDWAY: Friendship, my dear Ma'am, sometimes assumes a tenderer name—When a man entertains it for a woman, young and charming as you are, what ought it then to be called?

LADY FLUTTER: Why friendship, to be sure—what should it be else?

LORD MEDWAY: Shall I tell you?

LADY FLUTTER: No, I won't be told.

LORD MEDWAY: Then you guess—

LADY FLUTTER: Not I, indeed, my Lord—

LORD MEDWAY: 'Tis love! love! is not that a sweeter sound?

LADY FLUTTER: 'Tis a sound with which I am very little acquainted. [*Sighs.*]

LORD MEDWAY: Then let me be your tutor, to teach you a science, in which Sir Harry is not worthy to instruct you.

LADY FLUTTER: Oh, my Lord, if I had met with you before I was married, and before *you* were married—But it is too late now—

LORD MEDWAY: You must not say so. What are marriage ties, if the hearts are not joined? 'Tis that alone which makes the union sacred.

LADY FLUTTER: That is the chief thing, I grant.

LORD MEDWAY: Oh it is all in all!—With regard to Lady Medway now; she is a good woman, it is true, and I esteem her as such; but there is no love in the case, so that I consider myself absolutely as a single man. 'Tis just the same with you; there has a ceremony indeed passed between you and Sir Harry; but he slights you, and you very justly despise him: so that, to all intents and purposes, you are a single woman.

LADY FLUTTER: I wish I were, I'm sure, my Lord.

LORD MEDWAY: Why so you are, my dear Ma'am, if you would consider the thing rightly—If I thought otherwise, tho' I confess I love you to adoration, I would sooner stab myself to the heart, than endeavour to win your affections.

LADY FLUTTER: Indeed, my Lord, I believe you.

LORD MEDWAY: Then, since we are equally unhappy in wedlock, what crime can there be in our mutual endeavours to console each other?

LADY FLUTTER: I am sure I don't intend any harm.

LORD MEDWAY: Then why will you talk of leaving me? You know Sir Harry is too indifferent to be concerned at a separation; the grief, the disappointment, will all be mine.

LADY FLUTTER: Indeed, my Lord, I should be very unwilling to make you uneasy, to whom I owe so many obligations.

LORD MEDWAY: Then speak no more of parting. [*He takes her hand.*] I have a thousand things to tell you. The delightful subject we are upon is inexhaustible, but I can never get you for half an hour to myself.

LADY FLUTTER: Why no, Sir Harry is so perpetually whiffling[13] backwards and forwards, one can't be alone a minute for him.

[*Lady Medway comes to the door, and steps back on seeing Lord Medway and Lady Flutter in such familiar conference.*]

LORD MEDWAY: I have thought of an expedient, which, if you will agree to, will secure us against all interruptions for the future.

LADY FLUTTER: What is it?

LORD MEDWAY: You know Lady Lovegrove, who sat in the box with us at the play the other night (a very worthy woman.) I am sure she would be glad of your acquaintance. I'll introduce you to her, and there, you know, when you go of an evening to drink tea, I can meet you, and we can enjoy an hour's conversation without being interrupted.

LADY FLUTTER: I protest that will do very well. But we must not let Sir Harry know a word of my acquaintance with her, or may-be, some evening, he'll be for thrusting himself in.

LORD MEDWAY: By no means, he shall never be of our party. Come, Ma'am, I fancy, by this time, the ladies have done with their sober studies— Suppose we were to join them.

LADY FLUTTER: As you will, my Lord.

LORD MEDWAY: Not a word more of parting, remember.

LADY FLUTTER: I'll try what I can do to oblige your Lordship.

[*Exit Lord Medway, leading her out. Lady Medway comes out.*]

LADY MEDWAY: Oh, Lord Medway! this is beyond what I thought you capable of; but I will, if possible, prevent the destruction that you have plan'd. [*Exit.*]

END OF ACT II

ACT III

Scene changes to the Widow Knightly's.
Enter Colonel Medway and Miss Richly.

COLONEL MEDWAY: I would not have mentioned it at all, if I thought you could have suffered it to make so serious an impression on you.

MISS RICHLY: It ought not, I confess, knowing as I do the truth and generosity of your heart—and yet I cannot help being alarmed—an immense fortune, and a fine woman, as my sister really is—the temptation is so great! that were it any one but you—

COLONEL MEDWAY: Indeed, my dear Clara, these fears of yours reproach, at the same time that they flatter me. Is it necessary that I should tell you, over and over again, for the thousandth time, that I never can love any woman but yourself?

MISS RICHLY: I do not want to be convinced—and yet I own I am pleased to hear you repeat even what you *have* said a thousand times; but your father's authority—I dread that.

COLONEL MEDWAY: Believe me, you have no reason; for, tho' no son was ever more observant of a father's will than I have always been of his; yet, in the particular concerns of my heart, I must be my own director. This my father knows, and I hope he will never urge me more upon the subject.

MISS RICHLY: But if he should?

COLONEL MEDWAY: Would you have me swear to you?

MISS RICHLY: Oh, not for the world!—I am ashamed of doubting, and yet I don't know how it is, I am full of apprehensions: the truth is, I am not very happy at home; my sister is, of late, grown cold and peevish to me—I never suspected the cause before, but 'tis now too plain.

COLONEL MEDWAY: Did she ever mention me to you?

MISS RICHLY: Never but in a careless way—and yet I think since your father's last visit to her, she has been in better spirits than before, tho' I am not used one bit the kinder.

COLONEL MEDWAY: You shall not long be subject to her tyranny. My father already knows the secret of my love; and I think that, notwithstanding the article of fortune weighs much with him, his regard to my happiness will even out-balance that.

MISS RICHLY: I wish it may—Bless me! here's my sister.

[*Enter Mrs. Knightly, she curtsies gravely to the Colonel.*]

MRS. KNIGHTLY [*Coolly.*]: I thought you had been alone, Miss Richly, and came to chat with you; but I see you are engaged.

COLONEL MEDWAY: I hope *my* being here, Ma'am, will not deprive Miss Richly of the pleasure of your company.

MISS RICHLY: I believe, sister, we shall both think our conversation very much improved by your making a third in it.

MRS. KNIGHTLY: I don't know that—A tête à tête is to the full as often disagreeably inter-*rupted,* as improved by another person.

COLONEL MEDWAY: That, Madam, I am sure, can never happen, where *you* make the addition.

MRS. KNIGHTLY: I should be sorry it were the case now, I own, Colonel; for, to tell you the truth, I have vanity enough to be mortified at the thoughts of being considered as an intruder.

COLONEL MEDWAY: Bless me, Madam! I know of but one circumstance in the world, which could possibly place you in such a light.

MRS. KNIGHTLY: What is that, pray Sir?

COLONEL MEDWAY: Where an inferior beauty was meditating a conquest, and you stept in to snatch it from her.

MRS. KNIGHTLY: An inferior beauty—I protest, Colonel, I don't well understand that—There is an appearance of gallantry in the compliment, and yet there is something a little mystical in it too. Clara, are you good at solving riddles?

MISS RICHLY: No, indeed, sister; you know I have a very literal understanding; besides, I think what the Colonel says requires no explanation.

MRS. KNIGHTLY: Then, my dear, I won't affront you by making any application.

MISS RICHLY: If you should, sister, I am very ready to acknowlege my part in it; but you should consider that by the remainder, you would draw on yourself that imputation, which but now you wished to avoid.

MRS. KNIGHTLY: You see, Colonel, the mysterious speech you have made has the fate of all oracles, to be interpreted different ways, and, perhaps, none of them right—Nay, I am inclined to think it bears a still nearer resemblance to them, and that you, like the priests of old, delivered what you said without any inspiration of a god.

COLONEL MEDWAY: There, Madam, your comparison fails, for I assure you I am at this instance under the influence of a very powerful one.

MRS. KNIGHTLY: I vow I don't believe you; do you, Clara?

MISS RICHLY: I never had any reason to doubt the Colonel's veracity, sister.

MRS. KNIGHTLY: What, then, you think he is really in love?

MISS RICHLY: Don't you hear him acknowlege it?

COLONEL MEDWAY: Nay, Madam, if you won't take *my* word for it, I can't see what reason you have to believe any one's else.

MRS. KNIGHTLY: Why no, that's true—But where a matter of faith doesn't concern one's self, infidelity, you know, can be of no great consequence one way or another.

COLONEL MEDWAY [*Aside.*]: That's pretty home.

MISS RICHLY: Very true, sister; but scepticism is a dangerous, as well as an uneasy state, in *some* cases.

MRS. KNIGHTLY: And a state of *security,* Miss Clara, the casuists in *love,* as well as religion, are agreed, is not always the safest. But I don't know how we fell upon this odd topic.

MISS RICHLY: Nor I, I am sure.

COLONEL MEDWAY: I don't know how we came to talk of it; but I am convinced the man must be very insensible who could avoid thinking of it in this company.

MRS. KNIGHTLY: Clara, you are a monopolist; but I will have my share in that compliment—I don't know, Colonel tho', what your mistress would say if she were to hear you say so.

MISS RICHLY: She'd forgive him, I dare say.

COLONEL MEDWAY: Come, come, Ladies, I see by your pursuing this subject, that you have a design of getting my secret out of me; and, as I am sure I could not withstand your united force, I think my safest way is to make my retreat before I betray myself— [*Bows to both and exit.*]

MRS. KNIGHTLY: How long was the Colonel here before I came in, Clara?

MISS RICHLY: Not above a quarter of an hour—Pray, sister, why do you ask?

MRS. KNIGHTLY: Because it is quite astonishing to me, how a man of his vivacity can be entertained by such a piece of still-life as you are.

MISS RICHLY: Why, sister, it is not an in-*falli*-ble maxim, that we most admire those who are exactly of our own disposition. I, now, for example, who am naturally grave, do, notwithstanding, admire sprightliness in other people.

MRS. KNIGHTLY: Umph, so it seems—

MISS RICHLY: And the Colonel, tho' extremely lively himself, may, however, not disrelish the conversation of a serious woman.

MRS. KNIGHTLY: Indeed, Clara, you are a very conceited girl. I dare swear, if the Colonel says fine things to you, you believe every word of them.

MISS RICHLY: Indeed, sister, I have as humble an opinion of myself, as you, or any one else can possibly have of me.

MRS. KNIGHTLY: I am very glad to hear it, child; for I own I think vanity would not be a very desirable companion in your situation.

MISS RICHLY: What have I done, sister, to deserve these severe taunts from you?

MRS. KNIGHTLY: Oh, Clara, if you accuse me of severity, I must tell you that you are an ungrateful girl, and I fancy we shall not continue much longer together.

MISS RICHLY: **I am not quite so destitute, Madam, but that I can still be received by that friend who had the care of me from my childhood.**

MRS. KNIGHTLY: **Very well, Madam, I shall consider of it; but perhaps I may find out some more eligible place for you.**

MISS RICHLY: I see, sister, you are resolved to disapprove of every thing I say or do; my company is become irksome to you, and, for the present at least, I'll rid you it it— [*Exit.*]

MRS. KNIGHTLY: I was very unlucky in ever taking her into my house; had it not been for that, I should never, perhaps, have seen the only man who probably could have given me a minute's uneasiness.—I am puzzled at his conduct—and yet I suspect now more than ever that they love each other—If it be so, I shall know it too soon, for I am sure Lord Medway is thoroughly in my interests.—Yet my suspense is insupportable.—Who's there?

[*Enter a Maid.*]

MAID: Madam, your chair is ready.

MRS. KNIGHTLY: Come hither—I desire you will give orders to the servants, that any letters directed to my sister should be brought to me—I suspect that girl has got into a silly intrigue.

MAID: I believe, Madam, Miss receives letters very often; but I shall take care, for the future, that you shall have them first.

MRS. KNIGHTLY: Be sure you do—

[*Exeunt.*]

Scene ii. Changes to Lord Medway's.
Lady Flutter at her Toilet. Enter to her Lady Medway.

LADY FLUTTER: Good morning to your Ladyship. [*Looks coolly at her.*]

LADY MEDWAY: I was afraid you were not well, Lady Flutter, as you lay abed so long this morning.

LADY FLUTTER: I rested ill last night, nothing more.

LADY MEDWAY: I hope I don't interrupt you, Madam.

LADY FLUTTER: Not in the least; but I vow you are so ceremonious, Lady Medway, that you will not allow me to think myself at home.

LADY MEDWAY: I should be sorry for that, Madam; but you know there are times when one would not chuse to be broke in upon by any one; yet, to shew you how free I make with you, I have brought my work with me, if you will let me pore a little at it.

LADY FLUTTER [*Aside.*]: I wish she and her work were far enough.—Your Ladyship is excessively obliging. You and Miss Medway are such house-wives, you quite shame me—This is prodigiously pretty; who are these ruffles for?

LADY MEDWAY: My Lord, to be sure—Where is Sir Harry this morning? I have not seen him yet.

LADY FLUTTER: Dear Lady Medway, don't ask me about him, for I know nothing of him.

LADY MEDWAY: What, not of your husband, my dear! Well, well, Lady Flutter, when your young necks are a little more inured to the marriage yoke, I hope it will sit easier on you both—This work blinds me, I'll lay it by—

LADY FLUTTER: Oh impossible! he grows worse and worse every day. There never was such an incorrigible ill-natured thing in the universe.

LADY MEDWAY: Now, really, there I must differ from you; I never took Sir Harry to be ill-natured; hasty and petulant, I grant you, he is.

LADY FLUTTER: Madam, I hope you will allow me to be the best judge.

LADY MEDWAY: You have reason to be so, I own; but a stander-by may form an opinion.

LADY FLUTTER: I don't know what your *Lady*-ship's opinion may be; but I am sure it is the opinion of others, and some that I could name of un-doubted good judgement, that there never *was,* since the creation, a woman so unfortunate in a husband as I am.

LADY MEDWAY [*Aside.*]: Oh, Lord Medway, what have you to answer for!—I must say, Lady Flutter, that if it even *were* so (which, heaven knows, is far from being the case), they are not *your* friends, no more than Sir Harry's, who would endeavour to persuade you to such a belief.

LADY FLUTTER: Bless me, Ma'am! Why, isn't it visible to all the world? Doesn't all the town ring of his ridiculous behaviour, and wonder at my patience in bearing it?

LADY MEDWAY: Indeed, Lady Flutter, I believe you are mistaken. The town have something else to mind beside little domestic quarrels that no way concern them; and I dare say, no-body but your particular friends trouble their heads about it. Tho', I must observe, that had both you and Sir Harry been a little less communicative, even to some of your *friends,* on the subject of your disagreement, it might have been happier for you.

LADY FLUTTER: Oh, dear ma'am! I know there are some tame wives in the world, who can submit in silence to any usage; but I am not one of those, I assure you. I have not been used to controll, nor I won't be controll'd, that's more.

LADY MEDWAY: Softly, dear Lady Flutter, I don't mean to offend you; I would argue with you as a friend. Pray speak lower; I would not have any of our servants hear on what subject we are discoursing.

LADY FLUTTER: Gracious! why, every servant in the house knows how we live.

LADY MEDWAY: But, Madam, don't you think your unguarded complaints without doors, and perhaps your unadvised choice of confidants within, may lead you into some inconvenience?

LADY FLUTTER: I don't well understand your question, Lady Medway; my choice of confidants within—

LADY MEDWAY: Yes—male ones, I mean; for example now, if a young married lady should make choice of a gentleman to whom she should open her heart, and let him so far into her confidence as to tell him she despises her husband, what do you think must be the consequence?

LADY FLUTTER: What! why, I suppose he'd think—he'd imagine—I don't know what he'd think—

LADY MEDWAY: I'll tell you; he'd think, perhaps, that a liking to *him* had as great a share in the lady's contempt for her husband, as any real fault of the husband's.

LADY FLUTTER: If he thought so, I could not help it; but I am sure there is no one to whom I complain will draw any such inference.

LADY MEDWAY: There is nothing but what is very natural in all this, Lady Flutter; and the gentleman, on this supposition, will think himself bound to make an offer of his love to the lady; she, perhaps, receives it—

LADY FLUTTER: Lord, ma'am! these are strange conclusions— [*Aside.*] What can she mean?

LADY MEDWAY: If this should be the case, what must ensue! Oh, Lady Flutter, an innocent young creature like you, should start at the thought.

LADY FLUTTER: Upon my word, Lady Medway, I don't understand such insinuations. If Sir Harry insults me, I am not obliged to bear it from every one.

LADY MEDWAY: I am sorry, Madam, that you construe a friendly caution into an insult. I *am* your friend, perhaps the only one who has the power of saving you from destruction.

LADY FLUTTER: Destruction! Madam, I could not have expected this from you, in your own house. I believe my Lord would not thank you for treating me thus—but if you are tired of me, Madam—

LADY MEDWAY: Oh, my dear Madam! you are in a very great error, my Lord is the greatest enemy you have in the world.

LADY FLUTTER: You may happen to be mistaken in that, Lady Medway, as well as in other things.—[*Aside.*] Poor woman, she little knows—

LADY MEDWAY: Come, not to play at cross-purposes with you any longer, I must tell you that I am no stranger to my Lord's designs on you—

LADY FLUTTER: His *designs* on *me!*

LADY MEDWAY: Yes, Madam, his cruel, his (I grieve to say) infamous designs on you. Oh, Lady Flutter, you stand on a dreadful precipice! do not reject the kind hand that would snatch you from certain ruin.

LADY FLUTTER: This is such extraordinary language, Lady Medway, that really—I don't know what to say to it—I little imagined I should have created any jealousy when I came into your family.

LADY MEDWAY: Indeed, my dear, you intirely mistake my motive. I own there was a time when I might have been influenced by jealousy, but I have out-lived it; and am not now actuated by so selfish a passion. Pity to your inexperienced youth, friendship to your worthy parents, regard to the honour of your husband, joined to the tenderness and duty I owe my Lord, are the sole motives which urge me to save you all, if possible, from ruin. I know my Lord makes love to you; and that you have, unwarily, been drawn in to make an assignation with him.

LADY FLUTTER: If he has been so treacherous as to tell this!

LADY MEDWAY: He has not, I assure you; yet I am certain of the fact; I know too well the nature of his connections with Lady Lovegrove—And now, my dear, if you would escape the snare which is laid for your undoing, be advised by me, who am your true friend.

LADY FLUTTER: I don't think I have a friend in the world.

LADY MEDWAY: You are mistaken; I am sincerely so. My Lord is a man of pleasure, and is perhaps less scrupulous in affairs of gallantry, than in any other vice. Your youth and agreeable person were alone sufficient to attract him; but when superadded to this, he found you despised your husband, and made no difficulty of owning it to him, it almost amounted to an invitation.

LADY FLUTTER: An invitation, Lady Medway! you use me very ill.

LADY MEDWAY: To a man of his cast, Madam, it certainly does. Your unacquaintedness with men of intrigue makes you blind to your own danger; but indeed, Lady Flutter, there is but one step between you and inevitable shame and misery. What do you think must be the consequence, if Sir Harry should discover that you have appointed a private place of meeting with my Lord? What must he think of the nature of a correspondence thus meanly carried on by stealth? Ask your own heart if you can justify this to your husband and to your friends?

LADY FLUTTER: Lord bless me, Lady Medway!—you terrify me—I am amazed how you came to the knowlege of this.

LADY MEDWAY: 'Tis a happiness to you, Madam, that I have, if by it I can be the means of saving you.

LADY FLUTTER: I own I was a fool for consenting; but sure, Madam, you won't be so barbarous as to tell Sir Harry; it would give him such an advantage over me, I can't bear the thoughts of it.

LADY MEDWAY: Why really, my dear, I should be sorry to be under the necessity of taking so disagreeable a step; and if I thought I could rely on your honour and discretion, in your future conduct, I certainly should keep your secret.

LADY FLUTTER: Madam, I'll quit your house directly, if that will satisfy you.

LADY MEDWAY: By no means, Madam; how would you answer that to your friends, if they should enquire the reason? Here you came to town to stay the winter with me, and before a month's elapsed you quit my house!

LADY FLUTTER: Why I can tell them that Sir Harry is so insufferable, I can't live with him.

LADY MEDWAY: If you will be ruled by me, Lady Flutter, for one week, nay but for three days, I'll engage that Sir Harry and you shall be as happy a couple as any in England.

LADY FLUTTER: Oh gracious! you could as soon convert us into angels.

LADY MEDWAY: But will you promise to be guided by me, but for a little while?

LADY FLUTTER: Oh dear Lady Medway, I know you would recommend patience and submission, and all that; but I never can, nor never will submit to his humour.

LADY MEDWAY: Why then, Madam, I shall think it my duty to write to your father immediately, and let him know the danger of your situation; **for though I am sure the parting you from your husband would afflict him, yet 'tis better he should receive you while you are innocent.**

LADY FLUTTER: What is it you would have me do, Madam?

LADY MEDWAY: Your task is not hard, if you are disposed to set about it. You are married to a very young man, Lady Flutter; who, though he is warm and volatile, does not want sense, and I am sure is good-natured in the main.

LADY FLUTTER: Dear Lady Medway—you are enough to turn one's brain.

LADY MEDWAY: Hear me out, Madam. You, on the other hand, who have as much sense, and as much good-nature as he, are at the same time a little too quick and impatient of contradiction. He I will allow is too ready to *give* offence; but you in your turn must grant, that you are as sudden in *taking* it. Now, my dear, 'tis in your power, and give me leave to tell you 'tis your duty also, to correct yours. And I'll answer for it that Sir Harry will follow your lead; for I am sure that he loves you a great deal better than my Lord does, let him tell you what he pleases.

LADY FLUTTER: I wish I could see any proofs of it.

LADY MEDWAY: Will you make the experiment?

LADY FLUTTER: What and give up to *him?*

LADY MEDWAY: Only for once, just for a trial; if he does not receive it as he ought, I will never desire you to repeat it—I think I hear his rap at the door.

LADY FLUTTER: Well, Madam, to shew you that it is not *my* fault that we live so uneasily, I will do as you would have me; you yourself shall be the judge; but then remember you are not to write to my papa.

LADY MEDWAY: I will not, and remember you are not to have any private conferences with my Lord.

LADY FLUTTER: Agreed.

[*Enter Sir Harry.*]

SIR HARRY [*To Lady Medway.*]: How does your Ladyship do this morning?—I am tired to death, I have been at my banker's, and jolting all over the detestable city.—Defend me! Why your head is dressed so barbarously, Lady Flutter, you look like ten furies; by my life, an absolute Medusa; prithee who gave thee that formidable appearance, child?

LADY FLUTTER: I am sorry you don't like it, Sir Harry; I'll not employ that Frenchman any more.

SIR HARRY: Then I am sure you don't like it yourself; for Sir Harry's judgment has not the happiness of having any great weight with you.

LADY FLUTTER: No, I protest I think it quite becoming and genteel.

LADY MEDWAY: Then it *must* be to oblige *you,* Sir Harry.

SIR HARRY: Undoubtedly, ma'am, that's her study.

LADY FLUTTER: Upon my word, Sir Harry, I would make it so, if you would let me.

SIR HARRY: My dear! say that over again pray; it sounds vastly pretty, if it were but true.

LADY FLUTTER: Why then seriously I would rather dress to please you than any body.

SIR HARRY: Hark'ee, Lady Flutter, irony is a mighty ticklish weapon, and you handle it very awkwardly, upon my soul; lay it by, or you'll cut your fingers.

LADY FLUTTER: I declare and vow I am in earnest.

SIR HARRY: Oh dear ma'am, your most obedient—but you're a bungler, take my word for it.

LADY MEDWAY: But, Sir Harry, why should you doubt that Lady Flutter is serious?

SIR HARRY: Why really, ma'am, because I never knew Lady Flutter serious in any thing, but her endeavours to make herself disagreeable to me.

LADY MEDWAY: In which I fancy however she has not succeeded, Sir Harry.

LADY FLUTTER: If that be the case, then I am resolved to take another course, and try what my endeavours to please him will do.

LADY MEDWAY: What do you say to that, Sir Harry?

SIR HARRY: Say! 'gad, I don't well know what to say to it. There is something devilish pleasant in hearing her talk so, if the humour would but last.

LADY MEDWAY: Take my word for it, Sir Harry, it will be your own fault if it does not.

SIR HARRY: Faith, ma'am, I should be glad to keep up the ball as long as I could.

LADY FLUTTER: Indeed, indeed, Sir Harry, I will never quarrel with you again.

SIR HARRY: Upon your honour.

LADY FLUTTER: Upon my honour.

SIR HARRY: Nor I with you, upon my soul—And shall we grow fond of one another?

LADY FLUTTER: Immensely.

SIR HARRY: Agreed—I'll never find fault with any thing you do.

LADY FLUTTER: Nor I with any thing you say.

SIR HARRY: I'll never contradict you.

LADY FLUTTER: Nor I you.

SIR HARRY: Sweet rogue!

LADY FLUTTER: My dear Sir Harry!

[*He takes her hand and kisses it.*]

LADY MEDWAY: Well now is not this charming?—I congratulate you both on your happiness, and leave you to the enjoyment of it. [*Exit Lady Medway.*]

SIR HARRY: Duce take me but I should think you prodigious agreeable, if you were always in good humour.

LADY FLUTTER: And, upon my life, I should think the same of you.

SIR HARRY: How came we not to discover this sooner?

LADY FLUTTER: Because we never tried to find it out. Lady Medway was the first that told me we might be happy if we pleased.

SIR HARRY: Faith then she has more sagacity than my Lord; for he was of a contrary opinion, and used to pity me of all things.

LADY FLUTTER: For what?

SIR HARRY: For being married to you.

LADY FLUTTER: Really!

SIR HARRY: Truth, upon my word.

LADY FLUTTER [*Aside.*]: I see his treachery.—Then, Sir Harry, I will convince him of his error, by making the best wife in the world, in spite of him.

SIR HARRY: Charming creature! I shall grow too fond of you—I won't let you be so engaging, hussy—

LADY FLUTTER: You shall tho'—

[*Enter Lord Medway, who stops on seeing Sir Harry.*]

SIR HARRY: Pray, my Lord, come in—I have a sad complaint to make to you. This is certainly the most perverse girl!—

LORD MEDWAY: Oh Sir Harry, that is the old story—I won't hear what you have to say.

SIR HARRY: But, my Lord, this is a new, a quite spick and span new affair. She has taken *such* a resolution!

LORD MEDWAY: Not to part I hope!

SIR HARRY: No, no, my Lord, a much stranger thing.

LORD MEDWAY: Ay! what can that be?

SIR HARRY: You will be amazed when I tell you—We were disputing about it when you came in—

LORD MEDWAY: I am sorry, Sir Harry, to find you always in disputes with your Lady. I wish from my heart I could compose your differences—

SIR HARRY: Oh she is the very spirit of contradiction, my Lord.

LADY FLUTTER: Depend upon it, Sir Harry, I will have my own way in this.

LORD MEDWAY [*Aside to Sir Harry.*]: And in every thing else, I'll be sworn.

SIR HARRY: You must not.

LADY FLUTTER: I will.

LORD MEDWAY [*Aside to Lady Flutter.*]: That's right.—What is the matter in debate?

SIR HARRY: Why, my Lord, 'tis the oddest thing in the world; she is resolved right or wrong in spite of all I can say—to be very good—and make me love her whether I will nor not—Don't you think that is monstrously provoking?

LADY FLUTTER: And he, my Lord, has taken up as unaccountable a design—of never contradicting me in any thing—Is not that *as* provoking?

SIR HARRY: A'n't we a couple of fools, my Lord?

LORD MEDWAY: Why really, Sir Harry,—if this could be—I can't say—I am sure I sincerely wish to see you both on good terms—and if you have found out a way—with all my heart.

[*Sir Harry and Lady Flutter both burst out a-laughing.*]

LORD MEDWAY: I am glad to see you so merry, my young gentry—I wish it may last, that's all. Sir Harry, I have a word to say to you. [*Aside to Sir Harry.*] Why you are undone, man, if once you let her turn matters to ridicule.

SIR HARRY [*Aside to Lord Medway*]: Oh my lord, you are quite mistaken, all this is serious.

LADY FLUTTER: Come, I'll have no plotting.

LORD MEDWAY [*Aside to Sir Harry.*]: Poh, poh, she will get the better of *you* I see. Let *me* speak to her—Lady Flutter! [*Advances towards her.*]

LADY FLUTTER: The tables are turned, my Lord; I'll whisper with no-body but Sir Harry.

LORD MEDWAY [*Aside.*]: But two words—When shall we meet?

LADY FLUTTER [*Aside to Lord Medway.*]: Never— Sir Harry, now that you intend to be very fond of me, I desire that you will grow a little jealous, and tell my Lord that he must not come into my dressing-room in a morning.

SIR HARRY: Faith, my Lord, that's true, I begin not to relish the Spartan scheme as well as I did.

LORD MEDWAY: Mighty fine! this is an extraordinary metamorphosis, if it holds—but of that I own I have some doubt.

LADY FLUTTER: You need not fear, my Lord—We have *your* good wishes that it should, I know.

LORD MEDWAY [*Aside.*]: That's home.

LADY FLUTTER: Come, Sir Harry, I want to go to an auction this morning; will you be so good as to give me your company?

SIR HARRY: With all my heart, my dear, I'll attend you; and see here I received all this to-day! [*Takes out a purse, which she snatches from him.*] Oh you little plunderer! give me a kiss for it—I'll have another—

LADY FLUTTER: Go, you extortioner—day, day, my Lord.

[*They go out romping together.*]

LORD MEDWAY: What can be the meaning of all this? damned little coquet— So much art at her years!—or is it owing to my wife's interposition? Yet she knew not of my design—Any way I am ashamed to be baffled so ridiculously—And that puppy Sir Harry too—

[*Enter Servant.*]

SERVANT: Sir Anthony Branville's come to wait on your Lordship—

LORD MEDWAY: Shew him into my study—Here's another fool that don't know his own mind; but I'll fix him one way or another if I can.

Scene changes to Lord Medway's study.
Enter Sir Anthony and Lord Medway, meeting.

LORD MEDWAY: Sir Anthony, I am glad to see you; I was really in great pain for you yesterday, when I was obliged to leave you in the magic circle of Mrs. Knightly's charms; I wish you joy of your escape.

SIR ANTHONY: My Lord, I humbly thank you; 'tis a felicity to me I acknowlege; for, my Lord, there never was such a Syren, such a Circe! Sylla and Charybdis (of whom we read in fable) were harmless innocents to her; but, Heaven be praised, I am my own man again; and now, my Lord, I am come, agreeably to the intimation I gave you before, to make a most respectful offering of my heart, to the truly deserving and fair Lady, Louisa.

LORD MEDWAY: Sir Anthony, I have already told you I shall be proud of your alliance, and my daughter I make no doubt is sensible of your worth!— Therefore, Sir Anthony, the shorter we make the wooing—women are slippery things—you understand me!

SIR ANTHONY: Your Lordship's insinuation, though derogatory to the honour of the fair-sex, (which I very greatly reverence) has, I am apprehensive, a little too much veracity in it. *I* have found it so to my cost; for would you believe it, my Lord, this cruel woman (Mrs. Knightly, I mean, begging her pardon for the epithet) is the eighth lady to whom I have made sincere, humble, and passionate love, within the space of these thirteen years.

LORD MEDWAY: You surprize me, Sir Anthony; is it possible that a gentleman of your figure and accomplishments could be rejected by so many?

SIR ANTHONY: I do not positively affirm, my Lord, that I was rejected by them *all;* no, my Lord, that would have been a severity not to be survived—

LORD MEDWAY: How was it then?

SIR ANTHONY: Blemishes, my Lord, foibles, imperfections in the fair ones, which obliged me (though reluctantly) to withdraw my heart.

LORD MEDWAY: Ho ho, why then the fault was your's, Sir Anthony, not theirs.

SIR ANTHONY: I deny that, my Lord, with due submission to your better judgment, it was their fault; for the truth is, I never could get any of them to be serious. There is a levity, my Lord, a kind of (if I may so call it) instability, which runs thro' the gentler sex (whom nevertheless I admire) which I assure you has thus long deterred me from wedlock.

LORD MEDWAY: Then, Sir Anthony, I find you have been peculiarly unfortunate in the ladies whom you have addressed.

SIR ANTHONY: Supremely so, my Lord; for notwithstanding that they all received my devoirs most indulgently, yet I do not know how it was, in the long run they either absolutely refused making me happy, or else were so extremely unguarded in their conduct, even before my face, that I thought I could not, consistently with honour, confer the title of Lady Branville on any one of them.

LORD MEDWAY; Your lot has been a little hard I must confess. I hope however *that* honour has been reserved by fate for my daughter. She is your ninth mistress, Sir Anthony, and that you know is a propitious number.[14]

SIR ANTHONY: My Lord,I take the liberty of hoping so too; and that she is destined to recompence me for the disappointments and indignities I have received from the rest of woman kind.

LORD MEDWAY: Why then, Sir Anthony, I suppose I may now present you to her in the character of a lover.

SIR ANTHONY: My Lord, I pant for that happiness.

LORD MEDWAY: I'll call her, Sir Anthony—

SIR ANTHONY: As your Lordship pleases—but, my Lord, this widow Knightly—

LORD MEDWAY [*Aside.*]: Was there ever such a phlegmatic blockhead!—what of her, Sir Anthony?

SIR ANTHONY: I own I loved *her* better than any of her predecessors in my heart—Matters indeed had gone farther between us, for my Lord (not to injure a lady's reputation) I must tell you a secret—I have more than once pressed her hand with these lips.

LORD MEDWAY: Really!

SIR ANTHONY: Fact upon my veracity; I hope your Lordship don't think me vain: **and as she had indulged me such lengths, could I be censured for raising my wishes to the possession of this beauty?**

LORD MEDWAY: By no means, Sir Anthony; but then her ill behaviour to you—

SIR ANTHONY: Oh, my Lord, it has blotted, and as I may say totally erased her image from my breast—

LORD MEDWAY: Well, Sir, I'll bring my daughter to you, whose image I hope will supply hers in your breast. [*Exit.*]

SIR ANTHONY [*Solus.*]: I hope this tender fair one will not be too easily won—that would debase the dignity of the passion, and deprive me of many delightful hours of languishment—There was a time when a lover was allowed the pleasure of importuning his mistress, but our modern beauties will scarce permit a man that satisfaction. Pray heaven my intended bride may not be one of those—If it should prove so—I tremble for the consequences;—but she comes, and the condescending nymph approaches.

[*Enter Louisa, led in by Lord Medway.*]

LORD MEDWAY: Louisa, you are no stranger to Sir Anthony Branville's merit.

SIR ANTHONY: Oh my Lord! [*Bowing low.*]

LORD MEDWAY: That he is a gentleman of family and fortune, of most unblemished honour, and very uncommon endowments.

SIR ANTHONY: Oh, my good Lord, ordinary, slight accomplishments.

LORD MEDWAY: You are therefore to think yourself happy in being his choice preferably to any other lady. And now, Sir Anthony, I'll leave you to pursue your good fortune. [*Exit Lord Medway.*]

LOUISA: Sir, won't you please to sit?

SIR ANTHONY: Miss Medway, madam—having obtained my Lord your father's permission, I humbly presume to approach you in the delightful hope, that after having convinced you of the excess of my love—

LOUISA: I hope, Sir Anthony, you will allow me a reasonable time for this conviction!

SIR ANTHONY: Madam, I should hold myself utterly abandoned if I were capable at the first onset (notwithstanding what passes here) of urging a lady on so nice a point.

LOUISA: I thank you, Sir; but I could expect no less from a gentleman whom all the world allows to be the very pattern of decorum.

SIR ANTHONY: 'Tis a character, madam, that I have always been ambitious of supporting, whatever struggles it may cost me from my natural fervor; for let me tell you, madam, a beautiful object is a dangerous enemy to decorum.

LOUISA: But your great prudence, Sir Anthony, leaves me no room to suspect—

SIR ANTHONY: I am obliged to call it to my aid I do assure you, madam; for spite of the suggestions of passion, I by no means approve of those rash and impetuous lovers, who, without regard to the delicacy of the lady, would, (having obtained consent) as it were rush at once into her arms, you'll pardon me, madam, for so grossly expressing my idea.

LOUISA: Oh, Sir Anthony, I am charmed with your notions, so refined! so generous! and I must add (though it may appear vain) so correspondent with my own.

SIR ANTHONY: Madam, I am transported to hear you say so! I am at this minute in an absolute extacy! Will you permit me, dear madam, the ravishing satisfaction of throwing myself at your feet?

LOUISA: By no means, Sir Anthony; I could not bear to see a gentleman of your dignity in so humble a posture; I will suppose it done if you please.

SIR ANTHONY: I prostrate myself in imagination, I assure you, madam.

LOUISA: Now, Sir Anthony, as you see my papa is impatient for the honour of being related to you, and that I am bound to an implicit obedience, I am afraid, unless your prudence interposes, that we shall both be hurried into wedlock, with a precipitancy very inconsistent with propriety.

SIR ANTHONY; I declare, madam, I am of your ladyship's opinion, and am almost apprehensive of the same thing.—

LOUISA: How is this to be avoided, Sir?

SIR ANTHONY: Be assured, madam, I too well know what is due to virgin modesty, to proceed with that rapidity, which my Lord (with whom I have not the honour of agreeing in this particular) seemeth to recommend.

LOUISA: You are very kind, Sir Anthony.

SIR ANTHONY: Oh, madam, I should pay but an ill compliment to your transcending merit, if I did not think it worth sighing for a considerable time longer, I assure you.

LOUISA: That's very noble in you, Sir Anthony—So passionate! and yet so nice—if all lovers were but like you!

SIR ANTHONY: The world I will presume to say would be the better, madam—but then I hope your rigours will not extend too far, my dear lady—a few months or so—longer than that I should be very near tempted to call cruel, I can tell you.

LOUISA [*Aside.*]: **As my passionate lover seems so well disposed to wait, I may chance to escape him.**— Your extraordinary merit, Sir Anthony, will undoubtedly shorten your time of probation—Mean while as I hinted to you before, that my papa is rather in haste to call you son, I would not have him imagine that *I* give any delay to this union. He may call my duty in question, which he expects should keep pace with his own wishes—you apprehend me, Sir?

SIR ANTHONY: Perfectly, my dear madam, and if I may presume to interpret what you have so charmingly insinuated to my apprehension, you would have me just hint to my Lord, that you are not *quite* averse to honouring me with your fair hand.

LOUISA: That I am *ready* to do so, if you please, Sir Anthony.

SIR ANTHONY: Very good, but at the same time I shall give him to understand that I am not as yet intitled to receive that very great happiness.

LOUISA: To that purpose, Sir, for I would not have this necessary delay appear to be of *my* chusing.

SIR ANTHONY: You little know, madam, the violence I do myself to repress the ardor of my flames; but patience is a prime virtue in a lover, and Scipio[15] himself never practised self-denial with more success than I have done.

LOUISA: I rely intirely on your discretion, Sir Anthony, to manage this affair with my papa.

SIR ANTHONY: Oh, madam, I shall convince my Lord, that it is from very sublime motives I submit to postpone my felicity.

LOUISA: I am much obliged to you, Sir Anthony, for this generous proof of your passionate regard to me.

SIR ANTHONY: You'll find madam, *I* do not love at the ordinary rate—but I must not indulge myself too long on the tender subject. I doubt it is not safe.

LOUISA [*Rising.*]: Sir, I won't detain you.

SIR ANTHONY: I must absolutely tear myself from you, madam, for gazing on so many charms I may grow unmindful of the danger.

LOUISA: Sir, I will no longer trespass on your time.

SIR ANTHONY: I must fly, madam, lest I should be tempted to transgress those rigid bounds I have prescribed to myself.

LOUISA: Sir, You have my consent to retire.

SIR ANTHONY: I am so overpowered with transport, madam, that I hold it necessary to withdraw.—

LOUISA: 'Tis the best way, Sir.

SIR ANTHONY: Dear madam, vouchsafe one gracious smile to your adorer.

LOUISA: Sir Anthony, your humble servant. [*Smiles and curtsies.*]

SIR ANTHONY: Madam, your most devoted—oh dawning of ecstatic bliss! [*Exit.*]

LOUISA: Ha, ha, ha, I think I may now go, and very safely assure my papa, that I am ready to take my adorer whenever he pleases—this is fortunate beyond my hopes. [*Exit.*]

END OF ACT III

ACT IV

Scene i. A Study.
Lord Medway alone, reading.

LORD MEDWAY:There's nothing good or ill but by comparison—Confound your dry maxims, what are they good for? [*He throws away the book.*][16] Yet there is some truth in *that* too.—Yesterday I thought myself an unhappy man—but what am I this morning? *So* much worse, that when I compare the two conditions, I *now* think I was *happy* yesterday—

My affairs are in a hopeful condition truly! Ruined in my fortune, jilted by my mistress, disobeyed by my son, insulted by my wife's superior worth; and last night (thanks to my dear indulgent stars!) to sum up all, I was forced to pawn the only stake I had left, my honour; which when I shall redeem, heaven knows.—*All* is now lost; and if my son continues obstinately to refuse this match, I am irretrievably undone—**What can these chits want? [*Enter Sir Harry and Lady Flutter, arm in arm.*]**

SIR HARRY: **My Lord, I am in the greatest surprize in the world!**

LORD MEDWAY: **At what, Sir Harry?**

SIR HARRY: **At something my wife here has told me!**

LORD MEDWAY [*Aside.*]: **Sure she has not blabbed!—What is it?**

LADY FLUTTER: Something of your Lordship, I can tell you.

LORD MEDWAY: Of *me*, Ma'am! I hope I have done nothing, Ma'am, that—that deserves censure.

SIR HARRY: 'Egad, my Lord, you have tho', and very severe censure too.

LORD MEDWAY: Sir Harry, I am ready to answer any charge against me.

LADY FLUTTER: Ha, ha, ha, neither Sir Harry nor I come to challenge you, my Lord.

SIR HARRY: Ha, ha, ha, faith my Lord looks as grave as if he were afraid of it though.

LORD MEDWAY: *Afraid* of it, Sir Harry! pray change that word for a better.

LADY FLUTTER: I vow, my Lord, you look as if you had a mind to beat us both—doesn't he, Sir Harry?

LORD MEDWAY: Sir Harry, I have really some serious business on my hands, and should be glad if you would dispatch what you have to say.

SIR HARRY: What *I* have to say, my Lord, why all the world have it to say, as well as *I*.

LORD MEDWAY: What is it, pr'ythee?

SIR HARRY: Why, that you are going to force Miss Medway to marry an old hero in tapestry hanging.

LORD MEDWAY: Is that all!

SIR HARRY: *All!* and enough too, in conscience, I think; why what the duce; my Lord, it is the jest of the town already, Lady Flutter and I have *so* laughed at the thoughts of it this morning. We call him the Knight of the inflexible countenance.[17]

[*Here Sir Harry and Lady Flutter burst out a-laughing.*]

LORD MEDWAY: Oh! I am mighty glad to see you so much of one mind.

LADY FLUTTER: My Lord, as we are intirely indebted to *your* good offices for that union, I am sure it must give you pleasure.

SIR HARRY: Sarcastical gipsey! but come, we won't banter his Lordship about it; he meant us well, I believe, though he was a little out in his politics—for faith, my Lord, I think she is much the better since I have given her her own way.

LORD MEDWAY: I am glad of it, Sir.—Have you any thing farther to offer?

LADY FLUTTER: Nothing, but our good advice, my Lord; as we have received so much from you, I think we owe you some in return; and, I am sure, if you would take *mine*, you would not think of my uncle for a son-in-law.

SIR HARRY: Oh fy, fy! ridiculous to the last degree.

LADY FLUTTER: Positively, my Lord, I won't give consent.

LORD MEDWAY: I suppose your uncle's at age, Ma'am.

LADY FLUTTER: Oh la! he has been that these hundred years.

LORD MEDWAY: Why then—excuse me, I am not at present in a humour to trifle.

LADY FLUTTER: But *we are*, my Lord; an't we, Sir Harry?

SIR HARRY: Oh eternally, my dear.

LORD MEDWAY: Be so good, then, as to enjoy it without my participation—I am really busy.

LADY FLUTTER: Come, Sir Harry. He's so splenetic, there's no bearing him. Let's go and laugh by ourselves.

SIR HARRY: Oh there's no pleasure like it!

LADY FLUTTER: My Lord could tell us of others, I warrant; well, don't look so cross; we'll dance at the wedding, if it must be a match.

SIR HARRY: I dare say your uncle will have jousts and tournaments; I'll learn to handle a target, my Lord, against the time.

LADY FLUTTER: My Lord don't think us worthy of an answer, so we will leave him to his wise reflections.

[*Exeunt laughing.*]

LORD MEDWAY: A couple of impertinents.—He alarmed me at first, but I find she is too cunning to tell him all.

[*Enter Colonel Medway.*]

COLONEL MEDWAY: I met Sir Anthony just going to my sister, my Lord; I suppose matters are in a favourable train between them.

LORD MEDWAY: He is such an out-of-the-way fellow, there is no knowing what to make of him; he has been with me and quite tired me with his romantic absurdity; but I think it will be a match. Your sister has at least condescended to accept of him for a husband.

COLONEL MEDWAY: I am glad of it, my Lord, since it was a thing you wished.

LORD MEDWAY: I thank you, son.

COLONEL MEDWAY: Something has ruffled you, my Lord.

LORD MEDWAY: I have an affair, George, that lies heavy on my spirits—'Tis in your power, and I think—I hope, at least—in your inclination, to extricate me from the greatest difficulty in which I was ever yet involved.

COLONEL MEDWAY: My Lord, you know you may command me; I am ready to hazard my life for your service, if it be any thing of that nature.

LORD MEDWAY: No, no, no; I am not so old, Medway, as to require the assistance of your sword.—You mistake my meaning quite.

COLONEL MEDWAY: You seemed moved, my Lord—[*Lord Medway walks about.*];—pray explain yourself.

LORD MEDWAY: Faith, son, I am almost ashamed to tell you the distress I have brought both upon myself and you.

COLONEL MEDWAY: Dear my Lord, don't think of me in the case.

LORD MEDWAY: Last night, George, I lost two thousand pounds, which I was obliged to pay this morning, and my honour is engaged for almost as much more.

COLONEL MEDWAY: My Lord, I thought you had determined never to venture on such deep play again.

LORD MEDWAY: I had so; but something happened yesterday that vexed and disconcerted me, and I went to the old set, just to amuse myself for an hour; but I don't know how it was—they drew me in for half the night.

COLONEL MEDWAY: My Lord, I am exceedingly concerned; but what can *I* do now?

LORD MEDWAY: Why, there's the point—I am very loth to revive a subject, that I know is disagreeable to you; but you see to what distress I am driven—there is but one way left.—You remember what we talked of yesterday; if my curst ill fortune had not pursued me last night, I thought never to have mentioned it to you again.

COLONEL MEDWAY: My Lord, I flattered myself you never would.

LORD MEDWAY: I thought I should not have occasion. I had another thing in view; but this last blow has crushed all my hopes at once.

COLONEL MEDWAY: Is it not practicable, my Lord, to devise some other way?—

LORD MEDWAY: Oh impossible! I am overwhelmed with debts, and worried like a stag at bay; but with regard to this last, for which my honour's pawned, I must be speedy in the means of payment.

COLONEL: Indeed, my Lord, I am exceedingly shock'd at what you tell me.

LORD MEDWAY: And is that all I am to expect from you? Look ye, Medway, it does not become a father to *entreat* a son; neither is it suitable to your age, or the character you bear in life, to be threatened, like a sniv'ling girl, with parental authority; *mine* is impotent, for I have nothing left to bestow; but as you would wish to prosper hereafter, save your father from disgrace, your mother (a good one she has been to you) from penury.

COLONEL MEDWAY: My Lord, I call Heaven to witness I would give up my *life* to preserve you both; but you require what is infinitely more precious!

LORD MEDWAY: Oh fy! fy upon it! how like a woman this is!—Your sister, a romantic girl, could do no more than sooth me with fine speeches; I expected a more substantial proof of filial love from you.

COLONEL MEDWAY: My Lord, you wound me deeply by such a cruel charge. What have I not already done to shew my duty, or, what with me was much stronger, my *love* for you, my Lord? Have I not given up my birthright? put it wholly in your power to alienate for ever, if you please, my family inheritance, and leave me a beggar? Is not this a substantial proof? My Lord, I beg your pardon; but you have wrung my very heart.

LORD MEDWAY: And you have wrung mine—for, Medway, with equal grief and shame I speak it, I *have* made you a beggar; I have mortgaged the last foot of land I was possessed of in the world, and the only prospect I had of redeeming it, was by this lady's fortune; that would have recovered all, and restored you to the estate of your ancestors. I thought a boyish passion might have been overcome, when such important motives for it were united, as your own interest, and the honour of your family.

COLONEL MEDWAY: As for my own interest, my Lord, it is but a feather in the scale; and for the rest, I think my own honour (which you yourself taught me to prize) is more concerned in this event, than that of my family can possibly be.

LORD MEDWAY: You told me you were not engaged by promise to the lady.

COLONEL MEDWAY: I am not, my Lord; but are there no ties but what the law can vindicate? Oh my Lord, you forget the lessons you have given me on other occasons!

LORD MEDWAY: Well, well—I acknowlege the justness of your reproach; but it comes like a bearded arrow from a child's lips—But I have done—I give up the cause—Had this affair, on which I had set my heart, succeeded, I should perhaps have been happier than I desire to be.—I had this morning been laying down a plan—but no matter, it is all over—I am sorry your mother should be a sufferer with me—I have not been the kindest husband—but I did intend, after I had seen you and my daughter settled, to have retired into the country on a moderate annuity; and there, Medway, I might perhaps have led a very different life from what you have been used to see; but I must struggle with ill fortune as well as I can—You have been a worthy son, I acknowlege it—You have done enough—You shall not charge me with making you miserable for life.

COLONEL MEDWAY: Oh, my Lord, I wish you had kept up your resentment; I cannot bear to hear you talk in this strain.

LORD MEDWAY: Why not, man? 'tis nothing but the truth.

COLONEL MEDWAY: My Lord, I would do any thing to prevent—

LORD MEDWAY: What? Speak, George.

COLONEL MEDWAY: I can't, my Lord.

LORD MEDWAY: A father's ruin, you would say—I know the tenderness of your nature, Medway, and therefore I will not urge you; your father is not such a tyrant; I have always considered you as my friend.

COLONEL MEDWAY: My Lord, to deserve that title still, I must not see you unhappy.

LORD MEDWAY: Why *will*-ingly, I think you would not—nor would I make you so for the world—I have already hurt you but too much. I will not wrong you *every* way. *I* deserve the ruin I have brought upon myself, and am content to sink under it.

COLONEL MEDWAY: My Lord, that must not be while I have power to help it.

LORD MEDWAY: I cannot ask it, son.

COLONEL MEDWAY: I'll give up all—even my *love,* to save you.

LORD MEDWAY: You cannot mean it sure!

COLONEL MEDWAY: I'll do as you would have me.

LORD MEDWAY: What! marry Mrs. Knightly?

COLONEL MEDWAY: I will, my Lord.

LORD MEDWAY: Give me your hand—Oh, George, what a triumph is yours!—You make me ashamed. [*Breaks away.*]

COLONEL MEDWAY: My Lord, since your affairs are urgent, I will not trust to the wavering of my own heart; I will visit her this morning; but it will be proper first to apprize poor Miss Richly of this sudden change.

LORD MEDWAY: By all means; but take my advice, Medway, and do not trust yourself to see her. Write what you have to say, for sighs and tears are infectious things. But all I hope will soon blow over; and when you are married, you may then have it in your power to make her amends for the fortune she has lost.

COLONEL MEDWAY: Oh, my Lord, you little know the heart of Clara, it is not in the power of riches to heal a wounded mind! But I must not trust myself to think upon the subject; I'll write to her whilst my resolution's warm. If she lives and can forget me, 'tis all I dare to hope. [*Exit.*]

LORD MEDWAY: Worthy creature! it almost goes against me to let him complete this match. Yet what other resource have I left? I hope this lady may make him happier than he expects—But I must haste and write to her directly, to request that as a favour, which I am sure she will think her greatest happiness. [*Exit.*]

Scene changes to Mrs. Knightly's house.
Mrs. Knightly, as just coming in, giving her capuchin,[18] &c. to her Maid.

MRS. KNIGHTLY: Has any one been here since I went out?

MAID: No, madam.

MRS. KNIGHTLY: Nor any letter or message?

MAID: Not that I know of, madam.

MRS. KNIGHTLY: Go and send Miss Richly to me. [*Exit Maid.*] What a mortifying situation am I in! to have made advances to a man, who, instead of stepping forward to receive them, shrinks back—My Lord Medway I know would gladly promote a union between his son and me. The backwardness on his side then, can proceed from no other cause, but a pre-engagement of his heart. Yet that may be got over; but if (as I fear) my sister loves him, I must not come to any explanation with her; for whilst I seem ignorant of it, I am not obliged to compliment her at the expence of my own quiet—I begin to wish her out of my sight. [*Enter Miss Richly.*] Have you done the work I left with you, Clara?

MISS RICHLY: I did not imagine you had given it to me as a task, sister—I have done nothing to it yet.

MRS. KNIGHTLY: I cannot conceive what you have got into that head of yours, child; for of late you never do any thing that I desire—I think I never saw so strange an alteration.

MISS RICHLY: Excuse me, sister, the alteration is in you.

MRS. KNIGHTLY: Oh your servant, Ma'am, you have learnt to contradict too—but it would become you, Clara, to remember I am your elder sister; and tho' there is no great difference in our years, yet I think the state you are in should teach you a little more respect to me.

MISS RICHLY: Indeed, sister, I do not want to be hourly reminded of that; I am sufficiently humbled already.

MRS. KNIGHTLY: Upon my word, Clara, I believe you will find humility the most useful virtue you can practice; and that you may have a better opportunity of doing so, I have thought of placing you in a sober retired family in the country; and who knows but you may captivate some rural squire, and then you may live according to your own taste you know.

MISS RICHLY [*Aside.*]: I'll tell her at once to punish her for her cruelty.— Perhaps, sister, I may have it in my power to do so without captivating a rural 'squire—

MRS. KNIGHTLY: I am glad to hear it; but we won't talk of your visionary schemes at present. [*Aside.*] I won't let her explain herself.

MISS RICHLY: There is a gentleman, sister—

MRS. KNIGHTLY: Well, well, keep him to yourself; I'll hear none of your love-secrets.

[*Enter a Servant, and delivers a note to Mrs. Knightly.*]

SERVANT: From my Lord Medway, Madam; the servant waits for an answer.

MISS RICHLY [*Aside.*]: Lord Medway! what can this mean?

MRS. KNIGHTLY: My compliments to his Lordship, and shall be glad of the Colonel's company. [*Exit Servant.*] You were going to say something of a *gen*-tleman, Clara, ha, ha, pray who *is* the gentleman? But before you tell me *your* secret, I'll intitle myself to the favour by making you *my* confidant. I have made a conquest you must know, of which this billet informs me.

MISS RICHLY: A conquest, sister! I thought this note had come from Lord Medway.

MRS. KNIGHTLY: Why so it does, and the conquest is, though not *of* Lord Medway, yet of one who I hope *will* be Lord Medway—I'll read you the note.

"Madam,
" 'Tis sometimes as great a fault to be too modest as too bold; my son is "charmed with you, yet durst not tell you so. I told him that *I* would, and "even went so far as to promise him a favourable reception. You see, "madam, my credit as a man of sagacity is at stake on this occasion, and I "am sure you have too much goodness to let me forfeit it. I flatter myself "you will allow Colonel Medway the honour of kissing your hand. He will "wait on you in half an hour if you do not forbid him.

"I am, Madam, &c.
"Medway.

"P.S. I hope you will be alone."

What do you say to this, Clara! Is your lover as pretty a fellow as Colonel Medway?

MISS RICHLY: Oh, sister, this is too much! but I give you joy.

MRS. KNIGHTLY: What's the matter, child! Why surely, my dear Clara, thou couldst not have any design upon the Colonel! Could you suppose that a man of family like him would marry without a fortune to support his rank and title?

MISS RICHLY: I am satisfied I was mistaken, madam, and shall now be obliged to you if you will send me into the country directly.

MRS. KNIGHTLY: Why really, my dear, I think you judge right. I am sorry you have been so imprudent as to suffer any little gallantries, with which the Colonel might have treated you, to take a serious hold on you; but since it has happened so unluckily, I own I think it will be rather awkward for you to be in the house on the occasion; for, to tell you the truth, I intend to marry him.

MISS RICHLY: Then, sister, I will, if you please, retire for the present, to the house of my friend who brought me up, till you are at leisure to dispose of me otherwise.

MRS. KNIGHTLY: You are perfectly right, my dear; I am pleased at this mark of your discretion—We don't part in anger, Clara; I shall always be your sincere friend, I assure you.

MISS. RICHLY: I hope so, sister—I will just go and give a few directions to the servant, and then come to take my leave of you.

MRS. KNIGHTLY: You will not then be long in giving your orders, for I suppose you would not chuse to meet the Colonel here. Besides, you find he desires to see me alone.

MISS RICHLY: I shall not interrupt you. [*Exit.*]

MRS. KNIGHTLY: Poor Clara! I pity you, and am sorry to build my happiness on the ruin of *yours;* but I'll make you amends. I see she loves, but 'tis plain she is not beloved. Perhaps 'tis really as I said, and he has won her affections by a few compliments, meant only in gaiete de coeur. I hope that may be the case; for, notwithstanding my tenderness for him, I have delicacy enough to be unhappy, if I did not wholly possess his heart.

[*Enter Maid, and gives Mrs. Knightly a letter.*]

Why this is for my sister!

MAID: Madam, you ordered they should all be brought to you. [*Exit Maid.*]

MRS. KNIGHTLY: Oh, I had forgot—It is of no great consequence now; but let us see who this is from—George Medway! I am almost afraid to read it, but I will know the worse. [*Reads.*]

"Within this hour, my Clara, the faithless despicable man, who called "himself *your* lover, will supplicate your sister for her hand, and with a "heart long devoted, and never, never to be recalled from you, offer mean, "deceitful vows to her." (Heaven's! what's this?) "I know not what I "write, for despair dictates to my trembling hand. Hate me, despise me, I "conjure" (I wish I could do so too) "yet hear the reasons for this fatal "change—"

Oh; this has given me an ague fit!

[*Enter Miss Richly.*]

MISS RICHLY: I am come now, sister, to bid you farewell.

[*Mrs. Knightly rushes out of the room.*] Bless me, what can be the matter with my sister! she seems strangely agitated—she was reading a letter—it was not that which she just now shewed to me.—What can it be? but I'll not intrude to ask her; I believe she can dispense with the ceremony of an adieu, and I can depart without one.

[*As she is going out, Colonel Medway is shewn in by a servant, both stop short, and look at each other.*]

COLONEL MEDWAY: I did not expect this, Clara! I thought you would have spared me the pangs of such a meeting.

MISS RICHLY: It was not designed, Sir, believe me; yet, if you had vouch-safed to have given me but a little notice of this visit, it would have been but kind.

COLONEL MEDWAY: I thought my letter, distracted as it was—would at least have prevented an interview.

MISS RICHLY: What letter?

COLONEL MEDWAY: Did not you receive one from me within this half hour? it was the earliest notice I could give you.

MISS RICHLY: I received none; but now you mention it, I am afraid it has fallen into my sister's hands.

COLONEL MEDWAY: If so, then, Clara, what a monster must I appear to you? ignorant as you are of the motives of my strange conduct, which in that letter I explained at full.

MISS RICHLY: Indeed, I am but ill prepared for such a sudden shock—yet I am willing to believe you must have had strong reasons for what you have done.

COLONEL MEDWAY: Can the generosity of your heart admit it as an excuse for my leaving you, that it is to save from utter and immediate ruin, a father that I dearly love?

MISS RICHLY: It can, Sir, and honour you for the motive; for I am sure that nothing else could have brought about such an event; and I should little deserve that esteem which I hope you still retain for me, if I could not give up *my* feeble claim to your tenderness, for ties of so much more importance.

COLONEL MEDWAY: Oh Clara, why did I give you up? what have I got to compensate for your loss!

MISS RICHLY: Your virtue! the consciousness of having acted right—You have broke no oaths, no promises to me; nay, I have often told you I would never be your's but with your father's consent; for sunk as I am in fortune, I would not meanly creep into a family that rejected me. And for this reason, I would neither give, nor receive a vow; but left you at full liberty to make a better choice, when your duty or your interest should urge you.

COLONEL MEDWAY: That last word, madam, carries a reproach in it, which I cannot bear from you.

MISS RICHLY: Do not mistake me, Sir; I have not the least suspicion, that interest has the smallest share in this action—I wish it had—for then perhaps I should part with you with less reluctance, than now I own I have power to do—but we must not touch upon this string—My sister loves you, and I hope will make you happy.

COLONEL MEDWAY: *Happy* do you say! no, Clara, no, happiness and I have shaken hands; what I have done today has made a wretch of me for life.

MISS RICHLY: Oh Sir—shew more indifference, if you would not have me repine too much, at my own sad fate.

COLONEL MEDWAY; And what is mine then, Clara, condemned to losing what is dearer to me than life; with the superadded grief of giving up my days to one I cannot love—*Your* condition is not quite so wretched; *you* still are free, and time may incline you to bestow your heart upon some happy man.

MISS RICHLY: Never, never.

COLONEL MEDWAY: Do not say so—I had but that hope left to keep me from desperation—If I lose it, I shall forget all obligations, and give my father up to poverty and shame.

MISS RICHLY: No more I beseech you, Sir—you have made a noble sacrifice of your love—do not lose the merit of your filial goodness, by repenting of an act, that raises you higher even in *my* esteem.

COLONEL MEDWAY: Clara—the tears stand trembling in your eyes while you speak—pray give them vent, for I am ashamed to weep alone. [*He turns from her.*]

MISS RICHLY: See—mine are dispersed already—Collect yourself I beg of you, you have a noble character to sustain—.

COLONEL MEDWAY: Oh Clara, I am unequal to the task— I have no fortitude left—

MISS RICHLY: Think of your unhappy father, Sir! let that keep up your resolution. **I grant you have a difficult task, for my sister may possibly think herself affronted by the explanation you have made in that letter, which has fallen into her hands.**

COLONEL MEDWAY: **I hope she may!**

MISS RICHLY: **Nay, do not indulge in such a vain hope, 'tis but a surmise of mine, and may have nothing in it.—I know she suspected our attachment to each other, yet that did not check the progress of her love.**—I am going to quit her house directly, and this, sir, for my own, for my sister's, and for your sake, is the last time we must ever meet—forget me, sir, and try—I conjure you try to be happy— [*Exit.*]

COLONEL MEDWAY: Clara—stay—stay!—So! all's at an end—and the hope I had nourished for years is vanished like a dream.—This trial was more than I thought I could support; but her noble firmness, I believe, made me ashamed to sink quite under the blow that has parted us for ever—I wish I were out of this fatal house—for I am very unfit to act the lover's part. [*Enter Lord Medway.*]

LORD MEDWAY: How now, Medway! what is the meaning of this? alone, and with a countenance of despair! I bid you wear a better face. Where's Mrs. Knightly? have not you seen her yet? I thought, by this time, to have found you at her feet, and as I passed by the door, stepped in to help you to make love; for I know your heart is not warm in the business.

COLONEL MEDWAY: My Lord, I am very glad you are come; you must, indeed, make love for me; for I assure you I am in no condition to speak for myself.

LORD MEDWAY: Why, what's the matter man! I suppose Miss Richly and you have been whining over one another; did not I warn you against that, George, and bid you write to her?

COLONEY MEDWAY: So I did, my Lord; but unfortunately she did not receive my letter; so that by accident we met just now, not, I assure you, with the least design on either side.

LORD MEDWAY: That was unlucky; but how came she to miss of your letter?

COLONEL MEDWAY: By a circumstance still more unlucky, for she is afraid her sister got it.

LORD MEDWAY: What a curst untoward accident, if that be so! yet her love for you will make her overlook all this. 'Twas but a thing of course, mere gallantry.—I'll lead you to her, and turn it off.

COLONEL MEDWAY: I beg you, my Lord, to see her first alone; she does not yet know that I am come; the servant conducted me to this room, supposing she was here, and lucky was it for me that it happened otherwise; her sister's presence so disconcerted me, that I should have acquitted myself but very ill towards *her.*

LORD MEDWAY: But she expects you by this time; a lover and out-stay his appointment! for shame, George!

COLONEL MEDWAY: Let me beseech your Lordship to dispense with my seeing her just now; I'll take a turn or two in the Park,[19] and endeavour to compose myself; and if my passion for her sister should be mentioned, *you*, my Lord, can, with a better grace than I, give it what turn you please.

LORD MEDWAY: Well—perhaps it may be better so. I own I had rather she should speak of that to *me* than to you: get you gone quickly—I'll prepare the way for you—She admits me to her toilet.

[*Exeunt different ways.*]

END OF ACT IV

ACT V

Scene i. Lord Medway's House.
Lord Medway alone.

LORD MEDWAY: By what a strange fatality are all my actions governed!— Nothing that I can devise but what ends in disasppointment and vexation.—Yet in this last instance, I ought to be thankful for my disappointment; for had my design been accomplished, into what a horrid gulph should I have plunged my children. It makes my blood run cold to think of it.—I was born for destruction, and the ruins I have made myself are now come tumbling on my head. No hope left for avoiding them—no prospect before me but disgrace.—And the life of shame I have to look back on! To think how I have abused and perverted every gift bestowed on me for a blessing! How I sicken at my own reflections—

[*Enter Colonel Medway.*] George! What now, George!

COLONEL MEDWAY: My Lord, I have been endeavouring to assume such a frame of mind, as will, I hope, enable me to go through with the task in which I have engaged. I am ready now to wait on Mrs. Knightly.

LORD MEDWAY: I—did not expect you back so soon.

COLONEL MEDWAY: I thought, my Lord, the sooner I returned, it would be the more aggreable to you, as well as respectful to the lady.

LORD MEDWAY: Can you feel nothing more than respect for that lady, son?

COLONEL MEDWAY: My Lord, you know I cannot. My heart is given to another. *I* must be unhappy, yet I hope I shall not make Mrs. Knightly so.

LORD MEDWAY: Poor woman—she is already too much so.

COLONEL MEDWAY: Have you had any conversation with her, my Lord?

LORD MEDWAY: I have.—You cannot be her husband.

COLONEL MEDWAY: I am willing, my Lord, if the lady will accept of me.

LORD MEDWAY: You know not what you say—Oh, George, George—you will start when I tell you the strange discovery I have made.

COLONEL MEDWAY: What is it, my Lord?

LORD MEDWAY: Mrs. Knightly—she to whom I would have joined you—I find is—

COLONEL MEDWAY: What?

LORD MEDWAY: Oh Medway!—my own daughter.

COLONEL MEDWAY: You amaze me, my Lord—how did you discover it?

LORD MEDWAY: When I went to sollicit for you, I found her in her closet, under great agitation, on account of the letter you had written to her sister.—I pleaded for you, but found her averse and cold.—In a little pause of discourse, I happened to cast my eyes on the picture of a lady, which hung just before me, and was struck with the resemblance of a beauty whom, in my early days, I loved, and cruelly betrayed.

COLONEL MEDWAY: I remember, my Lord, to have heard you speak of some such thing—a lady, who, when you made your first campaign in Portugal, gave you her love.

LORD MEDWAY: The same—I thought the injured countenance seemed to frown upon me. Surprized at the sight, I hastily demanded whose the picture was, and was told by Mrs. Knightly 'twas her mother's.

COLONEL MEDWAY: That must, indeed, my Lord, have shocked you.

LORD MEDWAY: Oh, 'twas nothing to what I suffered after, when farther urging her to satisfy my curiosity, she told me her mother's name and family! The apparent confusion this threw me into, rouzed her in her turn to ask me some questions, which brought about this amazing explanation.

COLONEL MEDWAY: She could not know you by your name, my Lord, as it was since my birth you assumed *that* with the title of Medway.

LORD MEDWAY: True.—She had heard of me by my own family name, and asked me, with a faltering voice, whether I had not formerly been at Lisbon, and borne the name of Selby. My acknowleging that I had, threw her into agonies, from which I, with difficulty, recovered her.

COLONEL MEDWAY: Did you never know, my Lord, that you had a daughter by that lady?

LORD MEDWAY: Oh no, no! I was recalled to England early in my amour with her. I married soon after my return, and, thoughtless and young as I then was, never enquired after her more.

COLONEL MEDWAY: How then, my Lord, can you be certain of this fact?

LORD MEDWAY: Oh, Medway! by too sure an evidence—The penitence and deep remorse of a dying woman! The unhappy lady confessed the secret, with all its circumstances, to this her daughter, when she was on her deathbed.

COLONEL MEDWAY: Mrs. Knightly, then, had passed for Mr. Richly's daughter?

LORD MEDWAY: She had; the match between him and her mother was hastily concluded by her friends, immediately after my departure. At the time of this lady's birth, Mr. Richly was absent on his affairs in the Indies; and tho' she came into the world in less than seven months after the marriage, yet (this circumstance being carefully concealed from him) he never doubted of her being his own.

COLONEL MEDWAY: Poor Clara! she then has been doubly wronged, in being deprived of her birth-right, as well as in losing the unequal portion which her father left her.

LORD MEDWAY: That was the cause which wrung the secret from her dying mother's breast. Her deceased husband had, through a partial fondness for his supposed eldest daughter, left her such a disproportionate share of his wealth; and the mother, in divulging the secret, charged Mrs. Knightly, with her last breath, to do justice to her sister. This she herself, in the hurry of her shame, surprize, and grief, acknowleged to me.

COLONEL MEDWAY: I long to know, my Lord, what resulted from this extra-ordinary interview.

LORD MEDWAY: Mrs. Knightly's agitations are not to be described. She wept and wrung her hands. I mixed my tears with her's; and, while she fell on her knees before me, I involuntarily dropped on one of mine, and begged of her to accept a blessing from her repentant father. She strained me to her bosom; then rising with a noble air, she made a sorrowful and silent motion with her hand that I should leave her. I did so; and hastened home, to brood over my own reflections—Oh such reflections! such reflections, George!

COLONEL MEDWAY: My Lord, there is something so extraordinary in this event, that it looks as if Providence itself had interposed.

LORD MEDWAY: Oh, Medway, 'tis for your sake then; I do not deserve the care of heaven!

COLONEL MEDWAY: I beg, my Lord, you will not entertain such desponding thoughts, but hope the best.

LORD MEDWAY: George! there's no foundation *here* for hope; I want that *within* which should support me. It is not the flashiness of wit, or vanity of superior talents, that can avail me in an hour like this. I'd give them all, nay, the whole world, were I master of it, to be possessed of such a virtuous self-acquitted heart as yours.

COLONEL MEDWAY: Your *thinking* thus, my Lord, makes you almost the very man you wish to be.

LORD MEDWAY: Oh, George, George! words cannot describe the anguish which I feel. I should be resigned to it, did it concern myself only, as the just punishment of a life of folly and vice; but when I think of you and of your mother, I am distracted.

[*Enter Lady Medway.*]

LADY MEDWAY: My dear! [*Lord Medway turns from her.*] Medway, why do you let your father sink thus under his apprehensions?

COLONEL MEDWAY: Do you speak to him, madam, he wants your tenderness to sooth the troubles of his mind.

LADY MEDWAY: My dear, you have no cause to be thus affected; I come a happy messenger of joyful news to you.

LORD MEDWAY: Joyful, do you say! that would, indeed, surprize me.

LADY MEDWAY: Mrs. Knightly is in my chamber, my Lord. We have had a long conversation. She has told me the strange event which this day has unfolded, and begs to speak with you—shall I bring her in?

LORD MEDWAY: Ay, pray do, my dear. [*Exit Lady Medway.*]

COLONEL MEDWAY: Reassume your spirits, my Lord; I dare promise you a happy issue to this affair.

LORD MEDWAY: I own this unexpected visit from Mrs. Knightly has a little revived me; and the generous frankness with which she has communicated the secret to my wife, shews she has a noble and enlarged mind.

[*Enter Lady Medway and Mrs. Knightly.*]

MRS. KNIGHTLY: My Lord, I thought to have found you alone. I cannot, without confusion, look up to Colonel Medway.

LORD MEDWAY: *You,* madam, have no cause; but, if my son's presence creates in you any uneasiness, he shall withdraw.

MRS. KNIGHTLY: He need not, my Lord; for as he is materially concerned in what I have to say, 'tis fit he should be present at my explanation. I presume, sir, you are by this time no stranger to my story.

COLONEL MEDWAY: I think myself happy, madam, in finding I have so near and tender a claim to your regard.

MRS. KNIGHTLY: I hope to give you one still nearer, Sir. I will not now apologize for the means by which I came at the knowlege of that mutual love which I find there is between my sister and you.

LADY MEDWAY: It needs no excuse, Madam; it was a happy event, as it gave my Lord the opportunity of making a discovery so fortunate for us all.

MRS. KNIGHTLY: My Lord, I owe my sister a large amends for the distress I have occasioned her on more accounts than one; and you in your turn, I think, should recompense your son for the sacrifice he was willing to make to you. Has he your permission to make Clara his bride?

COLONEL MEDWAY: Oh, madam, you are too, too good.

MRS. KNIGHTLY: You have but little reason, Sir, to say so yet. My Lord, the Colonel's *love* for my sister ensures *his* happiness, and, to render her acceptable to you, I am ready to share half my fortune with her.

LORD MEDWAY: Oh, Medway, what an exalted mind is here!

LADY MEDWAY: My dear, do not keep your son suspended; he seems to check the transports that I see rising in his heart, till he has his father's sanction to his love.

LORD MEDWAY: Take, take your Clara from this excellent creature's hand, and may you both be blessed!

MRS. KNIGHTLY: No thanks, Colonel— [*The Colonel advances to Mrs. Knightly.*]—restrain your raptures till you see my sister. I have sent to desire her company here—And now, my Lord, I hope I have, by this one act of justice (for it is no more) made happy, the nearest, and dearest relations I have on earth.

LORD MEDWAY: Son! Lady Medway! help me to praise and to acknowlege as I ought, such unexampled goodness!

LADY MEDWAY: Oh, my dear, I want words—Medway's gratitude, you see, has stopt his utterance.

[*Enter a Servant.*]

SERVANT: Miss Richly, Madam, is below.

MRS. KNIGHTLY: My Lord, and Lady Medway, will you let me have the pleasure of presenting the Colonel to my sister without any other witness?

LORD AND LADY MEDWAY: By all means.

COLONEL MEDWAY: You, madam, have the best right to dispose of me.

MRS. KNIGHTLY: Come, Sir. [*She gives him her hand, and he leads her out. Lord and Lady Medway alone.*]

LORD MEDWAY: Oh, Lady Medway, I have not merited the benefits which are thus showered down upon me.—But it is *your* goodness, your's and my children's virtue, have been the care of Providence, and *I* am blessed but for *your* sakes. Yet, my dear, I have the satisfaction to assure you, that what has passed this morning, joined to some other late incidents, has so thoroughly awakened reflection in me, that from this day forward you will find me a new man.

LADY MEDWAY: My Lord, if you are sensible of any thing in your conduct that you would wish to rectify, I rejoice that you have taken your resolutions from the feelings of your own heart; for it would grieve me if I thought I had even by a look reproached you.

LORD MEDWAY: You never did, Madam; I acknowlege you have been the best of wives; 'tis time now that I should in my turn study to deserve that constant and tender regard from you, which I have hitherto but too much slighted. And now, best of women, receive my hand a second time; and with it an assurance, which I could never make before, that you possess my heart entire. [*They embrace.*]

LADY MEDWAY: Oh, my dear, I never was truly happy till this instant.

LORD MEDWAY: You'll find my conduct as perfectly reformed as your heart can wish; assure yourself you will.

LADY MEDWAY: Pray, my dear, no more—you are *now* every thing that I would have you to be. I have but one wish left, which, *could* it be accomplished, would render me completely happy—Poor Louisa!

LORD MEDWAY: I understand you, my dear—I hear young Branville is returned.

LADY MEDWAY: He is, my Lord, he arrived last night—I do not presume to mention *him;* but indeed she cannot be happy with Sir Anthony.

LORD MEDWAY: I would willingly gratify you in every thing; but how can I acquit myself with honour to Sir Anthony? You know he has my promise.

LADY MEDWAY: I know it, my dear; yet am I sure he is still so much in Mrs. Knightly's power, that with her assistance, I make no doubt but you could be easily disengaged from it.

LORD MEDWAY: If that could be done—

LADY MEDWAY: We shall certainly have a visit from him presently; suppose, my Lord, Mrs. Knightly were to try her influence on him when they meet, it will be a good opportunity—

LORD MEDWAY: Well, my dear,—you shall take your own way.
[*Enter Colonel Medway, Mrs. Knightly, Miss Richly, and Louisa; while Lord Medway and the Colonel talk apart. Mrs. Knightly presents her sister to Lady Medway.*]

MRS. KNIGHTLY: Madam, receive a sister from my hands.

MISS RICHLY: Oh, sister, my obligations to you—

MRS. KNIGHTLY: No more, sister; I have but acquitted myself of a duty—

LADY MEDWAY: Louisa, I have been petitioning for you once more; my Lord has yielded, if he can with honour get off from his word to Sir Anthony. Dear Mrs. Knightly, with a little of your help, I am sure it could easily be done.

MRS. KNIGHTLY: Madam, you may command me in any thing.

LOUISA: Oh, Madam, a word from you, nay a kind look, would I am sure recal your fugitive lover.

MRS. KNIGHTLY: I have not the vanity to think so; but since it will be agreeable to you, I'll try if I have still any interest in him.

LADY MEDWAY: This is about his time of visiting us. What if you were to make the experiment here?

MRS. KNIGHTLY: To oblige you, ladies—thus much I must tell you, I never mean to marry again; but I know it will content Sir Anthony barely to be restored to my good graces.

[*Enter a Servant.*]

SERVANT: Sir Anthony Branville is below, my Lord!

LORD MEDWAY: I'll wait on him.

LADY MEDWAY: Dear my Lord, suffer him to be conducted in here.

MRS. KNIGHTLY: My Lord, I have a design of stealing him from Miss Medway, I assure you.

LORD MEDWAY: Oh I see you have been plotting—Desire Sir Anthony to walk up—Louisa, on this joyful day I must not suffer you to wear a look of discontent—You owe all to this lady, and the best of mothers.

LADY MEDWAY: Louisa, you had best retire. [*Exit Louisa.*]

[*Enter Sir Anthony, bows low to Lord and Lady Medway, then looks round with surprize.*]

SIR ANTHONY: My Lord, I thought my eyes would have been blessed with the sight of my fair mistress.

MRS. KNIGHTLY [*Half aside.*]: Then I find it is all over.—What, Sir Anthony, not a look! Have you quite forgot me?

SIR ANTHONY: Ah, madam, that enquiry comes a little of the latest, I do assure you.

MRS. KNIGHTLY: I am sorry for it, Sir Anthony.

SIR ANTHONY: My Lord, I hope your Lordship is of opinion that I do not deviate from that fidelity which I owe your excellent daughter, in entering into conference with this lady.

LORD MEDWAY: By no means, Sir.

SIR ANTHONY: I flatter myself I am indulged with your ladyship's favourable construction on the same occasion.

LADY MEDWAY: Without doubt, Sir Anthony.

SIR ANTHONY: Colonel, I would entreat the favour of being uncensured by you likewise.

COLONEL MEDWAY: Oh, Sir Anthony, the laws of good-breeding are not to be dispensed with.

MRS. KNIGHTLY: Sir Anthony, I am glad of the opportunity of asking your pardon, in presence of this worthy family, for any part of my behaviour which you may have taken amiss.

SIR ANTHONY: Madam, I am not worthy of so great a concession; would to heaven there had never been any occasion given for it!

MRS. KNIGHTLY: I wish so too, Sir Anthony; but I find my repentance comes too late.

SIR ANTHONY: Repentance! heavens, madam, do you condescend to feel any compunction on the occasion?

MRS. KNIGHTLY: I do indeed, Sir Anthony.

SIR ANTHONY: Then, madam, I apprehend it will not be so adviseable for me to abide within the reach of your influence; I think I cannot do a wiser thing than to stop my ears against your allurements.

MRS. KNIGHTLY: Not till you have first heard me, dear Sir Anthony.

SIR ANTHONY [*Aside.*]: *Dear* Sir Anthony!—I had best depart, Lady Medway.

LADY MEDWAY: No, pray stay, good Sir Anthony.

SIR ANTHONY: There is a great peril in it, I assure your ladyship.

COLONEL MEDWAY: I thought your love for my sister, Sir Anthony, would be a sufficient guard against your relapsing.

SIR ANTHONY: Her charms, Colonel, I am ready to acknowlege should be an armour of proof; but give me leave to tell you, if there be a vulnerable part about me, this sorceress (craving her pardon for the expression) will certainly find it out.

MRS. KNIGHTLY: Sir Anthony, I confess I have been to blame in trifling with a man of your worth; yet I own I did not think you would have taken my little capricious coyness for an absolute refusal of your addresses.

SIR ANTHONY: Madam, madam, take care; I am *but* a man; though I hope not without fortitude to sustain those trials of my virtue and my patience.

MRS. KNIGHTLY: 'Tis *I*, Sir Anthony, who have most need of fortitude—but go, ungrateful as you are.

SIR ANTHONY: Do you hear that, my Lord? Before heaven, there never was such an inchantress since the days of Armida.[20]

LORD MEDWAY: I am surprised, I confess, Sir Anthony.

SIR ANTHONY: Well you may, my Lord—she is hung round with spells—I do aver it to you I am rooted here; I have not power to stir, my Lord.

COLONEL MEDWAY: Bless me, Sir Anthony, that's very strange.

SIR ANTHONY [*Walks about.*]: I use the word but metaphorically, Colonel; I have not absolutely lost the use of my limbs, thank heaven.

LORD MEDWAY: Then, Sir Anthony, you had better retire, before it be too late.

MRS. KNIGHTLY: Ay do, and carry that love, which was my right, to Miss Medway; but let me tell you, Sir, as a punishment for your inconstancy, that her heart is already given away to another.

SIR ANTHONY: 'Tis unlawful in you, madam, to slander an innocent lady's reputation.

MRS. KNIGHTLY: I speak nothing but the truth, Sir Anthony; and what is more, I know your nephew Branville is the man, and that she is equally beloved by him.

SIR ANTHONY: My nephew Branville! oh heavens, madam, what do you tell me! my Lord! my lady Medway! may I believe what this incomprehensible fair one says?

LADY MEDWAY: Sir Anthony, I must own that I believe there is an affection between your nephew, and my daughter.

SIR ANTHONY: I am thunder-struck—petrified—converted into stone.

LADY MEDWAY: I think, Sir Anthony, there is nothing so extraordinary in the circumstance.

SIR ANTHONY: Madam, there is such a degree of impurity, in the bare imagination of a nuptial so circumstanced, as has, I assure you, totally subverted my whole system.

COLONEL MEDWAY: I am sorry, Sir Anthony, you were not informed of this sooner.

SIR ANTHONY: Sir, 'tis not too late to prevent my honour from being stained.

LORD MEDWAY: You must judge for yourself in this case, Sir Anthony.

SIR ANTHONY: My Lord, passionately as I admire the lady, I would suffer martyrdom, rather than solemnize a marriage under such inauspicious influence.

COLONEL MEDWAY: Sir Anthony, you are not pressed to do it.

SIR ANTHONY [*Apart to the Colonel.*]: Colonel, I am not a man of a sanguinary spirit, but if such a measure is deemed necessary—I am at your service either afoot or on horseback—you understand me.

COLONEL MEDWAY: There is no occasion, I assure you, Sir.

SIR ANTHONY: I am ready—that's all—my alacrity is pretty notorious on those occasions.

COLONEL MEDWAY: For my part I approve of your punctilio intirely.

SIR ANTHONY: I am proud of your approbation; my Lord, I hope I am honoured with yours, in giving up my pretensions to the fair lady, your daughter.

LORD MEDWAY: Sir, you have my free consent.

MRS. KNIGHTLY: Then, Sir Anthony, I am sure you have too much generosity not to promote your nephew's happiness, if my Lord is willing.—

LORD MEDWAY: I have no objection to Mr. Branville, Madam,—but Sir Anthony knows my inability to give my daughter a fortune equal to her rank—

MRS. KNIGHTLY: Oh, my Lord, I am sure, Sir Anthony is too noble, to let the sordid consideration of money be a bar to the happiness of two faithful lovers—

SIR ANTHONY: On the contrary, Madam, I am charmed that my nephew has such an opportunity of shewing the generosity inherent in the family of the Branvilles, by contemning riches, in comparison of beauty.

COLONEL MEDWAY: Indeed, Sir Anthony, he deserves all your affection; for tho' I know he doats on my sister, yet hearing that you addressed her, he resolved to give her up.

MRS. KNIGHTLY: Generous young man!

SIR ANTHONY: Ah ladies, see what delight the little sportive god takes in persecuting us true lovers!—My Lord, if my nephew has your consent, I assure you I will render him in point of fortune, worthy of the lady of his heart.

LORD MEDWAY: Sir, after an instance of such generosity, your alliance must be doubly acceptable to me.

MRS. KNIGHTLY: And now, Sir Anthony, I hope you will return to your lawful sovereign.

SIR ANTHONY: Arbitress of my fate, thus I reassume my happy bondage— [*He kneels and takes Mrs. Knightly's hand. Enter Sir Harry and Lady Flutter.*]

SIR HARRY: What the duce is all this! my uncle in heroics at my widow's feet! every thing's topsy-turvy I think—My Lord! Lady Medway! an explanation quickly, for heaven's sake! Miss Medway gave us a hint of some strange things that were going forward here—What are you all about?

LADY FLUTTER: Dear Mrs. Knightly, I absolutely die with curiosity!

SIR HARRY: My dear, *that's* a disease that will never kill you, for you have been wonderfully subject to it ever since you and I were acquainted.

LADY FLUTTER: Prithee, Sir Harry, let your tongue keep pace with your wit, and then you will not talk so fast.—Tell me, do, Mrs. Knightly.

SIR HARRY: No, don't Mrs. Knightly—My dear, you really put me in mind of the cat in the fable,[21] who was metamorphosed into a fine lady; but upon the first temptation—slap—egad she was a cat again.

LADY FLUTTER: And you put me in mind—

LADY MEDWAY [*Draws her aside.*]: Take care, my dear, take care.

LORD MEDWAY [*Aside to her.*]: Beware of a relapse, lady Flutter, you are now happy if you are inclined to continue so.

LADY FLUTTER: So, my Lord! who has metamorphosed *you,* pray?

LORD MEDWAY: Lady Medway.

MRS. KNIGHTLY: My dear Lady Flutter, you shall know all at another opportunity. For the present, I am sure it will give you pleasure, to wish the Colonel and my sister joy on their happy union, to which my Lord has consented. You are to congratulate miss Medway too on her approaching nuptials with Mr. Branville.—

SIR ANTHONY: And you are to felicitate *me,* niece Flutter, on being permitted the transcendent happiness, of once more basking in the sunshine of this lady's favour.

LORD MEDWAY: And you are all to congratulate me, upon a double occasion; first, on that of being perfectly blessed in domestick joys; and next, that of seeing me a thoroughly reformed man. [*Exeunt omnes.*]

END OF ACT V

EPILOGUE.[22]

What strange odd maggots fill an author's pate!
A female court of justice—rare conceit!
Ladies, I give you joy of your new stations,
I think you've had a trial—of your patience.
What, five long acts, and not one pleasant sally!
But grave Sir Anthony's attempt to rally—
No sprightly rendezvous, no pretty fellows,
No wife intriguing, nor no husband jealous!
If to such innovations you submit,

And swallow tame morality for wit;
If such dull rates you let a woman teach,
Her next attempt, perhaps, will be to—preach.
I told her (for it vexed me to the heart)
Madam—excuse me—I don't like my part—
'Tis out of nature—never drawn from life,
Who ever heard of such a passive wife?
To bear so much—'tis not in flesh and blood—
Such females might have liv'd before the flood.
But now the character will seem so flat,
Give me threats, tears, hysterics, and all that—
If this don't work upon my Lord, I hope
You'll so contrive the plot—I may elope.
Take my advice, I think I know the town,
Without such aids your piece will scarce go down.
Hold, friend, she cry'd—I think I've hit the way
To reconcile both sexes to the play;
For, while the prologue bids our own be sov'reign,
The scenes instruct the other how to govern.
A harmless plot—with credit to dismiss
The piece—you know the Ladies never hiss.
And tho' they should condemn it, yet the men sure
Will leave a woman's faults to women's censure.
They, prone to meekness, charity, and love,
Are always silent where they can't approve.
But if at loud applause we dare to aim,
It is the men must ratify our claim.

FINIS.

The Dupe

A Comedy

PROLOGUE. *Friendly*

The paths of Truth with Fancy's flowers to strow,
To teach improvement from delight to flow,
The bards of old first bade the Comic strain
With mirth instruct, with moral entertain.
No vice or folly that disgrac'd the age
Escap'd the daring Poet's honest rage;
But Satire, uncontroll'd, pursu'd her plan,
Nor stopp'd at general lines, but mark'd the Man;
Ev'n features, voice, dress, gait, the scene display'd,
And living characters to scorn betray'd.

Such rude attacks be banish'd in our times,
Be persons sacred, but exposed their crimes:
For wise, and good, and polish'd as we are,
We still may find some vices—here and there.
And if a Modern, in this prudent age,
Dares to obtrude a Moral on the Stage,
Critics be mild: tho' unadorn'd our Play,
Nor wisely grave, nor elegantly gay,
How rude soe'er, it shocks not Virtue's eye,
Nor injures the chaste ear of Modesty;
Nor with soft blandishment bids Vice allure,
Nor draws the Good in odious portraiture.
Our Son of Folly is of Vice's brood,
And willingly bids evil be his good.

Is there a wretch that views, without remorse,
The better path, and yet pursues the worse;
Proud of imputed guilt, yet vainly blind,
Call's folly, sense; vice, knowledge of mankind;
Dup'd by the knave, he scorns and ridicules,
Rul'd by the Wanton, *whom he thinks he rules;*
This, this is folly: a determin'd fool
Provokes and justifies our ridicule.

DUPE

Sir John Woo   Ir. Yates.
Friendly,   Ir. Havard.
Wellford,   Ir. Packer.
Sharply,   Ir. King.

Mrs. Etherd   Mrs. Pritchard.
Mrs. Friendl   Mrs. Clive.
Emily, niece   Mrs. Palmer.
Rose,   Mrs. Lee.

ACT I

Scene i. A Chamber in Sir John Woodall's House.
Emily enters, Rose following her.

EMILY: Must I be persecuted by every one in the family? Has your mistress ordered *you* to be [**thus**] rude to me too?

ROSE: I don't know what you mean by rude, not I; so you always call me, when I would advise you for your good.

EMILY: I desire you will not concern yourself about me, Mrs. Rose.

ROSE: I only tell you as a friend, Miss, that if you provoke my mistress, it will be the worse for yourself.

EMILY: This is most astonishing insolence! I wish your master were come home.

ROSE: I wish he were, and we'll see whose story will be believed. [**I am sure**] I only speak for peace-sake. This house will be too hot for some of us before a week's over, that's for certain.

EMILY: If you mean for me, I am above your malice; and so my uncle be disabused, I care not what is my lot.

ROSE: Mighty well! If young ladies will be so froptious,[3] let them suffer; but remember I tell you—

EMILY: I'll hear no more of your impertinence. Begone—

ROSE: Ha!—a conceited set-up thing! who cares for you? [*Exit Rose.*]

EMILY: Into what vile hands am I fallen! And my uncle, unhappy infatuated man! to give me up to the conduct of this wicked woman.—Yet let me not carry my accusation too far.—He thinks at least she is faithful to *him,* and devoted to his interest; but I *will* undeceive him, let the consequence be what it may.

Scene ii.
Enter Mrs. Friendly.

EMILY: Dear Mrs. Friendly! I thought you had quite deserted me; I am very glad to see you.

MRS. FRIENDLY: One would not think so, my dear; when you could be a whole month without coming near me:—And you are never at home neither.—

EMILY: Never at home! Bless me, Madam! Why I never—

MRS. FRIENDLY: Nay, nay; young people love young company: And to be sure, diversions, and plays, and balls, and shews, and sights, and such things—

EMILY: Oh! Madam, you are quite mistaken—

MRS. FRIENDLY: Why, I don't blame you, child.—Youth loves pleasure, and if one does n't enjoy it when one's young, why—

EMILY: But that's not the case, Madam—If you'll hear me—

MRS. FRIENDLY: When you come to be of my age, I can tell you, Miss—

EMILY [*Aside.*]: There's no stopping her.—But, dear Madam, hear what I have to say. I have never stirred out since I saw you last, nor never knew you call'd on me.

MRS. FRIENDLY: Bless me! you surprise me! utterly amaze me! What has been the matter? Have you been sick? I have call'd at the door a dozen times: I am quite in a labyrinth—a wilderness! I can't for my life imagine—

EMILY: I'll tell you, if you'll allow me—

MRS. FRIENDLY: Ay, pray do—By all means, I would hear it; though I have very little time to stay with you, and I have a great deal to tell you too, Miss, I can assure you—But one thing at a time; and so what were you going to say?

EMILY: Why, not to trouble you with particulars, I have discovered such irregularities in Mrs. Etherdown's conduct—

MRS. FRIENDLY: A notorious creature I warrant her, though Sir John thinks her a saint—Heaven help the poor man, he is bad enough himself.

EMILY: I declared I would tell my uncle of her [behaviour], and from that time I have never spoken to her.—In resentment for this (as she pretends) I have been made a prisoner; but I fear she has some other wicked view; for ever since, Sharply, her brother, that audacious fellow, dares to persecute me with his impudent addresses.

MRS. FRIENDLY: Sharply! A bold man, or I'm mistaken. There's another of Sir John's favourites;—but it's no business of mine; I never meddle in other people's affairs; but to be sure it was an unchristian thing, and a barbarous thing, and a very unconscionable thing, in Sir John:—But Sir John *has* no conscience, that's what I blame him for.

EMILY: Indeed, Madam, his errors as much deserve pity as his faults do blame.

MRS. FRIENDLY: To send a young creature, an orphan as I may say, hand over head to town here, into such a family! Little did his poor sister think when she was dying—

EMILY: Dear Mrs. Friendly,—spare me on that topic. I cannot bear to think of it.—

MRS. FRIENDLY: [I see you have but just changed your mourning. La,] my dear, I beg your pardon! I did not think to draw tears from you; but I'll make you amends for it:—I have such news to tell you!—Who do you think is arrived from Germany?

EMILY: Dear Madam!—how could you keep this from me so long?—and now to surprise me so.—You are very good, but indeed you have put me all in a flurry.

MRS. FRIENDLY: *I* put you in a flurry! Lord, child, for what? If I had been abrupt, indeed, and said any particular person was come, you might say so;—but so far from that, I intend to make you guess half-a dozen times, perhaps, before I tell you.

EMILY: Oh! 'tis easy to guess:—I am interested in too few to be suspended.—Captain Wellford is returned.

MRS. FRIENDLY: The very man, as I am alive.—I never was so surprised since the hour I was born.—I was combing my hair at the glass—

EMILY: When did he arrive?

MRS. FRIENDLY: You shall hear—I was combing my hair—

EMILY: Do tell me; how does he look?

MRS. FRIENDLY: I'll tell you by-and-bye; but I can't stay with you two minutes, for I have a world of business to do before dinner.

EMILY: Well, I'll not detain you;—only tell me, if he can devise any means to see me:—You know I dare not admit him here.

MRS. FRIENDLY: Have patience, I was going to describe—

EMILY: Not *now,* my dear good creature; only answer my question, and leave out the rest of your narrative till another time.—

MRS. FRIENDLY: I declare and vow, now, that is so like Mr. Friendly! He can't bear to hear a regular narrative, and when I want to be a little intelligible, with proper explanations, and circumstances, and so forth, he always interrupts me.—

EMILY: That's hard.

MRS. FRIENDLY: To be sure, Mr. Friendly is a very good man, and a very good husband, and all that, and we have been married now—let me see—

EMILY [*Aside.*]: So she talks, 'tis no matter on what subject.

MRS. FRIENDLY: Two and-twenty—ay, two-and-twenty years;—but no matter for that. What were we saying before?

EMILY: We were speaking of Captain Wellford.—I am surprised he has not writ to me.

MRS. FRIENDLY: Why, he arrived but this morning, child, and did not know you were in town till he came to my house. He was posting down to the country to see you, till we stopp'd him. I vow and swear I think he is grown taller than he was.—Bless me! 'tis almost one o'clock; I must run away, for I have a thousand things to buy.—What do you think I have to buy, now?

EMILY: Nay, I can't tell.

MRS. FRIENDLY: Well, I'll reckon them up to you,—In the first place—

EMILY: Are you going to count over the thousand articles on your fingers? For goodness sake, don't lose so much of your time.

MRS. FRIENDLY: Lord! I shall be too late as it is; but I was in such a hurry to tell you the news.

EMILY: I wonder you were admitted.

MRS. FRIENDLY: One of the servants was just going out,—and in I brush'd, and up I ran, without asking any questions.—

EMILY: But did Wellford express no impatience to see me?

MRS. FRIENDLY: To be sure, child, did not I tell you so? Why, he would fain have come with me, only Mr. Friendly hindered him. He said he'd write too. And Mr. Friendly bid me tell you, he'd send the chariot for you this evening, to bring you to my house.

EMILY: Ay, but the difficulty is to get thither; for it will be impossible to go out without leave, and I cannot bring myself to ask it of such a wretch.—I wish you could contrive some means.—

MRS. FRIENDLY: Dear child, I am the worst in the world at contriving; I am not one of those that have words at will, and can make a long Canterbury tale out of nothing, and can contrive, and invent, and say this and that and t'other.—I am quite in a dilemma for my part.

EMILY: I own it goes against me to condescend so far as to ask permission of such a creature; but on this occasion I will get the better of my pride, and desire leave to go to your house. If she refuses me, I must be patient till my uncle comes to town, and then I am determined to quit this house at all events.

MRS. FRIENDLY: When do you expect Sir John? I wonder he is not impatient to see the son that his mistress has brought him since he left town.—I'll lay my life he's as fond of it as if it were born in honest wedlock; a naughty man!

EMILY: When he sent me to town, he went on a visit to an old acquaintance of his, where it seems he was seized with a fit of the gout, which has detain'd him so long; but he is now well, and we expect him every day.

MRS. FRIENDLY: Drinking, and rioting, and ranting, no doubt. Poor man! he has no shame in him.—Well, I must bid you good-by.—The Captain will be on thorns till he sees me.

EMILY: True; and therefore I will keep you no longer.

MRS. FRIENDLY: I had a great deal more to say, if I could remember it.

EMILY [*Aside.*]: I shall never get her away.—You'll excuse me, my dear Madam, but I have letters to write into the country, by a person who waits for them.

MRS. FRIENDLY: Oh! to be sure, you have your correspondents, child; why not?—Well, I won't interrupt you;—and I am so hurried, I have not had time to say a word;—and so day, day;—for I must go.—You'll be sure to send word tho', if you can't get leave to come.—

EMILY: Oh! undoubtedly.

MRS. FRIENDLY: Come, come, you shan't stir.

EMILY: I must wait on you down. [*Exeunt.*]

Scene iii.
Changes to Mrs. Etherdown's Chamber, she drinking Chocolate, Rose
attending.

MRS. ETHERDOWN: I tell you, something must be thought of directly to prevent it.

ROSE: I am sure I have thought and thought, and argued and argued, and begg'd and pray'd, as if I had been begging an alms, [and all to no purpose.]

MRS. ETHERDOWN: A perverse little vixen!

ROSE: As I said to her this morning, what signifies telling Sir John such a silly thing, only to make mischief in the family? You know my mistress is a great deal younger than him, and it is a common thing for ladies that live with elderly gentlemen to go astray a little now and then, and think no harm.

MRS. ETHERDOWN: Psha—Was that an argument? You should have frightened her by telling her my influence over Sir John, and that she had best not provoke me to revenge.

ROSE: Why so I did at last, [Madam.]

MRS. ETHERDOWN: [Well,] and what did the unlucky prying hussy say to that?

ROSE: Say! why she said [truly] she did not care, not she;—[and] that she would not have her uncle deceiv'd, and so she could but see you and your brat (as she called the poor innocent babe) fairly out of the house, she did not care what became of her.

MRS. ETHERDOWN: Oh! that brat shall be gall and wormwood to her yet.

ROSE: Ay, if it would induce Sir John to marry you, Ma'am, as you think it will.

MRS. ETHERDOWN: And a poor reward enough, Rose, for my three years slavery to his caprice and silly humours:—In short, I am so sick of him, and the continual disguise I am obliged to wear, that if I should once accomplish my point, I should rejoice to part from the beast.

ROSE: I wish it were come to that, for then you could leave him with credit: Lady Woodall, and a separate maintenance. Oh, that I could see that day!

MRS. ETHERDOWN: Why, you don't fancy [that] I have made so bad a use of my time as to depend on that, I hope.—No, no, Rose, make the most of the present hour, is my maxim.

ROSE: If you have done so then, what need you trouble your head about consequences, but march off and leave him to shake his ears?

MRS. ETHERDOWN: How do you think I have made my money? Why by dipping him over head and ears in debt; appropriating every shilling he gave me for other purposes to my own use.—This, by Sharply's management, has hitherto been kept from his knowledge: but if I were to leave him now, he would not pay sixpence for me, and I should lose the fruits of my industry.

ROSE: And how unluckily things have fallen out! I wish Miss Emily had never come into the house, for my part.

MRS. ETHERDOWN: I wish I durst strangle her.—I have kept her hitherto from tatling to her croney Mrs. Friendly; but something must now be done to hinder her from blabbing to Sir John: Can you think of nothing? I never saw you so stupid in my life.

ROSE: Why, I have found out something that may turn to account, I think, with good management.

MRS. ETHERDOWN: And what an ill-natur'd toad are you to keep it to your-self—out with it quickly.

ROSE: No—it's a secret.

MRS. ETHERDOWN: Prithee, dear Rose!

ROSE: 'Tis a secret worth gold.

MRS. ETHERDOWN: Well—here's gold for it.

ROSE: See here,—this letter I intercepted a little while ago.

MRS. ETHERDOWN [*Snatches it from her and reads.*]: Which way, good girl?

ROSE: A footman in a smart livery brought it to the door, and enquired for Miss Emily; I suspecting something, was resolved to find her out, and said I was her own maid, and he might give it to me: he still pressed to see her; I told him she could not be seen; but says I, looking very slily, don't you think now, I know who you came from?—Oh, Oh, cries he winking, then I suppose you expect a fee for delivering this? I laughed and twitch'd it from him, and away he went, mightily pleas'd with his own archness.

MRS. ETHERDOWN: Clever wench! 'tis from a lover indeed, and you shall hear the contents. [*Reads.*]

"My impatience to hear from my ever dear Emily, will not suffer me to "wait Mrs. Friendly's return. I am permitted to hope for the happiness of "seeing you to-day at her house. If nothing should prevent your coming, "the chariot will attend you at five o'clock.—I will not, till I see you, utter "one of the thousand tender things of which my heart is full.—Adieu— "your ever faithful,

"R. W."

Here are only the two initial letters of his name.—Who can he be?

ROSE: Nay, I can't tell—You know I could not ask his man any questions, as that would be shewing him I was not in the secret.

MRS. ETHERDOWN: And so that prating gossip, Mrs. Friendly, is a go-between after all.—Has she been here to-day?

ROSE: Ay, that she has, and slipp'd in unknown to any body, and Miss and she had a long confab.—Don't you think you can strike something out of this?

MRS. ETHERDOWN: Certainly.—How she purposes to get to her rendezvous tho', I can't imagine; I believe she will hardly ask my leave, and I think she will scarce venture to go without it.—

[*Enter a Maid and gives a Card to Mrs. Etherdown.*]

Ha! ha! ha! A pretty air truly! "Miss Emily sends her compliments to me, "and begs I will permit her to pay a visit to Mrs. Friendly this evening." Humph—tell Miss I will consider of it.—[*Exit Maid.*] A visit to Mrs. Friendly! yes, yes, we understand your visits; an equivocating little slut;— this letter, then you see, was a mere work of lover's supererogation, and she may never know that it was sent, for the plan seems to be settled already between her and Madam Clack.

ROSE: And do you intend to let her go?

MRS. ETHERDOWN: Yes,—at least she shall think I do.—Where is Sharply? He is never in the way [, **I think,**] when I want his assistance.

ROSE: Mr. Sharply! What assistance do you want from him? I am certain Mr. Sharply will give himself no trouble about her.—He must be brought into every scrape.

MRS. ETHERDOWN: You seem warm! What, he is a gallant of yours, I suppose?

ROSE: Well,—if he be, I have as free liberty to have my gallants as other people, I suppose?

MRS. ETHERDOWN [*Aside.*]: Provoking hussy, but I'm in her power.—Oh! to be sure, Rose, I am far from finding fault with the thing itself, only I thought you wiser than to throw away your favours on such a beggarly fellow.

ROSE: There's nothing in that, if I like him.

MRS. ETHERDOWN: I'll be hanged if he ever knew who his father was, for I could never get him to tell me his real name.

ROSE: What signifies his name,—he is a pretty man, I am sure of that.

MRS. ETHERDOWN: Ha! ha! a pretty man!—Hist,—I think I hear his voice in the next room.—He is talking loud to Emily;—laughing too;—I'll step to the door and listen to what they are saying.—Go you and get things ready for me to dress:—make haste, good Rose. [*Exit Mrs. Etherdown.*]

ROSE [*Alone.*]: So! you want to get me out of the way, do you? What new piece of roguery can she be contriving, that *I* am not to be let into?—Some wicked trick, I am sure; and Mr. Sharply is to be her tool, her cat's paw.— Now would I give one of my fore-teeth to know what she has to say to him.—Ay and I *will* know too.—I have followed your example many a time to keep you in countenance:—but I'll make bold to practise the *last* you have set me, to please myself.—I think I can *listen* with you for your ears.— [*Exit Rose.*]

Scene iv.
Enter Sharply laughing, Mrs. Etherdown following.

MRS. ETHERDOWN: I thought your impudence was not to be parallel'd, but I find your absurdity is even an over-match for it.—An idiot to suppose the girl would *marry* you!

SHARPLY: [**Ha, ha, ha,**] upon my soul I can't help laughing at your folly, as much as that little rustic's impertinence, in rejecting my *honourable* addresses.—How she did rant, and pout, and swell, when I proposed marriage! I thought I should have split my sides.—

MRS. ETHERDOWN: Why, you sot! to throw away your time upon such an idle project.—Did I ever propose any thing but your getting her for a mistress, puppy? that I might have her as much in my power, as I am now in hers.—Was not that the plan I laid down for you, and told you how to behave?

SHARPLY: And you have really taken me for a puppet all this while, that was to be moved by your pretty finger and thumb!—A reasonable expectation to be sure! and because I have hitherto been your instrument to cheat that fool Sir John, you modestly suppose I am to have no will of my own.

MRS. ETHERDOWN: Why, how dare you talk thus to me? *You* a will! that owe the cloaths on your back, nay the very bread you eat to my bounty.—Do you remember the figure you cut when I took you up first?

SHARPLY: A damn'd shabby one.—What then?

MRS. ETHERDOWN: With an old tatter'd regimental, a rusty black crape about your neck to hide the want of a stock, and a pair of greasy high-topp'd gloves to look as if you had a shirt.

SHARPLY: I *was* rather bare of linen at one time of my life,—that's certain: these premises granted, what would you infer from thence?

MRS. ETHERDOWN: And have not I dress'd you out like a gentleman, and taken you into the house, and have not you the credit of passing for my brother?

SHARPLY: Ha! ha! ha! Credit quotha.—Ho! ho! ho! that kills me quite!

MRS. ETHERDOWN: Yes! credit, jackanapes!—greater than any of your kin ever had; I am a gentlewoman born.

SHARPLY: Oh yes! and bred too.—We all know that.

[*He makes signs of* [*washing and*] *clapping cloaths with his handkerchief.*]

MRS. ETHERDOWN: You are a slanderous coxcomb. I was as well educated—

SHARPLY: You were an inimitable clear-starcher, that's certain; and *iron'd* like a cherubim.

MRS. ETHERDOWN: You are the most audacious—

SHARPLY: Dear Ma'am, you flatter.

MRS. ETHERDOWN: The most daring—

SHARPLY: Dear Mrs. Etherdown, you quite overwhelm me!

MRS. ETHERDOWN: The most impudent rogue!

SHARPLY: Nay, prithee now, don't make one blush!—such *extravagant* praise!—and to a friend too, fy!—

MRS. ETHERDOWN: What! you pique yourself on it?

SHARPLY: And with reason too—'Twas the former of those good qualities first procured me the honour of your ladyship's acquaintance—the other recommended me to Sir John: since which it has been my business to flatter him, lie to him, applaud his nonsense, act the ninny to his face, and laugh at him behind his back:—so much for my roguery.—And for my impudence, besides the use[s] aforesaid, 'tis by that I keep you in awe in spite of your insolence, and by that I expected to get Emily for wife in spite of her pride.

[MRS. ETHERDOWN: **And would it not have serv'd you as well in trying to get her for something else, puppy?**

SHARPLY: **To be sure—**] but it was not worth while to squander such a precious talent on an intrigue; an heiress was my object, not an amour.

MRS. ETHERDOWN: You are a rare projector, to be sure; your impudence has defeated your *own* purpose, and undone my hopes. What had you to recommend you as a *husband* to such a proud minx?—

SHARPLY: Front—front,—which has carried many a wiser woman.

MRS. ETHERDOWN: 'Tis that has shock'd her.—Had you play'd the humble lover, she would have thought it was her person only, not her fortune, that you aimed at; and by this time she might have fallen into the snare; for I think a woman might like you well enough as a gallant.

SHARPLY: I am rather tolerable, you are of opinion?

MRS. ETHERDOWN: Deuce take you, you have fool'd away your time to no purpose.—Things are now come to an extremity: Sir John will certainly be at home to-morrow, perhaps to-night; and if Emily's mouth is not stopp'd, I am undone.

SHARPLY: And I too, by my soul! for all must out together; so e'en shift for yourself. [*He offers to go.*]

MRS. ETHERDOWN: But, dear Sharply, sure you can't be so cruel as to leave me thus, standing upon the very brink of ruin. If that vixen cou'd be got out of the way for one week, nay but for two or three days, I shall, by that time, be above the reach of her little spiteful tongue.

SHARPLY: Toss her into the Thames!

MRS. ETHERDOWN: Psha!

SHARPLY: Or suppose I were to run away with her now, and be hang'd, to do you a pleasure.

MRS. ETHERDOWN: Suppose I were to convince you that you hazard nothing in running away with her, have you address and courage enough to undertake the business?

SHARPLY: Courage, you know, is not amongst the accomplishments I value myself *chiefly* upon.

MRS. ETHERDOWN: You will have no farther need of it than to overcome some trifling obstacles;—danger there is none at all.

SHARPLY: Explain, explain.—Barbara Etherdown, none of thy tricks will pass upon me.

MRS. ETHERDOWN: Emily is no heiress:—Sir John has another heir.

SHARPLY [*Sneeringly*]: Really!

MRS. ETHERDOWN: Dare I trust you with an important secret?

SHARPLY: If it be for my interest to keep it, I am mute as a fish—if not, out it comes, by my soul!

MRS. ETHERDOWN: Well—I must trust you.

SHARPLY: [*Walks about and whistles.*] Well—where's the secret?

MRS. ETHERDOWN: I hate that audacious* cool indifference: prithee, be serious a minute, and hear me.

SHARPLY: Well!

MRS. ETHERDOWN: I am married to Sir John. [*Sharply laughs in her face.*] I knew you would not believe it; but as I have a soul to be saved† it is true.

SHARPLY: This is to me now, Barbara, to me, that knows you so well!

MRS. ETHERDOWN: I have been his wife above a twelvemonth; why don't you think him sot enough to be drawn in?

SHARPLY: Yes.—Yet I am slow, wonderfully slow of faith in this article.

MRS. ETHERDOWN: I took him in a fond hour, and pretending scruples of

---

*Dublin edition reads "impudent."
†Dublin edition reads "but by all that's good."

conscience, declared I would live with him no longer, if he did not marry me.

SHARPLY: And he took you at your word?

MRS. ETHERDOWN: Sooner than part with me he at last consented; but so contrived it, that to have the *credit*, as he called it, of passing for a keeper, rather than a husband, 'tis impossible for me to prove our marriage; for I knew neither the parson nor the witness.

SHARPLY: If this be so,—pray what difference is there between your being his wife or his mistress,—*Conscience* out of the question?

MRS. ETHERDOWN: You shall hear,—he promis'd if I brought him an heir, of which I gave him hopes [just] before he left town, that he would own me for his wife; for the fool is not really so bad as he would fain be thought.

SHARPLY: Humph.—Well and you *have* brought him one?

MRS. ETHERDOWN: And therefore I expect he will acknowlege our marriage as soon as he comes home, provided he has not tales told him.

SHARPLY: But if he should; by my soul! he'd rather bastardize his whole generation, than bear to be laughed at for a cuckold; especially by Friendly, with whom he would fain pass for a man of great sagacity.

MRS. ETHERDOWN: You see therefore the present necessity of getting Emily out of the way.

SHARPLY: Get her out of the way then as fast as you can.

MRS. ETHERDOWN: How provoking this is now.—You know I can't without your help.

SHARPLY: [*Sings.*]: Tol, lol, lol.—

MRS. ETHERDOWN: —But, Sharply, if you'll assist me, I'll reward you beyond your hopes.

SHARPLY: Open your plan of operations.—Now you talk reason, I'll vouchsafe you a hearing.

MRS. ETHERDOWN; Thus it is then, Emily has desired to go* this evening to Mr. Friendly's, on pretence† of a visit, but in reality to meet a lover.

SHARPLY: A lover! some country booby I suppose, that has scampered after her from Hertfordshire.

MRS. ETHERDOWN: Most likely.—Friendly's chariot is to call for her at five o'clock; it will be then too dark to distinguish the difference, and there will be no difficulty in putting her into another chariot, and as she does n't know the streets, conducting her to another house, where you may be ready to receive her.

SHARPLY: The thing is not absolutely impracticable:—But what am I to get for undertaking this business?

MRS. ETHERDOWN: Have you thought of any place to which you can convey her?

SHARPLY: I'll not stir an inch under two hundred pound, one of which I will be paid before-hand.

MRS. ETHERDOWN: You have no more conscience in you—But you shall have it.—Whither do you mean to carry her?

---

*Dublin edition reads "is to go."
†Dublin edition reads "upon a sham pretence."

SHARPLY: Mrs. Private, our old acquaintance, has generally a spare room, where I sometimes meditate.

MRS. ETHERDOWN: The best place in the world.—Don't you appear till she is in the house; then give her into safe custody, return home, and leave it to me to charge her elopement on this lover, with the connivance of Friendly's family, which will exasperate Sir John against them, and hasten the acknowlegement I want him to make.

SHARPLY: Faith, I begin to relish the scheme; for besides the profit, it will gratify my revenge on that little coy puss, for refusing me.

MRS. ETHERDOWN: True; for when you have her there, you know—

SHARPLY: No farther instructions, dear Madam: I fancy I may be able to proceed without your help.

MRS. ETHERDOWN: One word more, Sharply, and then I've done. I think in a few days my fool and I must separate; for this is but a temporary expedient, and all must soon come to light.—The creditors too grow pressing; but before the storm comes, don't you think something might be done for me, by way of settlement?

SHARPLY: Ah! thou harpy!

MRS. ETHERDOWN: You shall have poundage, Sharply.

SHARPLY: You know how to work upon my good nature.

MRS. ETHERDOWN: Ay, and that you can lead Sir John with a silk thread.

SHARPLY: Oh! curse him; an obstinate mule.*—My way is to persuade him *against* the thing I want to insure the execution of.

MRS. ETHERDOWN: You know his trim; ha! ha!

SHARPLY: Then does he thunder out ten thousand execrations at me, for a stupid loggerhead; and then I drop my arms, and dangle them this way, and stare at him, and look mightily frightened, and bless myself at hearing such oaths, and stretch out my neck, and call him a sad *wicked* gentleman.—That always pleases him.—I am an honest ignoramus, he says, and wonders how the devil such a fool could ever be taught arithmetic.—Then I give a sheepish grin, and tell him he's so pleasant, and so comical, and so witty, there's no being angry with him.—He breaks into a horselaugh, I join in the chorus, and so we get lovingly drunk together.

MRS. ETHERDOWN: Ha, ha, ha! an admirable picture!—Well, you had best set about preparing your business, but take care not to let Rose know the least tittle of the matter; her jealousy would blow us all up.

SHARPLY: *Rose*'s jealousy!

MRS. ETHERDOWN: Come, come, I know what terms you are upon with her; you need not deny it.

SHARPLY: I don't intend to deny it.

MRS. ETHERDOWN: I am only amazed how you could like such a dowdy.

SHARPLY: Poh!—Any thing to pass away an idle hour.

MRS. ETHERDOWN: But such a vulgar creature! I thought you had a better taste.

---

*Dublin edition reads "no, he's as obstinate as a mule."

SHARPLY: Ah, poor devil! she haunted me perpetually, till I shew'd her a little pity.

MRS. ETHERDOWN: Well, I'll now go and give my permission to Miss Emily to go to her rendezvous, and at the same time I'll send Mrs. Friendly word she can't come.—I had best say Sir John is come home, and that will keep the busy body quiet for to-night.—Get *you* gone, we have no time to lose.

SHARPLY: There's a small point to be adjusted first between you and me.

MRS. ETHERDOWN: What's that?

SHARPLY [*Makes signs of counting money on his hand.*]: I budge not a foot* without it.

MRS. ETHERDOWN: Oh!—Come with me into my closet.—I had quite forgot.

SHARPLY: Your memory is prodigiously like a sieve;

> Your interest it preserves, like weighty grains,
> But promises are chaff, it ne'er retains.[4]

[*Exit.*]

[*Rose comes from behind a screen, where she had been concealed.*]

ROSE: Now a mischief light on you both, for a couple of false treacherous serpents as you are!—Rose's jealousy will blow us up!—Yes, yes; I'll blow you up with a witness!—That rogue Sharply! Any thing to pass away an idle hour!—And that other ungrateful upstart; a dowdy! a vulgar creature! I'll fit you for your fine contrivances!—If I don't make you both smart for this! [*Exit Rose.*]

END OF ACT I

ACT II

Scene i. Sir John's House. Mrs. Etherdown's Dressing-room.
Enter Mrs. Etherdown, a Maid following.

MRS. ETHERDOWN: What can become of Rose? Was there ever such assurance as this, to go out without saying a word to me?—Is Mr. Sharply come in yet?

MAID: No, Madam.

MRS. ETHERDOWN: The deuce take them both.

Scene ii.
Sir John without.

SIR JOHN: What the plague's the meaning of this? The house is like an inn, I think; all the doors open!

---

*Dublin edition reads "step."

MRS. ETHERDOWN: Here's Sir John, as I live!—Quick, quick, hide those things.* [*The Maid throws a veil over her toilet.*†]
[*Enter Sir John.*]

SIR JOHN: So, so, so; What, keeping your room still, Bab! Well; and how dost do, girl? [*She runs and falls on his neck.*] I thought you had been gone abroad, for the house seems to be flung out at the windows! Nobody in the way!

MRS. ETHERDOWN [*Speaking faintly.*]: Me! heaven help me! I abroad! I have not been able to go down stairs yet; and I'm s—o weak, and s—o faint, and so overpower'd with joy, that I ca—n't ca—n't speak my dear Sir John!

SIR JOHN: Well, well, well; here I'm for you again, you poor fond toad you:—and how hast thou done all this while?—whimpering, blubbering, like a fool, I suppose, for me.

MRS. ETHERDOWN: Oh Sir John!—three long months!—I would not live three months again without you!

SIR JOHN: That damn'd gout catch'd me by the toe just as I was coming home. If a man *will* play the devil, why he must pay for it; so there is no more to be said.—How does your bantling do?

MRS. ETHERDOWN: *My* bantling! he's your own dear picture.

SIR JOHN: Not the better for that, you know.—How does Sharply and Emily?

MRS. ETHERDOWN: And is that all you care about the poor dear child, your own flesh and blood, not to desire to see him, and he's so pretty, and so like yourself!

SIR JOHN: I wish he may make a better man, or Lord ha' mercy on your foolish sex, some twenty years hence!

MRS. ETHERDOWN: Ay, as you say, Sir John; if he should have your deluding ways.—

SIR JOHN: Poh! nonsense!—mere stuff!—prithee, talk a little sensibly, and give me some account of the family; every thing at sixes and sevens, I suppose, since I have been gone.—You snivling and moping up in your room; Sharply driv'ling and blund'ring on as usual; and Emily giggling and flaunting about the streets.

MRS. ETHERDOWN: I declare, Sir John, you know as well how it was, as if you had been at home.—I'll have Miss Emily call'd to you, if you please.—Go bid her come hither.
[*Exit Maid.*]

SIR JOHN: I don't want her.—I'm monstrously tir'd with my journey.—How do Friendly's family?

MRS. ETHERDOWN: La! Sir John, I never see any of them; they shun me as if I were a very rattle-snake!

SIR JOHN: Oh! Mrs. Friendly is one of your virtuous women; but I'd have her know, I can make you as virtuous as herself when I please.—'Tis but owning you for Lady Woodall, and let me see who'll dispute your virtue.

---

*Dublin edition reads "put these out of the way."
†Dublin edition reads "The Maid whips away some silks and other ornaments."

MRS. ETHERDOWN: Ay, my dear Sir John, you remember your promise, and my character now, you know—

SIR JOHN: Burn character!—What good does character do any body? give me a good estate and a good constitution, and let character go to—

MRS. ETHERDOWN: Ay, but your son, you know, Sir John.—

SIR JOHN: Well, well, the thing shall be own'd some time or other; but I can't bear the thoughts of that dogmatical fellow Friendly's grinning at me; and then the curs'd impertinence of his wife too, who is always meddling in other people's affairs. When her tongue is set a going, you may as soon stop a whirlwind. 'S-death I'd as lieve be married to a wild cat as to such a woman.

MRS. ETHERDOWN: Ay, Sir John, but they have more reasons than one for hating me. You must know Miss Emily is mighty great at their house of late; and to tell you the truth, I believe she is carrying on an intrigue there.

SIR JOHN: What, with Friendly?—Well—

MRS. ETHERDOWN [*Aside.*]: Brute!—No, no, not with Friendly himself.

SIR JOHN: Nay, I should not wonder; his wife is such a chattering devil, he must be sick of her. But who is it with then?

MRS. ETHERDOWN: Why, with a shabby young fellow, that is not worth sixpence; but he is a relation* of theirs, and Mrs. Friendly's in the secret.

SIR JOHN: What, she's a bawd too! I am glad of that; well—

MRS. ETHERDOWN: Why, as they know that in case you have no lawful issue, Emily is your heir, they think to snap her up, and are mightily afraid of your marrying me.

SIR JOHN: What the d—I should put it into their heads that I'd marry at all?

MRS. ETHERDOWN: I know from what he said to my brother, that Mr. Friendly has a notion you will, one time or other.

SIR JOHN: Curse his notions:—What does he take me for? Does n't he know that I abominate the very thoughts of matrimony?

MRS. ETHERDOWN: He knows it very well, Sir John; yet he said, many a man that hated it as much might enter into the state for convenience.

SIR JOHN: Did Friendly say so?

MRS. ETHERDOWN: He did indeed; and, says he, as Mrs. Etherdown has always behaved so well, and is so fond of Sir John—

SIR JOHN: Did he? Did Friendly say so?

MRS. ETHERDOWN: I am telling you his words; and she is such a careful, prudent woman, and knows her duty so well—

SIR JOHN: Ah, poor Friendly, poor Friendly! there the shoe pinches; he thought of his own wife there.

MRS. ETHERDOWN: That I should not be surprised, says he, if Sir John were to marry her.

SIR JOHN: Friendly said so!

MRS. ETHERDOWN: His wife was present; and she, forsooth, must put in her word; and said, it would be a base thing, and a wicked thing in Sir John; and Mr. Friendly took her up short, and said, all the world knew Sir John did not much value doing a wicked thing.—

*Dublin edition reads "a particular Friend."

SIR JOHN: Ha, ha, ha! Oh! he knows me well.

MRS. ETHERDOWN: But, says he, I'll give you leave to hang him, if you catch him doing a silly thing.

SIR JOHN: Ha, ha ha! he's no fool; Friendly's no fool; and he knows me well. [*Enter Maid.*]

MAID: Madam, Miss Emily is gone out.

MRS. ETHERDOWN: Gone out! Where?

MAID: I have been enquiring for her, Madam; and one of the men says, she went out in a chariot, a little while ago. [*Exit.*]

MRS. ETHERDOWN: Oh! Sir John, Sir John! I am afraid that girl is a young Hypocrite, Sir John.

SIR JOHN: By my soul, she can't be a better thing; for if I find her out, I'll so claw her.—

MRS. ETHERDOWN: I did not think to have shew'd it you, Sir John, but I can keep nothing from you;—look at this letter that Miss Emily dropt to-day.

SIR JOHN [*Reads.*]: "*Mr. Friendly's chariot will call for you*———*One of the thousand tender things.*"—ha, ha, ha! by the mass, the girl takes after me; she has spirit, and loves intrigue; I wish she don't come upon the town tho'.

MRS. ETHERDOWN: No, Sir John, Mr. Friendly's people have other designs; pretty friends they are indeed, to profess such a regard for you, and spirit your niece up to rebellion, and then entice her away; just when you were expected home too, to marry her, I'll lay my life, to their beggarly relation; but they think they can laugh you out of your resentment.

SIR JOHN: Laugh! 's-death, let me catch any one daring to laugh at me: laugh! how durst you say such a thing? how durst you *think* of such a thing?

MRS. ETHERDOWN: Dear Sir John, I think of no such thing; but I know Mr. Friendly's gibing way; and if he can but rail at me, and set you against me, he'll expect* to enjoy his fine plot in triumph.

SIR JOHN: Curse them and their plots too; I'll shew them I can out-plot them, with a vengeance—if the thing be as you suspect.—

MRS. ETHERDOWN: It is but too sure, Sir John.

SIR JOHN: Then I'll convince Friendly at once that he is a blockhead; for I'll tell him I am married, and have a son to inherit my estate; and then, pray, what becomes of his plot?

MRS. ETHERDOWN: Ay, there will be a thunder-clap indeed, as you say, Sir John.

SIR JOHN: I wanted something to provoke me to it; and if it had not been for this scurvy dog's trick of Friendly's—I don't think I should have own'd you; [*Half Aside.*]—not while I liv'd, by my soul.

MRS. ETHERDOWN: They'll deny it, as sure as I live, Sir John, and fancy they can impose on you.

SIR JOHN: [**Yes,**] Yes, I am a likely fellow to be imposed on! I have liv'd till this time of day, to be gull'd to be sure!

---

*Dublin edition reads "think."

MRS. ETHERDOWN: A probable story, as you say, indeed, Sir John.

SIR JOHN: I have thought of a way to mortify Friendly horribly. I'll go to him to-morrow; and, as if I did not suspect him to have any hand in this affair, I'll pretend to consult him about marrying.

MRS. ETHERDOWN: Ay, and then he'll begin to slander me.

SIR JOHN: And [then,] he'll come with his advice, and his objections, and his arguments against it; and when I get him to that point, I'll come slap upon him, with owning my marriage; ha, ha, ha!

MRS. ETHERDOWN: [Ha, ha, ha!] You have such a contriving brain, Sir John!

SIR JOHN: Then I'll laugh in his face, and leave him to consider who plots best, he or I—ha, ha, ha!

MRS. ETHERDOWN: Ha, ha, ha! and such a malicious wit!

SIR JOHN: Ha, ha, ha! how I enjoy the thoughts of plaguing the surly cur! he'll be ready to hang himself.—Come, I don't care if I do take a peep at this same brat of ours.

MRS. ETHERDOWN: I fancy he's asleep, but you may look at him: Oh! he's a little angel!

SIR JOHN: I am delighted to think of Friendly.

MRS. ETHERDOWN: My dear Sir John. [*Exit, with her arm round his neck.*]

Scene iii. Changes to a Room in Friendly's House.
Enter Friendly and Wellford.

WELLFORD: There never was any thing so vexatious! when my impatience, my wishes, and my hopes were all at the utmost stretch, to be disappointed thus! That unseasonable coxcomb to come home at such a juncture!

FRIENDLY: Well, I'll allow you it is a little mal-a-propos. I am glad, however, that he *is* come; and if we can but obtain his consent to your marrying Emily—

WELLFORD: Emily has not answered my letter neither! Not to afford me a line! nothing but a cold excuse by word of mouth; it's very strange.

FRIENDLY: Poh! there's nothing strange in it; but you lovers are such restless beings!

WELLFORD: I have loved her almost from my childhood, Friendly! I had her good mother's approbation: I think she loves me too—yet—

FRIENDLY: Yet—what now? You have a suspicion in your temper, Wellford, that will never suffer you to be happy.

WELLFORD: Why, to tell you the truth, Mrs. Friendly has alarmed me exceedingly with something she has told me.

FRIENDLY: Oh! my poor wife! that tongue of her's can never lie still. 'Tis her only fault; but I never expect to cure her of it, as she fancies herself the most silent woman in England.—She has told you, I suppose, of Sharply's addresses.

WELLFORD: The scoundrel—I'll cut his throat!

FRIENDLY: Bounce—there it goes off.—For shame, man, don't be so impetuous. You can't suspect Emily of favouring such a fellow; a mean hanger-on in Sir John's family.

WELLFORD: But your wife says, he's a handsome rascal, and of so plausible a tongue—

FRIENDLY: Oh! that's so like her! fy, fy, don't think of him.

WELLFORD: I am ashamed of it, I own, yet passionately as I love Emily, 'tis impossible my heart should be at ease, while she continues in that vile house.

FRIENDLY: Well, well, have patience.

WELLFORD: Patience!—Friendly, I believe you never knew what it was to love.

Scene iv.
Enter Mrs. Friendly, talking as she comes in.

MRS. FRIENDLY: I never was so amazed and astonished!—

FRIENDLY: Ha! ha! I wish Mrs. Friendly were to hear you say so.

MRS. FRIENDLY: What was he saying, my dear?

FRIENDLY: Only that I never was in love:—But what has thrown you into all this astonishment?

MRS. FRIENDLY: Something about Emily—But pray, Captain, let me ask you, what you mean by such an assertion?

WELLFORD: Oh, madam, I was only bantering Mr. Friendly.—For heaven's sake, what of Emily?

MRS. FRIENDLY: I don't pretend to be as young nor as handsome as Miss Emily; but I *have* been young, Sir, and perhaps Mr. Friendly thought me as handsome too; and for you to go and assert such a thing so roundly, Mr. Wellford—Till you explain your reasons, I shall keep my mind to myself, I assure you, Sir.

FRIENDLY: That I am sure is impossible, my dear wife.

MRS. FRIENDLY: Perhaps, Mr. Friendly, you'll find yourself mistaken; and that I am not so fond of communicating my thoughts, but that I can be silent, and not drop the smallest hint, that a person has behaved in an extraordinary and unexpected manner.

FRIENDLY: What! has Emily done this?

MRS. FRIENDLY: I named no name, Mr. Friendly.

WELLFORD: Dear madam, don't keep us in suspense; I beseech you, tell us what you mean.

MRS. FRIENDLY: If you'll answer my question, Sir, then I'll answer yours; if not, I'll let you see I can hold my tongue;—but for you to make so strange a declaration, and not to give a reason for it! I swear and protest—

FRIENDLY: That's her way of holding her tongue.—Why, I tell you there was nothing in what he said; if you'll not believe me, I can't help it. [*Aside to Wellford.*] Let her alone, we shall have it all out presently; she would sooner talk to herself than keep it in.—Make yourself easy, man; you may be sure you will see Emily to-morrow.

MRS. FRIENDLY [*Walking about.*]: Yes, yes; a likely story!—Heaven knows what is become of Emily!

WELLFORD [*Turns hastily to her.*]: Madam!

FRIENDLY [*Aside.*]: Don't mind her.

MRS. FRIENDLY: How young creatures can act so unaccountably, that have been educated with so much care!

WELLFORD: Dear Madam, explain yourself.

MRS. FRIENDLY: I was not saying any thing, Sir.—Such a contrivance! it's well if it is not with her own consent, after all.

WELLFORD: For goodness sake, madam, speak out.

MRS. FRIENDLY: You see, Sir, I can be as dumb as other folks when I please.

FRIENDLY: Yes, yes; that's clear: but there seems to be more in this than I apprehended.—Prithee, my dear, now, don't be in a tift about nothing. The whole of the business that you resent so much, was no more than this: I was laughing at Wellford's impatience; and he said, if I knew what it was to be in love, I would not make a jest of it.

WELLFORD: This was all, upon my word, Madam.

MRS. FRIENDLY: And why could not you have said so at first, instead of running on a rig-maroll.—I was afraid, indeed, he had observed something that might induce him—

WELLFORD: No—not in the least, good Madam: tell me now—

MRS. FRIENDLY: Oh! if that was all, why, I will tell you.—You know you expected to see Emily here this evening.—

WELLFORD: I know it.—

MRS. FRIENDLY: And you know she sent word she could not come, because—

WELLFORD: I know I am disappointed:—go on, Madam.

MRS. FRIENDLY: 'Tis a disappointment to be sure, as it is so long since you have seen her; fourteen months, I believe: it was in September that you went to—

FRIENDLY: What's all this to the purpose? Pray proceed.

MRS. FRIENDLY: Mr. Friendly, I wish you would not use that phrase so often; I never speak, but you come out with, "What's all this to the purpose?"

FRIENDLY: Well, well, my dear, go on.

MRS. FRIENDLY: I was sitting at work in the parlour just now, and to tell you the truth, I was thinking of you and Emily. What joy will it be, thought I—

FRIENDLY: Prithee, don't tell us your thoughts, my dear, but say what has happened.

MRS. FRIENDLY: Well, no matter then what my thoughts were; tho' perhaps they might be worth knowing too: But who should come in, in a violent hurry, but Rose, Mrs. Etherdown's maid.—Lord, Madam, says she, do you know any thing of Miss Emily? (Laying down my spectacles, for I can't work without them) Not I, indeed, says I. Then to be sure, says she, she is gone off with Mr. Sharply, and will be undone, if—

WELLFORD: Heavens! Madam! how could you delay telling this so long?— Oh! Friendly, what do you say to my suspicions now?

FRIENDLY: Where is the woman? is she in the house?

MRS. FRIENDLY: Ay, to be sure;—she's below stairs: I did not stay to ask her any more questions, but ran up directly, to tell you what she said.

FRIENDLY: Yes, and you have made wonderful haste to tell it, with your confounded round-abouts. I'll bring the maid* up, and let her speak for herself. [*Exit Friendly.*]

MRS. FRIENDLY: Why, this is one of the most strange, incomprehensible

*Dublin edition reads "woman."

affairs that ever was, Mr. Wellford. I am quite at my wit's end to unriddle
it.—Emily sends word she can't come, because Sir John is arrived. I
thought that might be true; but then again, it can't be true, because she is
actually gone out.—And then, that Sharply has had so many opportunities; and he is a very personable man, I can tell you; and young creatures
are so giddy now-a-days!—It was not so when I was a girl; it was not a
handsome face, nor a smooth tongue, that could win me.
WELLFORD: Good madam, you need not aggravate matters; my own apprehensions have already made me but too miserable.

Scene v.
Enter Friendly and Rose.

FRIENDLY: Come, repeat what you have said to me, before this Gentleman;
he is most concern'd to know it.
ROSE: Sir, I am sure Mr. Sharply has carried Miss Emily away; I overheard
my mistress and him talking about it. I would have warn'd Miss Emily
herself, but she is so proud and so scornful, she won't suffer me even to
speak to her.
FRIENDLY: Why did not you come to me directly?
ROSE: My mistress kept me so employed, Sir, I could not for my life get out
sooner.
FRIENDLY: Do you know where they are gone?
ROSE: Yes, Sir, I can bring you to the house.
FRIENDLY: Come, Wellford, we have no time to lose.
WELLFORD: No, Friendly, I'll not stir:—let her enjoy her infamy.—I have
done with her for ever.
MRS. FRIENDLY: Gracious! what do you mean, Captain?
FRIENDLY: Are you out of your senses, man? don't you hear it's a plot, a
wicked contrivance of Sharply's?
WELLFORD: Friendly, I hardly know what I say.—Come with me, and if I find
that villain has dared to— [*He takes up his Sword.*]
ROSE: Oh! dear Sir, sure you would not offer to kill him.
WELLFORD: Lead me directly to the house, or—
ROSE: I'll go down on my knees to you, Sir, not to hurt him.
FRIENDLY: What! then jealousy, it seems, has urged you to tell this?
MRS. FRIENDLY: A fine motive! I was wondering indeed what—
WELLFORD: Tell me [**directly**] where they are, or by all that's gracious—
FRIENDLY: Come, come, I'll answer for it there shall be no harm done; bring
us to the house.
ROSE: Well, Sir, [**then**] I'll depend upon you.
WELLFORD: Begone then, and lead the way.
MRS. FRIENDLY: My dear, you'll bring Emily home with you, if you find her;
I'll order a chamber to be got ready for her.
FRIENDLY: Certainly. [*Exit Friendly, Wellford, and Rose.*]
MRS. FRIENDLY [*Talking to herself as she goes out at the door.*]: To be sure it
is one of the [**strangest**] most perplex'd, unaccountable affairs, that ever
was in the world; and I am more surprized—

Scene vi. Changes to a room in Mrs. Private's house.
Emily walks about, Sharply following her.

SHARPLY: But, my dear Emily, now—prithee [but] hear me, child.

EMILY: Hear you! What can you say in defence of so much treachery?

SHARPLY: I'll tell you:—If I were guilty of treason, perjury, robbery, and so forth, all these things would I justify, to e'er a woman in England, by those three Monosyllables, I love you.

EMILY: And do you think that this act of violence won't make me hate you more than ever I did?

SHARPLY: No.

EMILY: No!

SHARPLY: No, I tell you n—o; I never knew a man hated for an act of violence of this kind in my life.—Besides, as I take it, I am not altogether an object of aversion.

EMILY: You are too modest, Sir.

SHARPLY: Middling as to that; tho' faith it is a fault too, as you observe, but then it's easily mended, my dear; for example now—[*Offers to throw his arms round her; she pushes him away.*]

EMILY: Intolerable impudence!

SHARPLY: Why, what the deuce would you be at? I wish you knew your own mind; just now I was too modest, and now I am too impudent; I would fain please you if I knew how.

EMILY: Audacious man!

SHARPLY: Come, come, I know you don't dislike me at the bottom of your heart: you think me saucy, but agreeable, a devilish agreeable fellow. Ah, you little rogue! there is an arch smile of assent under that angry brow, that makes you look so enchantingly!

EMILY: My contempt for you is so great, that it has banish'd even my fears of you.

SHARPLY: Fears! Lord, my precious, you have nothing to fear! I'll be as constant as a dove, and never tell a word of the matter to mortal; I scorn to blab.

EMILY: Thou most abandoned!

SHARPLY: Come, don't be peevish:—you can't imagine how much prettier you are when you smile.—Besides, child, you should consider that I am at present lord and master of thy destiny; and if you provoke me, who knows what may follow?

EMILY: You wretch,—how dare you talk thus! Alone and helpless as I am, I feel myself so superior to you, that I as much despise your threats, as if I were this minute arm'd with the power to crush you for them.

SHARPLY: Why, to say the truth, I had rather owe my happines to your own voluntary kindness; for mutual love you must know, Miss, is the prettiest thing in the universe, and when uncompell'd by duty, the source of ten thousand pleasures that lovers only know, and wives and husbands never dream of:—(By my soul, I believe you were in the right *not* to marry me). Think of the delightful billet-doux, the transports of meeting, and even in absence, the millions of little, sweet, charming anxieties! then when we happen to meet in publick, I, unexpectedly perhaps, strike your eyes; you with a beautiful consciousness withdraw them, and throw them round the company; your face in a fine glow all the while—probably you see the women coquettishly trying to engage my attention; Ay, ay, say you, you may ogle as much as you please, but he's all my own.

EMILY [*Crying.*]*: Detestable monster! [*He catches her in his arms.*]

SHARPLY: Adorable creature! how! in tears! Oh, would I were that lover whom you were to have met this evening at Friendly's, then would my visionary scene be realized!

EMILY: Do you then know whom I was to have met?

SHARPLY: Alas! not I.

EMILY: Know then, that it is one, who will make you dearly repent of this outrage.

[SHARPLY: **Indeed? ha, ha, ha!**

EMILY: **Yes,**] tho' you fled to the remotest part of the earth.

SHARPLY: Oh lud! oh lud! prithee, who is this mighty giant?

EMILY: Do you know Captain Wellford?

SHARPLY [*Aside.*]: Wellford! S'death!—Is *he* the man?

EMILY: Yes, wretch; and assure yourself, he will call you to a severe account for this.

SHARPLY: Ha, ha, ha!—now do you fancy I have been serious all this while? why Lord, Madam, Wellford and I are as intimate as two Brothers.—I had only a mind to startle you a little; but to convince you I had not the least design to injure you, I will immediately restore you to your lover.

EMILY: Is this possible! can I believe you speak seriously?

SHARPLY: As seriously as if I never were to speak more. Captain Wellford is the man in the world I should wish to oblige, and [**I**] shall be proud to deliver you up safe to him. I'll conduct you directly to Mr. Friendly's.

EMILY: Let me go then instantly.—Bless me! [*A noise of talking heard without.*] What noise is that? I wish I were out of this house. If you deceive me again—

SHARPLY: By this fair hand, I will not; we shall find chairs at the door, I'll lead you to one.

EMILY: You may depend on all the grateful returns I can make.

[*She gives him her hand, and while she speaks Wellford enters, followed by Friendly and Rose. He steps back on seeing her.†*]

EMILY: Ah! Wellford! [*She runs to him, and he turns from her.*] Is this your greeting, Sir? This *can't* be Wellford!

WELLFORD: Yes, it *is* he, who came hither to deliver you from the hands of a vile ravisher; but I see I wrong him by the epithet, and might have spared myself the trouble, light ungrateful creature!

EMILY: Injurious man!

WELLFORD: What! is it *you*, Randel? thou despicable wretch! how I blush for the woman who could thus debase herself.

SHARPLY: Captain—One word with you in private.

WELLFORD: Impudent ruffian, stand off. Look at this sword, it once pre-

---

*From the Dublin edition.

†The last sentence of the stage direction is from the Dublin edition.

served your coward life; it came now prepared to revenge my own, and that lady's wrongs; but the cause is beneath it, so I leave you to your fortune. [*Exit Wellford.*]

FRIENDLY: What, Sir; it seems that you don't value your neck, that you have ventured thus.—

SHARPLY: You are a reasonable man, Sir, and I'll talk with you, if you'll give me the opportunity.

FRIENDLY: Hold your tongue, rascal—you shall give an account of yourself in another place.

SHARPLY [*To Rose.*]: Thou unlucky devil!—Miss Emily, pray speak for me: was not I going to carry you to Mr. Friendly's house?

EMILY: He said he would [**indeed**] Sir, I must do him that justice.

FRIENDLY: A mere pretence, in order to decoy you, perhaps, to a more convenient place.

SHARPLY: Let me perish, if I did not mean to bring her safe to you; I was compelled to take the steps I have done, but I no sooner heard of Captain Wellford, than gratitude, as well as honour—

FRIENDLY: Gratitude and honour! how dare such a fellow as thou art pretend to either? Say rather your fears, if there be any truth in you.

SHARPLY: Call it what you please, Sir; but if you stand my friend, I have something to tell you perhaps—

FRIENDLY: This is no fit place to talk with you;—you shall come along with me, Sir, and you too, Mrs. Rose,—for I am determined to sift this black affair to the bottom. [*To Emily.*] Madam, I ordered my chariot to follow me, which shall carry you to my house; for these gentry, I shall take care to convey them thither myself.

[*He gives his hand to Emily.*]

SHARPLY: Sir, I am ready to attend you any where.

EMILY: And for me, Mr. Friendly, I am now indifferent whither I go.

FRIENDLY: Come, Madam, all, I hope, will be clear'd up.

[*He leads her out.*]

ROSE [*To Sharply as she goes out.*]: Oh, thou villain! [**thou villain!**]

SHARPLY [*Following her, shakes his fist at her.*]: A—h!

[*Exeunt.*]

End of Act II

ACT III

Scene i. A chamber in Friendly's house.
Mrs. Friendly and Emily sitting. Wellford leaning on the back of Emily's chair.

MRS. FRIENDLY: Well, but child, now that the Captain is convinced that his suspicions were foolish, and groundless, and idle, and ridiculous, and every thing; you ought to forgive him, and make up your quarrel.

EMILY: No, Madam, what I have declared, was but in justice to my own character; for the rest, I am little solicitous to satisfy a man, capable first of suspecting, and then of accusing me, as *he* has done.

MRS. FRIENDLY: Very true, my dear, capable of suspecting and accusing; but jealousy you know is of all things—

WELLFORD: Blind, blind and infatuated!

EMILY: To think I could favour* such a mean impostor! a cheat even to his very name!

MRS. FRIENDLY: Ay, a paltry subaltern fellow! that was broke for cowardice! after the Captain, as he tells me, had saved him from being killed by another officer.

WELLFORD: I acknowledge my fault with all its aggravations; yet I thought my penitence, my grief, for having so justly provoked this lady's resentment, might have attoned for an offence, which nothing but the strongest love could have occasion'd.

MRS. FRIENDLY: I can't think what Sharply—

WELLFORD: For heaven's sake, Madam! don't name a wretch any more, that has occasioned so much mischief, [any more—Emily!—]

MRS. FRIENDLY: Bless me, Captain! don't be so sudden! I declare you startle one in a manner!—I say, I wonder what can keep Sharply and Rose so long with Mr. Friendly! they have been lock'd up now almost—

EMILY: You'll soon know, Madam. Here is Mr. Friendly.†

Scene ii.
Enter Friendly.

MRS. FRIENDLY: Lord! Mr. Friendly, what have you been about all this while?

FRIENDLY: Sharply has told me something that has surprized me exceedingly.

MRS. FRIENDLY: Ay! what can it be? but pray, my dear, first tell me, were the candles lit in the drawing room as you came by? for I expect company [presently].

FRIENDLY: Psha;—I don't know.

WELLFORD: What has he told you?

FRIENDLY: Why, nothing less than that Sir John—

MRS. FRIENDLY: [Ay,] any body's question will be answered before mine.

FRIENDLY: I wish your drawing room and your company were—Sir John is married!

EMILY: Married!

WELLFORD: To whom, in the name of wonder?

MRS. FRIENDLY: Now don't tell him, Mr. Friendly, but let me guess; you know I have an excellent guess.

FRIENDLY: Prithee, my dear, give me leave;—why to that compound of mischief and wickedness, Mrs. Etherdown.

---

*Dublin edition reads "To suspect me of favouring."
†This line does not appear in the Dublin edition.

WELLFORD: You amaze me!

MRS. FRIENDLY: It does not amaze me in the least now; I knew it would come to that as well as if—

EMILY: Sure, Sir, this must be an invention of Sharply's?

MRS. FRIENDLY: Don't you remember, my dear, I told you about a month ago, when you and I were talking of Sir John*; don't you remember I said, says I—

FRIENDLY: Ay, ay, I remember your prophesy.

MRS. FRIENDLY: Now you see—just the same way I foretold Mr. Testy's marriage with the widow; and Mrs. Lofty's with—

FRIENDLY: For heaven's sake, good wife! give others leave to speak as well as yourself.—

MRS. FRIENDLY: Pray, Captain, do I hinder him? I declare one would imagine that—

WELLFORD: Dear Madam, let me ask Mr. Friendly a question or two.

MRS. FRIENDLY: There now again, as if *I* stopp'd you! would not one think that I kept all the discourse to myself? and now, pray Mr. Wellford, all the while that we were at piquet after dinner, did I say a syllable but what was absolutely necessary,† except two or three times that I ask'd you, What you were thinking of? And you said, Of your cards; and I said—

FRIENDLY: There's no bearing this; come with me into my study, Wellford; her tongue's wound up for an hour, and she must let it run down.

[*Enter a Servant.*]

SERVANT: The ladies are come, Madam.

MRS. FRIENDLY: I'll wait on them.—A fine character I should get indeed, if people were to take Mr. Friendly's word!

[*Exit Mrs. Friendly.*]

WELLFORD: How long does that fellow say Sir John has been married?

FRIENDLY: Above a year, he tells me; and if it be true, the son he has by Mrs. Etherdown is legitimate, and Emily's hopes are cut off at once.

WELLFORD: I am glad of it.

EMILY: How, Sir! that I'm not worth a shilling.

WELLFORD: No, Madam; but that I can now convince all the world, I love you for your own sake only. You, I hope, wanted no such proof of the sincerity of my affection. Oh! Friendly! I have offended, too justly provoked my Emily's resentment! persuade her to forgive my fault, and let me call her mine.—

FRIENDLY: What say you, Madam? This generosity deserves a kind return; and if Sir John consents—

EMILY: Hold, Sir! I own I have pride—perhaps too much; and cannot bear to lay myself under obligations, where I once hoped to have the power of conferring them.

FRIENDLY: But, Madam—

EMILY: Excuse me, Mr. Friendly: Let me only beg the protection of your roof till my uncle's return: I dare say, when he hears how cruelly I have

*Dublin edition reads "about Mrs. Etherdown."
†Dublin edition reads "but what was necessary in the Game."

been treated, he will provide for me somewhere: Perhaps I may trouble you but for a night or two.

WELLFORD: And whither will you then go? By heaven! you shall never be at the mercy of those abandoned wretches, while I have life or power to succour you.—Oh! Emily, this is not the return I expected from your tenderness! To whom ought you to fly for shelter, but to the man that loves you with such an honest and disinterested passion as I do?

EMILY: No, Wellford, no; you ought to know me better. The woman whom you have debased by your mean suspicions, will not, on such terms, condescend to be your wife. [*Exit Emily.*]

FRIENDLY: A noble girl, by my soul! 'twere pity you should lose her.

WELLFORD: Lose her! I'd lose my life as soon. Dear Friendly, if you would preserve *that,* do you and your wife use all your influence on her. That pride too, which would deform another woman, makes her still more beautiful.—What is fortune in comparison with such a mind?

FRIENDLY: Why, all this is very fine, I grant you; but the loss of a good estate is a damned baulk notwithstanding, Wellford.

WELLFORD: By all that's good, Friendly, I despise it; let me but possess my Emily, and—

FRIENDLY: You'll live in a cottage on love—determined like a true Arcadian swain; but it won't do in this part of the world, let me tell you, boy. But to be serious; what Sharply has told me, he has no other authority for, than Mrs. Etherdown's own word; though he adds, that Sir John, on account of this child's birth, means directly to own his marriage. However, I'll suspend my belief till I have it from himself.

WELLFORD: But have you let Sharply escape? I had forgot to inquire after him.

FRIENDLY: Oh! I have made him my own. I got him to draw up in writing a full account of Mrs. Etherdown's scheme concerted with him against Emily; together with some other curious anecdotes, to which Rose and he are privy: Which notable confession I have made them both sign.

WELLFORD: And what use do you purpose to make of it? 'Tis of little consequence now, methinks, to separate Sir John and his precious bargain.

FRIENDLY: I have a design in my head to bring that worthless puppy, if possible, to a sense of his folly. If he be really married to that woman, I shall soon get it out of him; and will then, and not before, lest he should deny it, lay open all her iniquities. I have engag'd Rose in my interest, as well as Sharply. I cannot now explain the whole of my plan to you, for I mean to go immediately to Sir John's, who they tell me is expected home every minute; but Emily shall not know this, as I wish for your sake to detain her a while.

WELLFORD: I have but little hopes, for I know the firmness of her temper.

FRIENDLY: Come, come, courage, man; you know you have a friend within; I'll venture to bring you to her.

WELLFORD: Do what you will with me.

[*Exeunt Friendly and Wellford.*]

SHARPLY: Its only one of your jokes, may be, Sir John: you are such a joker! But I don't believe every thing you say for all that.

MRS. ETHERDOWN: It's too true, as Sir John says.

SIR JOHN: I have found out the whole plot, tho', you must know; and to-morrow I intend so to work Friendly about it.

SHARPLY: Mr. Friendly! ay,—to be sure, he is a knowing man, and can give fine advice when a body's in trouble.

SIR JOHN: Confound your logger head! do you think I *want* advice, or would *take* advice, and from *him?* Why, he is the whole contriver of the thing, man.

SHARPLY: Who! Mr. Friendly, Sir?

MRS. ETHERDOWN: Yes: Mr. Friendly! as Sir John says.

SHARPLY: Lord! I'd never ha' thought that of him!

SIR JOHN: *You*'d never ha' thought! Why, you numscull, how the plague should *you* think, that mind nothing but dunning of tenants, and then excusing them their rent? A good joke, i'faith.

MRS. ETHERDOWN: That's true, indeed, Sir John; he knows nothing, poor soul, but the keeping his own books.

SIR JOHN: And a miracle 'tis to me, that he can do even that! Take him out of his figures, and my coach dog has more sagacity.

SHARPLY [*Laughs foolishly.*]: Ha! ha! ha! Well, well, I would not give my figures for all your wit:—now, Sir John, there's for *you*.

SIR JOHN: True! there you're right, Sharply. Every man has his talent. [*Enter a Servant.*]

SERVANT: Mr. Friendly's come to wait on you, Sir.

SIR JOHN: What the plague can Friendly want with me now?

MRS. ETHERDOWN: To try how the land lies, I suppose.

SIR JOHN: He'll find himself cursedly bit.—I think I am a match for Friendly. Give me but a clue, and let *me* alone to unwind a piece of knavery.—Get you both into the next room. Desire Mr. Friendly to walk in. Ha! ha! [*Exit Servant.*]

SHARPLY: I would not stand in Mr. Friendly's shoes, no, by the sun and moon, not for all the money in his pocket.—You'll work him, Sir John.

MRS. ETHERDOWN: Ay, Sir John, now's your time.

SIR JOHN: Yes, yes: I think I am a match for Friendly.
[*Exit Sharply and Mrs. Etherdown.*]

Scene vi.
Enter Friendly.

SIR JOHN: Your servant, Sir.

FRIENDLY: How do you do, Sir John? I heard, by accident, you were arrived, and just call'd in as I pass'd by.—

SIR JOHN: Oh, I thank you, Sir.

FRIENDLY: You seem out of humour, Sir John.

SIR JOHN: Perhaps I really *am* so, Sir.

FRIENDLY: I am sorry you have any occasion: but you need not shew it to your friends. Prithee, what has ruffled you so?

SIR JOHN: Nothing worth ruffling *my* temper, or any man's temper; women will be women.

FRIENDLY: Something about Mrs. Etherdown, I suppose.

SIR JOHN: No, Sir, it is not; you are always supposing in the wrong place.— There's my niece—

FRIENDLY: What of her?

SIR JOHN: Run away—that's all.

FRIENDLY: Run away! impossible! with whom!

SIR JOHN: How the d—l should I know? with a man, I suppose.

FRIENDLY: It can't be! When did she go? Have you sent to enquire after her?

SIR JOHN: Ounds! what a catechising is here! I don't know when she went, nor where to look for her.

FRIENDLY: I presume she'll come back again!

SIR JOHN: Ay, when she's ready for the magdalen-house,[6] I suppose she may.

FRIENDLY: Fy, fy, Sir John! how can you talk with so much levity of so good a girl, and so near a relation?

SIR JOHN: Prithee, Friendly, none of your sanctified airs. A good girl! and a near relation! I warrant you'd have me be mighty anxious about her *virtue* now, and try to recover her, for fear she should be *ruin'd,* as you call it. Not I, by the mass! if the wench has a mind to take her fling, e'en let her, for me.

FRIENDLY: But have you no regard for—

SIR JOHN: The *Honour* of my family, I hope you are going to say—uph, uph, uph*—Yes, I'll tell you how far I regard it: as I should not chuse to have my estate squandered away upon beggarly rascals, with handsome faces, (the use to which, I suppose, my hopeful niece would apply it) this frolic of hers has determined me—

FRIENDLY: To what?

SIR JOHN: To what goes plaguely against my stomach; but necessity—

FRIENDLY: What do you mean?

SIR JOHN: I'd as lieve be a slave in the gallies; but since the young hussy has provoked me to it, I am resolved—

FRIENDLY: On what, prithee?

SIR JOHN: To marry, Sir, if you must know.

FRIENDLY: The Deuce you will! you'd as soon hang yourself!

SIR JOHN: Ay, ay, that's true; I do hate the thoughts of it most *con*-sumedly, you know I do; but when a man's ill us'd in his own family—and to tell you the truth, Friendly, I don't find myself so young as I was some years ago.

FRIENDLY: No! that's strange!

SIR JOHN: And faith, I begin to think it's time to settle, and live a little honestly; a man can't hold out always, to drive such a career. I have been a sad dog, that's the truth on't.

FRIENDLY: Oh, you intend to mend then?

SIR JOHN: No, hang it, I don't say that neither; I don't know whether I *can*

---

*These exclamations do not appear in the Dublin edition.

mend or not;—what's bred in the bone, you know—the old leaven, I'm afraid; but a man may try.—Come, Friendly, let me have a little of thy advice. I have a mind to marry, as I told you; what sort of a woman, now, do you think would suit me?

FRIENDLY: Why, if you are actually resolved—

SIR JOHN: Peremptorily.

FRIENDLY: In the first place then, I would not have you marry one that's over young.—

SIR JOHN: Right—not a giddy girl. [*Aside.*] Bab's thirty at least.

FRIENDLY: In the next place, one whom you think doesn't marry you merely for the sake of your fortune; but a woman who can have some regard for your person.

SIR JOHN: Ah! good! [*Aside.*] Bab again, she adores me!

FRIENDLY: One of a mild and gentle temper, who can bear with all your odd humours.

SIR JOHN: Excellent! [*Aside.*] Still Bab.

FRIENDLY: One who would be prudent in the management of your family,* and not given to expensive pleasures.

SIR JOHN: Oraculous! [*Aside.*] Bab's the very thing.—Well, and what more?

FRIENDLY: Nay, I think that's enough, you need not desire money.

SIR JOHN: Give me your hand. [*Aside.*] Bab to a tittle; she's not worth a groat.—Egad, Friendly, you never talked so sensibly in your life; and now, who do you think answers this description in every point?

FRIENDLY: Nay, I can't tell; I suppose there are women enough to be found who do.

SIR JOHN: Suppose I were to name one: what think you of Bab?

FRIENDLY: Mrs. Etherdown! marry Mrs. Etherdown!

SIR JOHN: What! you don't approve of it?

FRIENDLY: I do not, indeed, Sir John.

SIR JOHN [*Aside.*]: Oh! I thought so. — But why not? I always intended to marry her, when I grew weary of her.

FRIENDLY: That's a strange paradox.

SIR JOHN: Not at all; for may be, in a cross fit, I might turn her off—and then I know I should repent it, I am so used to her little coaxing ways.

FRIENDLY: Why, do you know the consequence of marrying a kept mistress?

SIR JOHN: What! if I keep her myself, man?

FRIENDLY: That makes very little difference, Sir John.

SIR JOHN: No! [*Aside.*] Now it begins to work.

FRIENDLY: No! believe me, a woman who has been used to consider a man as a kind of property, of whom she is to make the most, while his inclination to her lasts, will not easily be brought to think, that there is but one common interest between them, as man and wife.

SIR JOHN: Ah! she won't?

FRIENDLY: Nor can she who has been accustomed to caresses, and flattery and stuff, as a mistress, descend to the meek, the tender, the complying duties of a wife.

*Dublin edition reads "House."

SIR JOHN: Indeed! [*Aside.*] How I'll surprize him just now. —Why, Bab has always been the most obliging, submissive creature in the world to me.

FRIENDLY: She finds it her interest to be so, but if once she were sure of you, she'd change her note.

SIR JOHN: You don't tell me so! [*Aside.*] How he'll stare presently!

FRIENDLY: Take my word for it, Sir John, if you were to marry that woman, you'd repent it before a week were at an end.

SIR JOHN: Ha! ha! ha! ha! poor Friendly! thou art, generally speaking, damnably out in thy judgment; but were never more so in thy life than now! For you must know:—ha! ha! ha! excuse my laughing at you, you must know, that I have been married to her above two and fifty weeks, and have never repented of it yet. Ha! ha! ha!

FRIENDLY: Oh, Sir John—enjoy your laugh; but that joke won't take.

SIR JOHN: Oh—the devil! what, because I am a facetious puppy, and now and then a little sarcastical, do you think I am *never* serious?

FRIENDLY: I understand you, Sir John;—you want to trick your niece out of her inheritance; and Mrs. Etherdown and you have entered into a confederacy to *say* you are married.

SIR JOHN: Ah! do you begin to feel?

FRIENDLY: Who do you think will take *your* word?

SIR JOHN: I'm an unlucky dog in point of character, that I own;—but I can prove this, honest Friendly.

FRIENDLY: I defy you.

SIR JOHN: Ah! does it sting? I can name the parson and the witness.

FRIENDLY: You may name a parson that has been transported, and a witness, may be, that has been hang'd.

SIR JOHN: What do you think of my little toping curate, of Woodall Green; is he transported? and our old friend in equity, Tom Shifter, is he hang'd?

FRIENDLY: Were they your operators?

SIR JOHN: Ask them.

FRIENDLY: Ha! ha! ha! ha!

SIR JOHN: Ha! ha! ha! Who's the fool now, Friendly?

FRIENDLY: 'Tis even so then—well, peace be with you.

SIR JOHN: Poor devil! how he's mortified! don't go, man.

FRIENDLY: What am I to stay for?

SIR JOHN: I want a little more of your advice.

FRIENDLY: Confound you. [*Exit Friendly.*]

SIR JOHN: I wish you joy of your heiress, Friendly!—ha! ha! a turbulent booby! I'll go and tell Bab tho'.

Scene vii.
Sharply and Mrs. Etherdown enter as he goes out.

SIR JOHN: Oh! are you there? come in.—He's gone.—E'gad I have given it to him!

MRS. ETHERDOWN: I could hear you, Sir John, laughing at him as he went out.

SIR JOHN: But the best joke of all is, he pretends not to believe what I told him.

MRS. ETHERDOWN: And here's this wiseacre does n't believe it neither.

SHARPLY: No, nor won't unless Sir John says it; ay, and swears to it too, that's more, for all you think me so easy.

SIR JOHN: And why not, Sharply? come, let's have your wise reasons.

SHARPLY: Sir John, now mind me; only mind what I am going to say—

SIR JOHN: Observe his important face.—Now, for a weighty sentence of sound argument! out with it, Sharply.

SHARPLY: Sir John, I have known you early and late; and tho' I am one that don't very well comprehend—that is, I am not very capable—I mean, I can't so very well express—

SIR JOHN: Ha! ha! poor Sharply! ha! ha! ha!

SHARPLY: There it is now, you always dash one in the middle of an argument; and because you have more learning, and can talk like a satyr, a body must not speak plain sense before you.

SIR JOHN: Call it a satyrist the next time, Sharply.

SHARPLY: You may call it what you please; but reason is reason, and truth is truth, and so I don't believe a word of the matter.

SIR JOHN: Fact tho', for all that, Sharply.

SHARPLY: My sister Lady Woodall! O—h!

SIR JOHN: The dog's proud of it, you see.

MRS. ETHERDOWN: My dear Sir John! you are so good!

SHARPLY: Good! by all the flesh of my back, I would not be such a sinner! no, not for all his land! Take that now, Sir John:—you find I can be smart when I please. Ha! ha! ha!

SIR JOHN: Ha! ha! ha! scurrilous varlet;—but you are right, Sharply, I have done such things in my time! Ha! ha! ha! did I ever show you my list? no, I believe not; hang it, I never loved boasting—there were not above nine of them that I did not turn off next day tho'.

SHARPLY: Nine! I don't know what nine you mean.

SIR JOHN: Only of the girls that I have had; none of them behaved like my old girl here.

SHARPLY: She's a sensible woman to be sure, for all she's my sister.

SIR JOHN: No, no, Sharply, no; not much of that neither: But she is docile; a teachable wench enough; and with a little of my training we do pretty well: e'nt it so, Bab?

MRS. ETHERDOWN: Ay, as you say Sir John.

[*They sit down at the table.*]

SIR JOHN: Come, here's your health. I can't but think of that booby, Friendly, how he must be gall'd! and his meddling fool of a wife, I wish she would cuckold him, that I might laugh at him about her virtue.—Here's his health tho', I have known him these twenty years.

[*Rose comes to the door.*]

ROSE: I'd speak with you, Madam.

SIR JOHN: Where now, Bab? [*Mrs. Etherdown rises.*]

MRS. ETHERDOWN: Only to give some orders to Rose, Sir John.

[*She makes signs of drinking to Sharply, and Exit.*]

SHARPLY: Married!

SIR JOHN: Faith, Sharply, I began to think it high time to wipe off the score.

SHARPLY: And my sister Lady Woodall!

SIR JOHN: Confound you, leave off your exclamations, and put the bottle about.

SHARPLY: And all unknown to me!

SIR JOHN: The dog's beginning to get drunk! and I shall be overwhelm'd with a deluge of folly and impertinence.

SHARPLY: And I'll warrant, you have settled the Lord knows what upon her!

SIR JOHN: What's that to you, Sir?

SHARPLY: Sir John, now mind what I say. You know, I am very apt to give a little good advice now and then, and tho' you rail at me so, I can't for the blood of me keep it.—Now, I would not have settled sixpence on her, were I you, for all she's my sister. I'd know how to manage a wife, I warrant: I am sharp enough in some things. She's as proud as Lucifer, tho' she's *my* sister.

SIR JOHN: That's a lie;—if she has any thing good, 'tis her humility and meekness, buzzard!

SHARPLY: And an extravagant woman, tho' I say it.

SIR JOHN: Another lie!—if she has any virtue, 'tis her good œconomy.—I'd trust her with all I'm worth.

SHARPLY: By the sun that shines then, so would not I, nor e'er a woman that ever wore a head; I have a little judgment too.

SIR JOHN: Judgment! *you* judgment!

SHARPLY: Sir John, listen to me now, and let me advise you—

SIR JOHN: By my soul, I'll break your head, if you begin to advise, Sharply.

SHARPLY: By this good day, I never was in such a humour for giving advice in my life.

SIR JOHN: You are ever so when you are drunk, you dog; tho' you can't speak a sentence of common sense when you are sober.

SHARPLY: Then 'tis my duty never to be sober; for I find myself at this minute as wise as any oracle that ever was born, and therefore my advice is *pro* and *con*—No settlement.—Mark what the oracle says.

SIR JOHN: I do, I do; and to shew what prodigious influence your sage counsel has on me, I intend—

SHARPLY: Ha, ha, ha! I knew you'd come about; you find I have judgment.

SIR JOHN: Tho' I never *thought* of doing it before, I shall settle a hundred a-year upon her, for all she's your sister.

SHARPLY: What, after all my arguments against it! By this hand of mine then, I'll have nothing to say to it. Mr. Friendly would no more do such a thing than he'd eat fire. Sir John, I say thirty pounds a year; observe me now; and that only during pleasure, do you mind?

SIR JOHN: Two hundred a-year, by the Lord! and that settled irrevocably, since you provoke me to it.

SHARPLY: Mercy upon me! Well, don't be too hasty now, Sir John, in this affair, but think a few days, and consult—

SIR JOHN: Burn you! whom should I consult?

SHARPLY: Mr. Frie——no,—not Mr. Friendly, I don't mean him—but argue, and think, and reason with yourself—

SIR JOHN: You know I always take your advice, and therefore—it shall be done directly.

SHARPLY: What, not to night, Sir John; you are not bewitch'd sure.—

SIR JOHN: Sharply—depart in a whole skin, and take a walk to Mr. Bustle's, you'll find him in his chambers at this hour.—

SHARPLY: Won't next week do as well, Sir John?

SIR JOHN: Utter one word more, and I break every bone in your body. The thing shall be done now, immediately, this identical night, and I'll surprise my Lady Woodall with it to-morrow. I'll write a line to my lawyer, and you shall carry it, to shew you of what importance you are.—So come to me in half-an-hour; in the mean while, go and sleep yourself sober, most oraculous Sharply. [*Exit Sir John.*]

SHARPLY: Ha, ha, ha, ha! thou incorrigible coxcomb! thou empty, vain, bragging sot! whose greatest boast is the being a rascal, whilst in reality your greatest vice is being a fool. [*Exit Sharply.*]

END OF ACT III

ACT IV

Scene i. Friendly's House.
Enter Wellford and Mrs. Friendly.

WELLFORD: I wish Mr. Friendly were returned, tho' I expect nothing but a confirmation of Sir John's marriage;—but anything is better than suspense.

MRS. FRIENDLY: I declare and vow, Captain, I am as restless, and as unsettled, and as perturbed, as I may say, on poor Emily's account; but Mr. Friendly will come at the truth, depend upon it he will.—I remember just such an affair once, it was the most dark intricate business, and so tedious;—I'll tell you the whole story—You must know—

WELLFORD [*Aside.*]: Oh! thank my stars, here's Friendly come to relieve me.

Scene ii.
Enter Friendly.

MRS. FRIENDLY: I'll tell you another time, Captain.—Well, my dear, what news?

FRIENDLY: 'Tis even as Sir John said; he is actually married. I have found out the person who was present.

MRS. FRIENDLY: And he own'd it to you?

FRIENDLY: He scrupled at first, but finding I was let into the secret, he confirmed every thing that Sir John told me. I am heartily sorry for it for Emily's sake. Have you seen her this morning, Wellford?

WELLFORD: Not yet;—but I purpose presently going to take my leave of her; for I am determined to set out this night in order to join my regiment;—and if nothing happens to change my fortune, why then—

FRIENDLY: What then, man, thou wilt not hang thyself on a willow![7]

MRS. FRIENDLY: Heaven forbid! you have more grace than to do so, I hope.

WELLFORD: I hope so too, Madam; but I shall be but little solicitous to preserve a life, that without her will be a burden.

MRS. FRIENDLY: I declare and protest I am so grieved for you I am ready to cry perfectly;—but who knows what may happen? Emily may still change her mind.

WELLFORD: Oh! I have not the least expectation of that; one thing however let me request of you both before I go.

FRIENDLY: What is it, Wellford? you know you may command us.

WELLFORD: That you will take Emily under your protection. To what must she be exposed in such a world as this? young and beautiful as she is—an orphan—without fortune—Let me now have the grief to add, without friends too.

FRIENDLY: You need not doubt my tenderness for her.

WELLFORD: Will you, my dear Mrs. Friendly, be a mother to my Emily?

MRS. FRIENDLY: Will I! my own daughter shall not be more welcome to me, I assure you, Mr. Wellford.—I protest I am so troubled; I never was more troubled in my life.

WELLFORD: I beg pardon for thus distressing you.—We'll talk no more on the subject; the few hours I have to stay ought not to be spent in fruitless vexation.

FRIENDLY: A few hours sometimes produces strange revolutions, especially in a woman's mind—Emily's may alter.

WELLFORD: Oh! you don't know her as well as I do.

FRIENDLY: Well, I'll not oppose you, only beg for the present you'll clear up your brow a little. I have a mind to have some mirth with Sir John this morning, which shall however only be a prelude to a more serious scene. I shall go to him presently, and pretending not to believe a syllable in regard to his marriage, I will, by way of prevention, lay open all Mrs. Ether-down's conduct.

WELLFORD: This may entertain you, Friendly; but what is it to me?

MRS. FRIENDLY: I wish, my dear, it was consistent for me to go with you, that I might help you to talk to him properly.

FRIENDLY: Oh! you shall have an opportunity: I find he is possessed with a belief that Emily has been inveigled away thro' mine and my wife's means.

MRS. FRIENDLY: Our means, my dear? Why, can he suppose—

FRIENDLY: Ay; but when he finds that his own dear Bab is at the bottom of it, I'll answer for it, that my Lady Woodall will be turn'd off with disgrace.

WELLFORD: What does that signify now? She has done all the mischief she could already.

MRS. FRIENDLY: For my part, I think it will be doing an act of charity to rid Sir John of such a notorious body.

WELLFORD: No doubt, Madam, it is a christian office to part a man and his wife.

MRS. FRIENDLY: From *such* a wife I think it is, Mr. Wellford.

FRIENDLY: Right, my dear, Wellford is out of humour, and would pervert our meaning.—Leave the management of the business to me; I think I shall entertain you.

WELLFORD: I fancy not; but take your own way.—You'll excuse me; I must go and give orders about my journey, and then I'll come, and bid Emily adieu.

FRIENDLY: Perhaps you don't go, Wellford.

WELLFORD: Certainly, Friendly. [*Exit Wellford.*]

MRS. FRIENDLY: Poor Man! I vow I pity him.—If you are going to Sir John's, my dear, I'll step up stairs to Emily.

FRIENDLY: Ay; go and comfort the sweet girl. [*Exeunt severally.*]

Scene iii. Changes to Sir John's.
Mrs. Etherdown at her Toilet, Rose attending.

MRS. ETHERDOWN: A penurious wretch! two hundred a year, and his estate as many thousand!

ROSE: You may thank your stars you have got so much, Madam.—I reckon Mrs. Friendly has blazed your marriage all over the town, for here have been I don't know how many people with their bills this morning already.—Here's a comfortable breakfast for him.
[*Rose takes out a parcel of papers.*]

MRS. ETHERDOWN: They are sent in by my own direction, lay them down there. I now only want to provoke him to part with me, but it shall be his own act and deed.

ROSE: Ay, for then, I suppose, he must give you a separate maintenance.

MRS. ETHERDOWN: Right; for if you are faithful, nothing can be proved against me; and then you and I, Rose, will live together, and so enjoy ourselves.

ROSE: Ay, that will be charming.

MRS. ETHERDOWN: Did you order the jeweller to call?

ROSE: I did, Ma'am; he will be here presently.

Scene iv.
Enter Sir John, speaking as he comes in.

SIR JOHN: Bab, Bab, my Bab!—What, what, what have we got here? What's all this bedizzening for? Patch'd! and painted *too,* I believe, by my soul!

MRS. ETHERDOWN: Sir John, you will oblige me, if for the future you will knock at the door before you come in.

SIR JOHN: Hey! knock at the door! it was not that you said, I hope?

MRS. ETHERDOWN: It is not manners to come so abruptly into a lady's dressing-room; 'tis not indeed, Sir John. And let me beseech you not to be so vulgarly familiar.—Lady Woodall hereafter, if you please.

SIR JOHN: Rose, can you tell what ails your mistress?

ROSE: There's nothing ails my lady, that I know of, Sir.

SIR JOHN: No! Why but, Bab?

MRS. ETHERDOWN: Bab, again! In two words, Sir John, I expect to be treated with a little more ceremony.

SIR JOHN: Hey day, mad, by my soul! fit for Bedlam! This comes of my owning her! I must take her down a peg or so.—Get you out of the room.—[*Exit Rose.*] I gave you a paper this morning; a little parchment, you know; a settlement on you, Bab. [*Aside.*] I'll take it from her, by the Lord.

MRS. ETHERDOWN: Well, Sir! what then?

SIR JOHN: Why, there was a mistake committed in the drawing of it up; let me have it again, that I may get it rectify'd.

MRS. ETHERDOWN: I have n't it about me, Sir John.

[*Enter Rose.*]

ROSE: Here's Mr. Brilliant, Madam.

MRS. ETHERDOWN: Bid him come in.

SIR JOHN: Mr. Brilliant! who the d—l's he?

ROSE: My lady's jeweller, Sir.

SIR JOHN: My lady's jeweller, quotha?—Well, I'll treat you with a ring, since you put me in mind of it.

[*Enter Jeweller.*]

MRS. ETHERDOWN: Servant, Mr. Brilliant—What have you got there?

JEWELLER: I made bold to bring your ladyship a few things, that I fancy will please you.

MRS. ETHERDOWN: Let's see.

JEWELLER: Here's a pair of ear-rings will come cheap; I can let your lady-ship have them for two hundred and eighty pound.

MRS. ETHERDOWN: Baubles! How do you like them, Sir John?

SIR JOHN: 'Pshaw!—If you have got ever a neat diamond hoop, of about nine or ten guineas, my wife may be a purchaser.

JEWELLER: None so low as that, Sir; I have from fifteen to twenty—will your ladyship please to look at these?

SIR JOHN: No, no; you have nothing here that we want.

JEWELLER: I have brought a bill, according to your orders, Madam.

MRS. ETHERDOWN: Give it to Sir John.

SIR JOHN: I have no occasion for it, Sir; I suppose I can furnish myself at any other shop as well as at yours. [*Throws down the bill, without looking at it.*]

MRS. ETHERDOWN: That's no reason you should not pay him, Sir John.

SIR JOHN: Pay him! for what?

MRS. ETHERDOWN: A few trifles that I have had of him.

JEWELLER: You'll find my charges very reasonable, Sir.

SIR JOHN: Well, well, Sir, you may carry your trinkets away.

JEWELLER: If Sir John does n't like the jewels, madam, I shall be very ready to take them again, with some allowance.

MRS. ETHERDOWN: Sir, I shall keep them—and Sir John will pay you for them another time—Next week you shall have your money.

JEWELLER: It's very well, Madam. [*Exit Jeweller.*]

SIR JOHN: So Bab! egad, this was a good bold push—and you really thought I was to be drawn in to buy you some of these gym-cracks!

MRS. ETHERDOWN: No, no; I know you too well for that; but I think you ought to be ashamed not to pay your honest debts.

SIR JOHN: Debts!

MRS. ETHERDOWN: Ay, there are all the people's bills.

SIR JOHN: Bills! [*He takes them up.*]

MRS.ETHERDOWN: And vastly reasonable they are, in my mind—I don't suppose the whole [*He examines them.*] amount to above fifteen hundred pound—You find I have not been extravagant, Sir John.

SIR JOHN: Why, what!—you don't mean, I suppose, that these are debts!

MRS. ETHERDOWN: Real debts—contracted by me your lawful wife.

SIR JOHN: And that I am to pay them! you don't mean that?

MRS. ETHERDOWN: Undoubtedly—who else should pay a woman's debts, but her husband?

SIR JOHN: And I am *your* husband, and you are *my* wife; and all these are real, actual debts, you say?

MRS. ETHERDOWN: All reality, substantial truth, as you will find to your cost—Ha, ha, ha! the farce is at an end between us; and you will find me quite a different creature from what you supposed, I assure you.

SIR JOHN [*Stands and stares at her.*]: Why—why—why—what the devil are you? a woman or a fiend?

MRS. ETHERDOWN: Ha, ha, ha! a woman, a woman of spirit, a woman of fashion, a woman of pleasure, expence, profusion, luxury! what do you think of me now?

SIR JOHN: Why, you are an imp of hell, I believe; where's your sawcer eyes, and your cloven feet—and, and, and, and—your horns, pray?

MRS. ETHERDOWN: Oh, I leave *them* for you, my dear Sir John.

SIR JOHN: Dear! damnable!

MRS. ETHERDOWN: Why, do you fancy I could ever have any regard for such a *thing* as you are?

SIR JOHN: Curse me, but I have a good mind to—to—

MRS. ETHERDOWN: To beat me, I hope: ha, ha, ha! do, at your peril! Who is it that you threaten with your anger? Do you take me for the tame fool I have appeared all this while? And do you fancy I'll submit to your absurd humours, merely for a maintenance? No, no, Sir; let me tell you, I shall enter upon a new system; I must have my separate purse, separate chariot, separate bed, my morning concerts, routs, visiting days—and if you expect I should live with you—

SIR JOHN: Live with me! fire and sulphur! I'd as soon—I'll lock you up in a dungeon—feed you on bread and water—bastinado[8] you!

MRS. ETHERDOWN: Ha, ha, ha, ha!

SIR JOHN: Starve you—make you lie on straw—

MRS. ETHERDOWN: I despise your menaces: I am your wife, acknowledged in the face of the world; and I'll make you know it too.

SIR JOHN: I'll turn you out of my doors; expose you, brand you! confound me if I don't.—And that scoundrel Sharply, I'll kick him out of my house too.

MRS. ETHERDOWN: Impotent threatening! we both laugh at you.

SIR JOHN: I'll make you an example to all the—
[*Enter Servant.*]

SERVANT: Mr. Friendly, Sir, is come to wait on you.

SIR JOHN: I won't see him, Sirrah.

SERVANT: He's coming up, Sir.

SIR JOHN: You dog, how dare you let him in? [*Exit Servant.*]
[*Enter Friendly.*]

FRIENDLY: Good-day to you, Sir John.

SIR JOHN: So, Sir.

FRIENDLY: Why so gruff, Sir John? What's the matter now?

SIR JOHN: Poh!—nothing at all.

FRIENDLY: Nothing at all! that can't be; you have too much sense and too much temper to be out of humour at nothing.

SIR JOHN: 'Pshaw—it is next to nothing—only a little foolish debate here, between Madam and me.

FRIENDLY: A *debate* between you!

SIR JOHN: Ay, she has been playing the wag a little with me this morning, that's all.—What sort of weather is it abroad, Friendly?

FRIENDLY: Nay, Sir John, I am afraid there's more in this; you don't use to wear so angry a brow.

SIR JOHN: 'Pshaw—I tell you I am not in the least angry:—will you drink a dish of chocolate, Friendly?

FRIENDLY: Not any, Sir John.—And you, Madam, seem extremely ruffled.

MRS. ETHERDOWN: Mr. Friendly, I'll appeal to you, whether Sir John uses me well: he has refused to pay a debt for me this morning, and has been so peevish about it!

FRIENDLY: Oh fy, Sir John! there I must take your lady's part; so prudent a woman as Lady Woodall! such an œconomist! 'tis but a trifle, I'll lay my life now.

MRS. ETHERDOWN: But seven hundred pound, I assure you.

SIR JOHN: Seven hundred devils!—don't believe a word she says, man.

FRIENDLY: Seven hundred pound! that's a good round sum! but I suppose my lady has made some pretty little purchase now, for your use; and you are so testy because you did not do it yourself—Come, own, is not that the case now?—What is it, Madam? a bit of land in the country? or a house in town?

SIR JOHN: Poh!—split your enquiries—Why, there's not a syllable of truth in the thing.

MRS. ETHERDOWN: Nay, Sir John, you can't deny that you refused the man payment; the jewels, I am sure, are cheap of the money; and if I am not to appear like other people of my rank, I might as well be Mrs. Etherdown still as lady Woodall.

FRIENDLY: Oh! what it was for trinkets then? humph; to be sure, Sir John, you ought to pay your wife's debts; and in my opinion—

SIR JOHN: Rot your opinion, Sir! keep it to yourself—'s curse, you are so inquisitive, and so troublesome, one would take you for your wife that had got into breeches.

MRS. ETHERDOWN: Lud! Sir John, how can you be so ill bred? you have not the least idea of good manners:—You can't imagine, how rude he was to *me* just now.

FRIENDLY: Rude to your lady! Oh monstrous! and to such a meek woman too!

SIR JOHN: S'death, Sir, I'll be angry when I please; and reconciled when I please; without asking your leave.

FRIENDLY: Come, come, if my lady has offended you, she'll ask your pardon; she's all submission and obedience.

MRS. ETHERDOWN: *I* ask his pardon! if he had any shame in him, he would down on his knees to ask mine.

FRIENDLY: And she has such little coaxing ways, you know.

SIR JOHN: This is damn'd hard, that a man must be besieged with such impertinence in his own house; prithee, Friendly, mind your own affairs.

FRIENDLY: Come, Sir John, all jesting apart; I will now do the office of a friend by you.

SIR JOHN: Sir, I want none of your offices.—

FRIENDLY: Look ye, Sir John, as I did not think you would have persisted in this ridiculous pretence of your being married, I would not, last night, add to the vexation of your niece's being stolen from you, the knowledge of this vile woman's conduct.

MRS. ETHERDOWN: You are an officious fellow, Sir; and if this be your business, I desire you will leave my house directly.

SIR JOHN: *Your* house!

MRS. ETHERDOWN: Yes, *my* house, Sir.

FRIENDLY: Madam, Madam! this affair is growing too serious:—I know Sir John is not married to you; we don't take him for such a fool neither.

MRS. ETHERDOWN: Sir, I shall call a servant to shew you the door.

FRIENDLY: I should not wish to expose you, bad as you are, if I were not afraid, that my friend's utter disgrace would be the consequence of his suffering you to pass for his wife.

MRS. ETHERDOWN: Are you not ashamed, Sir John, to stand by, and listen to his scurrility?

SIR JOHN: E'gad, I think you seem to be a match for him.

FRIENDLY: Sir John, this woman, I speak it before her face, has betray'd and deceiv'd you in every article.

MRS. ETHERDOWN: I scorn all that your malice can invent.

FRIENDLY: But I can prove it, Madam: nay, what's more, that it was by your contrivance Emily was spirited away by that rascal Sharply.

SIR JOHN: Ha! ha! ha! Emily spirited away by Sharply!

FRIENDLY: Yes, Sir John: that scoundrel, that vile tool, that abettor in all *her* iniquity, has conveyed your niece away, and married her by this time, for ought I know.

MRS. ETHERDOWN: Ha, ha, ha! much good may do him with her.

SIR JOHN: What, in the name of Beelzebub, *is* all this?

FRIENDLY: 'Tis all as I tell you, Sir John; this precious hypocrite here, you see, does n't deny it.

MRS. ETHERDOWN: Sir John, you are the greatest poltroon in Europe, if you don't fight him for abusing your wife thus.

SIR JOHN: Wife! the vengeance! I don't believe you *are* my wife, if you go to that;—I—I never was married—get out of my house this minute.

MRS. ETHERDOWN: Ay, deny me, if you dare:—I am Lady Woodall in spite of you, all the town knows it now.—Thanks to your wife, the publick cryer could not have proclaimed it more effectually.

FRIENDLY: Come, courage, Sir John; don't let the termagant frighten you, speak boldly and say at once, she is not your wife.

MRS. ETHERDOWN: Ay do, encourage him to expose himself, *honourable, honest* Mr. Friendly!

SIR JOHN: O—nz! I believe she is *not* my wife.

FRIENDLY: Believe! are not you certain of it, Sir John?

SIR JOHN: I wish I was;—but I am *not* certain, there's the curse of it.

FRIENDLY: What! married to such a creature as this?

MRS. ETHERDOWN: Yes—and this creature will force you, ay, *you* Sir, in spite of your turbulence, to the full proof of what he has acknowledged to you.

SIR JOHN: Get you out of my doors, thou fiend!

MRS. ETHERDOWN: Oh! it is mighty well, Sir!—remember you turn me out of your doors! yes, I *will* quit your house, and leave you to the scorn and laughter of mankind. When next you hear from me, it shall be with an authority that neither you nor your friend there, that meddling, cynical, *informing* coxcomb shall dare to dispute; and so, with the utmost contempt, I turn my back upon you both.

FRIENDLY: Is this really so, Sir John?

[*Exit Mrs. Etherdown.*]

SIR JOHN: Really so, Sir John! what the d—l signifies your coming with your queries now? could n't you have told me this before?

FRIENDLY: Before what? don't you say, you have been married above this twelvemonth?

SIR JOHN: Death and fire, Sir! it is enough to distract a man to hear such things—That woman is turned into a fury, I think—It's all magic and witchcraft.

FRIENDLY: I am very sorry, Sir John—

SIR JOHN: Burn your sorrow, Sir, keep it to yourself—Unfaithful to me!— Friendly, this is damn'd odd of you to say so.

FRIENDLY: True, believe me, Sir John.

SIR JOHN: And Emily ran way with by Sharply!

FRIENDLY: Fact—and by your wife's contrivance.

SIR JOHN: Oh the infernal sorceress!—but it can't be, man! the thing's impossible! the fellow's almost an idiot!

FRIENDLY: Oh, you are as much deceived in that as in the rest—I tell you, he has own'd it all.

SIR JOHN: A dog! but I have one comfort left, the rascal's bit in his hopes; he thought Emily was to be my heir—I have a son, tho' his mother may be a—But I don't believe a word you say, Friendly—Do now, own that it's all a confounded lye of your own inventing; do, dear Friendly.

FRIENDLY: I wish it were for your sake; but it's all too true, Sir John; and what is still worse, Sharply *will* possess your estate in spite of you. That boy which has been palm'd upon you for your own, is not even your wife's; but some brat brought in on purpose to induce you to own your marriage.

SIR JOHN: Death, Sir! do you take me for a stock,⁹ or an idiot! that you attempt to make me swallow such impossibilities?

FRIENDLY: Read this paper, Sir John—'Tis Sharply's full confession of the whole plot—Rose, who was her mistress's agent in the conveyance of the child, (tho' she herself was ignorant of the design) in her days of fondness for Sharply let him into the cheat—You will find the whole account there, when you are calm enough to peruse it.

SIR JOHN: And the villain knowing this, has married Emily!—I'll have him hang'd—as sure as fate he swings for this—That's a comfort—He has stolen an heiress, *knowing* her to be such.—And that wicked she imp—I'll be divorc'd from her.—You can prove her an adultress, you say?—You shall prove it, and I'll be divorc'd—that's another comfort.

FRIENDLY: There, I'm afraid, Sir John, we shall find a difficulty; for, tho' we have the strongest presumptive proof in the world against her, yet the law requires more in those cases.

SIR JOHN: Sir, it shall have all, and more than it requires.

FRIENDLY: There is not the least doubt of your being (I am sorry to say) a cuckold, Sir John; yet the crime can't be proved against your wife.

SIR JOHN: Furies, Sir! how dare you call me a cuckold? If any thing would make me fight you—You are a barbarous unworthy fellow, so you are.

FRIENDLY: Why is not your wife—?

SIR JOHN: Wife! Uph—uph—Oh! Friendly, that word is worse than ten thousand daggers.

FRIENDLY: Now, Sir John, you see the consequence of your foolish as well as criminal affectation, of wanting to pass for a worse man than you are.

SIR JOHN [*Walking about.*]: The fiends!—the vipers!—the monsters!

FRIENDLY: Do you think that a woman who could submit to live with you, under the infamous imputation of being kept, could have any principles?

SIR JOHN: Hell-hounds! robbers! and murderers!

FRIENDLY: Or that a low rascal, like Sharply, the mean flatterer of your follies, and the real practiser of your imaginary vices, whose sole business in your family was to prey on your fortune, and make a jest of your person, was to be bound by any ties of gratitude?

SIR JOHN: Scorpions! serpents! furies!

FRIENDLY: Or could you expect that an inexperienced young creature like Emily could be trusted in the house with two such wretches as I have described, and not be undone?

SIR JOHN: Oh! Friendly, Friendly, Friendly!

FRIENDLY: Do you see your folly?

SIR JOHN: My folly! my purgatory! my hell! Don't let your wife come near me, nor Sharply, nor Emily, nor my own everlasting torment—I'll cut my own throat—My estate shall be forfeited—I'd be burnt at a stake, rather than let them have it!

FRIENDLY: Will you at last submit to be advised by me?

SIR JOHN: What can advice do now? Am not I married to a strumpet?

FRIENDLY: Turn her off.

SIR JOHN: Suppose I do, I can't marry again, can't hope for an heir, and my estate will go to a scoundrel, that has ruined my poor niece.—Oh! Friendly, I am punished for the sins of my youth!

FRIENDLY: Indeed, Sir John, I pity you.

SIR JOHN: S'death! have I lived to be pitied too!—Sir, you sha'nt pity me; I wo'nt be pitied by e'er a man alive.—And now I am recovered from my surprise, you shall see the justice I will do myself on that crocodile and her brother.—Who's there!

[*Enter a Servant.*[

Bid your mistress come hither. [*The Servant goes out.*]††

FRIENDLY: Her brother! Why Sharply's no more her brother than he is mine; he has acknowleged that he was only a creature of hers entertained under that notion to impose on you.

SIR JOHN: Mercy on me! mercy on me!

[*Enter a Servant.*]

SERVANT: Sir, my lady is just gone out, and said she should not return.

SIR JOHN: What's to be done now, Friendly?

FRIENDLY: Why now, Sir John, I think we must see what can be done with Sharply; if you'll step with me to my house, I'll send for a friend of mine, a man deeply skilled in the law, whom we'll consult on the occasion.

SIR JOHN: Ha! good; I'll do it, Friendly.—I'll hamper him, by the mass!

FRIENDLY: Ay, Sir John, we'll teach him to run away with heiresses!

SIR JOHN: Come along, Friendly; I'll hamper him. [*Exeunt.*]

END OF ACT IV

ACT V

Scene i. A Room in Friendly's House.
Emily sitting alone reading. Enter to her Wellford. She rises.

WELLFORD: Forgive me, Madam, for thus intruding; but I am now come to take my leave of you, to bid you farewell, perhaps for ever.

EMILY: My good wishes, Sir, shall always attend you.

WELLFORD: And is that all, Madam?

EMILY: My prayers too, for your happiness.

WELLFORD: Unkind Emily! we met but yesterday, after a long, long absence; and is it *thus* we part to day?

††Added by the editors.

EMILY: *How* did we meet yesterday? Wellford, remember that.

WELLFORD: I thought, Madam, that a few rash words which jealous love forc'd me to utter might have been forgiven.

EMILY: Think how you reproached me!

WELLFORD: I was in hopes my sorrow for having offended you might—

EMILY: How you scorn'd, and left me!

WELLFORD: Since my crime is too great for pardon, Madam, I can plead no more in my defence.

EMILY: I could have born with patience every misfortune but that—the loss of parents, friends, fortune!

WELLFORD: And can you, Emily, let that stubborn cruelty banish for ever from your presence a man who loves you as I do? Cold unrelenting creature! but I have done—Fare-you-well—

EMILY: Wellford!—I forgive you.

WELLFORD: Speak that again!

EMILY: I pardon your unkindness to me; and now we'll part like friends.

WELLFORD: Part! did you say, part! sooner with my eyes, my life, my very soul! No Emily, no; since you forgive me, we never more will part!

EMILY: Indeed we must.

WELLFORD: By heaven, we won't! What is there now wanting to compleat our felicity?

EMILY: Ah! Wellford—your ardor makes you forget it now; but will you always speak thus, when the burden of a wife makes you feel the want of fortune?

WELLFORD: For shame, my love, what a thought is that to mix with our new-kindled flames?—No, Emily, the world contains not any thing that I would not give in exchange for you!—why do you hang your head?

EMILY: Wellford, this generosity of yours has quite conquered my resentment, but it shall not overcome my resolution.—My heart is yours for ever.—Were I mistress of a crown, you should share it with me; but you shall not be partaker of my poverty: And now fare you well at once. [*Exit Emily.*]

WELLFORD: Barbarous creature!

Scene ii.
Enter Mrs. Friendly.

MRS. FRIENDLY: What! not reconciled yet? Well, you lovers have such preposterous notions!

WELLFORD: Oh! Madam, all my hopes are now at an end! Emily has forgiven me, yet peremptorily refuses to be mine—

MRS. FRIENDLY: Well, that is to me now so unaccountable? Where is she? let me give her a lecture.

WELLFORD: She's just now retired to her chamber.—I thank you for your good intentions; but as I know your attempt will be in vain, I will not wait the issue.

MRS. FRIENDLY: You won't go till you see Mr. Friendly, sure?

WELLFORD: You'll pardon me, Madam; my own thoughts have rendered me unfit for any other company. I shall set out immediately on my journey, and so—my good old friend, adieu. [*Exit Wellford.*]

MRS. FRIENDLY: Now, as I live and breathe, I'll go to Emily, and rattle her for this!— [*Exit Mrs. Friendly.*]

Scene iii. Changes to the Street before Friendly's House.
As Wellford comes out, enter Sir John and Friendly.

FRIENDLY: Where now, Wellford?

WELLFORD: I am this minute going to leave town, Friendly; and am glad I have met you to bid you good-bye.

FRIENDLY: I have something to say to you; you must not go yet.

WELLFORD: Indeed you must excuse me.

FRIENDLY [*Aside.*]: Sir John, do you insist on his staying; this is the gentleman I mentioned to you.

SIR JOHN [*Aside.*]: What the d—l, a lawyer in militaries! he holds well; but I have been so masqueraded, that e'gad I am surprised at nothing I see.— Pray, Sir, step in with us, I have material business with you; my name is Woodall.

WELLFORD: I'll attend you, Sir. [*Aside to Friendly.*] Friendly, what can this mean?

SIR JOHN [*Aside.*]: Mind that, Friendly.—A whimsical dog I suppose.
[*They all enter Friendly's House.*]

Scene iv.
Mrs. Friendly and Emily.

EMILY: But, dear Madam, would you have had me, thus situated, throw myself on a young man who has nothing but his sword to carve him out a maintenance?—Suppose we should have a family?

MRS. FRIENDLY: Why, that's true too;—and to be sure you would have one; I was not near so young as you when I married, and yet I have had nine children, no less I assure you, all alive, and christened.

EMILY: Well, Madam, and does n't this—

MRS. FRIENDLY: I have but three left now;—the other six are better provided for, and very thankful I am that they are so.

EMILY: Why, does n't this strengthen my argument *against* marrying Wellford? You know he is liberal to a fault, he loves pleasure too—

MRS. FRIENDLY: Young men to be sure will be gay; I remember Mr. Friendly, when he was a young man, why he—

EMILY: But, good Madam, you will not hear *my* reasons against a thing that you urge me to comply with, and yet are offering strong ones against it yourself.

MRS. FRIENDLY: Lord, child, I have not said a syllable either for or against it!—To be sure, Wellford is as pretty a young man, and as good a young man—I have known him from his childhood; Mr. Friendly had the care of him when he was a boy; my Harry and he are just of an age.—I would be glad he were married to a princess for that matter;—but what must be will be;—and as you are a prudent young creature, you may have your reasons, and so—

EMILY: *May* have! Why, Madam, I have been endeavouring to give them to you, if you would hear them.

MRS. FRIENDLY: But I must needs say, if your rejecting him should drive the poor young man to desperation; for to tell you the truth he look'd so when he went away, that he made my very heart ake.

EMILY: Is he gone?

MRS. FRIENDLY: Gone! ay, to be sure, I thought I had told you so before.

EMILY: Poor Wellford!

MRS. FRIENDLY: You might well say poor indeed, if you had seen him. I warrant you could sit down now, and cry your eyes out for vexation.—This comes of being positive;—but all's for the best, and so, my dear, you must think no more of it, but be merry and chearful, and—here will be Mr. Friendly home presently, and we shall hear—all about Sir John.—I vow here he is! and Sir John with him, as I live!

EMILY: My uncle!

Scene v.
Enter Friendly and Sir John.

FRIENDLY: Now, Sir John, are you satisfied?

SIR JOHN: How came you here, Emily?

MRS. FRIENDLY: That's a very extraordinary question, Sir John; but I'll tell you.

SIR JOHN: Hang me if you shall.—I'd rather remain in ignorance till doom's-day.—Let the girl speak for herself.—Was it Sharply who carried you away from my house?

EMILY: It was, Sir; and by Lady Woodall's contrivance: I am sorry to add, she had reasons for it, very disgraceful to herself and you.

MRS. FRIENDLY: There's for you, Sir John; very disgraceful reasons you find—a blessed bargain you have made of it truly—to go to bring such a woman to be a mistress of your family, and an aunt to your poor niece, and a mother to—

FRIENDLY: My dear, don't teaze him.

SIR JOHN: Answer me one question, Emily, and speak truth: Did that same lady of mine ever entertain a gallant or so, in my absence?

EMILY: She did, indeed.

MRS. FRIENDLY: Several, I warrant.

EMILY: But, Sir, out of respect to you, I now wish the story to be buried in silence.

FRIENDLY: Why, she has turned out a very tygress, and behaved worse since he has own'd her, than she did before.

SIR JOHN: I have turned her off tho': why don't you tell that too, Friendly?

MRS. FRIENDLY: I am heartily glad of it. I knew it would come to this.

EMILY: I am sorry, Sir, that matters are gone so far, for the sake of your child.

SIR JOHN: Child! why, Friendly says it's none of mine.

MRS. FRIENDLY: There—I knew it.—Oh! Sir John, who would have thought you could have been made such a fool of! If you had taken Mr. Friendly's advice; but you were *so* obstinate, and *so* refractory, and thought yourself *so* wise—

SIR JOHN: Prithee, Madam, hold your tongue.—Friendly, have you no command in your own house?

MRS. FRIENDLY: And pray whose *is* this child, Sir John, that you are to father?

SIR JOHN: Your husband's, I believe.

MRS. FRIENDLY: My husband, Sir John! he have an intrigue! Mr. Friendly have a correspondence with a loose woman!

SIR JOHN: Why not? where would be the wonder, pray?

MRS. FRIENDLY: Sir John, you are very uncivil, let me tell you; and if you make nothing of such wickedness—

SIR JOHN: Heaven help me! *my* wickedness is a lasting topic with these good sort of gentlewomen.—Pray, Friendly, desire your wife not to abuse me.

FRIENDLY: My dear, you wrong Sir John; he is very far from being wicked; he has indeed been grossly deceived.

SIR JOHN: Don't provoke me, Friendly, don't!

FRIENDLY: Provoke you, Sir John! does the vindicating your character provoke you?

SIR JOHN: My character, Sir, is very well known; I want none of your palliations—if I have been an idle fellow, what's that to any man? perhaps I may reform, if I take it into my head.

FRIENDLY: As you please for that, Sir John.—In the mean while, you must give me leave to bring in a friend of mine.
[*Exit Friendly.*]

EMILY: Whom does Mr. Friendly mean? do you know, Madam?

MRS. FRIENDLY: Not I, I protest, my dear.

SIR JOHN: Wickedness, and wickedness! I must be twitted forsooth every where I go with my wickedness!

MRS. FRIENDLY: I can't say but I am very sorry for you too, Sir John; you have been sadly abused, no one can deny that; but many an honest man has been made a fool of before now.

SIR JOHN: O—ds, Madam, who do you call an honest man?

MRS. FRIENDLY: Why, to do you justice, Mr. Friendly says, there is no great harm in you after all.

SIR JOHN: Curse me, Madam, but you are very absurd, and I won't bear this!

MRS. FRIENDLY: Nay, Sir John, don't be in a passion; if you are a Dupe, it was not *I* that made you one.

SIR JOHN: Dupe! Dupe! 's-death, do you know what you are saying? do you know the meaning of that word, that you use as familiarly indeed, as if—as if you knew what you said?

MRS. FRIENDLY: Yes, Sir John, I do know the meaning of it; you see I do; it means being made a fool of; and it means that you are a weak man, and a credulous man, and one that is easily overseen, and one that does n't know the difference between right and wrong, and one that thinks—

SIR JOHN: That thinks you are possessed with ten thousand talking devils; and that I had rather be buried alive than listen to you.

Scene vi.
Enter Friendly and Wellford.

FRIENDLY: How now, Sir John! quarrelling with my wife!

SIR JOHN: By my soul there's no bearing her, Friendly; I wish you were as well rid of her as I am of my plague.

MRS. FRIENDLY: Your plague! I scorn the comparison, Sir John; and—Lord, Mr. Wellford, are you here!

EMILY: I thought he had been gone!

FRIENDLY: Why, I luckily intercepted him in his flight, and have, within this quarter of an hour, unravelled a mystery to Sir John, and made him acquainted with this gentleman.

SIR JOHN: Well, Captain, are you disposed to marry, notwithstanding the sad example you have before you, in me and poor Friendly here?

MRS. FRIENDLY: Poor Friendly! Sir John!

FRIENDLY: Don't worry him, my dear.

WELLFORD: Sir John, if this lady can be prevailed on to accept of me—

SIR JOHN: What do you say, Emily? Friendly has given me a good account of this young fellow; and since he is willing to take you without a fortune, I have no objection; I'll hinder no body from playing the fool that has a mind to it.

EMILY: Mr. Wellford, Sir, already knows my determination on that subject.

SIR JOHN: You won't have him then? a spirited wench, by my soul; I like her for that too.—How puzzled she looks tho', Friendly!

FRIENDLY: Come, I'll explain:—Emily, you are your uncle's sole heir. Sir John is convinced that his supposed son is an impostor, brought in by Mrs. Etherdown, to answer her own ends.—You will pardon me for making this experiment on your firmness of temper; and you, Wellford, for thus trying the sincerity of your love.

SIR JOHN: So now, there's a surprize, you! egad, I think I carried on the joke very well.

EMILY: Uncle, is it possible this can be true?

SIR JOHN: Faith I don't know whether it is possible or not; but I believe it to be fact. It has been a strange damn'd whimsical affair, from beginning to end.

MRS. FRIENDLY: Why, I am quite in amaze, Mr. Friendly!

FRIENDLY: Softly, my dear.

EMILY: Wellford, here's my hand; and since my uncle approves—

SIR JOHN: Ay, ay, with all my heart; and since I am my own master again, I'll try what living a little virtuously will do.

FRIENDLY: Well said, Sir John, resolved like a wise and worthy man; and let me tell you that is a better character than that of a fool and a rake; the first of which titles was all you got by affecting the last.

SIR JOHN: None of your grave saws, Friendly; the wisest man may be deceived, if he deals with greater knaves than himself.

EMILY: Uncle, if you will permit me to return to your house, I shall endeavour by the most dutiful behaviour—

SIR JOHN: Ay, ay, you are all fine promises.—I'll consider of it;—but let nobody interpose, you know I hate that.—I'll have a bonfire to-night, and get drunk, for joy that I am rid of my wife.

FRIENDLY: And here's Wellford and I will get drunk for joy with you.

SIR JOHN: Oh! brave Friendly! Ah! you rogue, you would not let me be good, if I had a mind to it! but I will in spite of your teeth; I'll let you see I can be just what I please.

FRIENDLY: There's no contending with you, Sir John, once you are resolved; that I know.

SIR JOHN: You allow *that,* I believe, Friendly; a determin'd dog, *that* you'll grant.

FRIENDLY: Here are two criminals without, Sir John, that are afraid to appear in your presence; but since they have been so instrumental in detecting your wife's baseness—

SIR JOHN: Oh! You mean Sharply and Rose—as precious a brace as ever were unhang'd—What would you advise me to do with them, Friendly? I can transport them, at least.

MRS. FRIENDLY: And I think you would do right, Sir John.—

SIR JOHN: You do! then to let you see I am a better Christian than you, I will forgive them both. What do you say to me now, Friendly?

FRIENDLY: Faith, Sir John, I think you are even with her. Shall I call them? Who's there?

[*Enter a Servant, Friendly whispers to him.*]

SIR JOHN: Ay, do—poor paultry devils not worth my resentment;—tho' that Sharply is a sad rascal too, for I was always kind to him.

FRIENDLY: And he has repaid your kindness, Sir John; for if it had not been for him, you would not be the free man that you now are.

SIR JOHN: Faith, that's true—[*Rose and Sharply come to the door.*] Come in, you sneaking scoundrel you.—

[*Sharply enters.*]

What, my oracle! my adviser!—Hey, how's this? what the plague's become of your fool's face?

SHARPLY: That was but a mask, Sir John, which I wore occasionally, for your entertainment, but have now no farther occasion for it.

SIR JOHN: The d—l ow'd me a spite, and he has paid me with a vengeance;— so I am not angry with *you,* I don't think you worth it.— [*Aside.*] Is not that right, Friendly?

FRIENDLY: Perfectly.—You see how much he's asham'd, poor bashful fellow.

SIR JOHN: As for you, Rose, you are a poor ignorant wench, and did as your mistress bid you. I suppose you did not think you were doing any great harm, so I forgive you too.—[*Aside.*] Am I right, Friendly?

FRIENDLY: Never more so in your life.—Come, Mr. Sharply, since Sir John has pardon'd you your crimes against him, the rest of the company must own themselves obliged to you.

EMILY: I have promised that he shall not find me ungrateful.

ROSE [*Apart to Emily.*]: Good Madam, if you would but make Mr. Sharply keep his promise to me!

EMILY: Did he promise you marriage?

ROSE: He did indeed, Madam, or I am sure I should never—

SIR JOHN: And you want him to keep his word, I hope?

ROSE: Yes, Sir, if you please.

SIR JOHN: Go, go, you silly slut, you are better as you are.—What do you think, Friendly?

FRIENDLY: I think, Sir John, the woman's a fool who subjects herself for life to a man who must despise her.

SIR JOHN: Right.—What do you think, Emily?

MRS FRIENDLY: I think, Sir John, the man's a greater fool that ventures to take a woman who he knows to be—

SIR JOHN: Stop, stop, stop; 's death! I have raised a wasp's nest about my own ears—What do you think yourself, Sharply?

SHARPLY: I think, that having many sins to repent of, Sir John, I'll throw my vows to Mrs. Rose in amongst the rest; but will not impose such a pennance on myself as to fulfil them.

SIR JOHN: Well said, Sharply. Egad he's no fool after all. Rose, you see the banns are forbid on all sides. No more matrimony, as you love me.

FRIENDLY: No, no; no wedding, Rose.

WELLFORD: By no means, it would spoil both their fortunes.

FRIENDLY: Come, Sir John, if you weigh the good against the bad, you will find that you are arrived at a happy period of your life; for you have, within these four-and-twenty hours, acquired a piece of knowlege that you were ignorant of all your days before.

SIR JOHN: I have paid devilish dear for my knowlege tho', Friendly, and have learnt nothing by it, but that there is no truth in man or woman.

FRIENDLY: You mistake me, Sir John; the knowlege I mean is that of knowing yourself.

MRS. FRIENDLY: Ay, Sir John, know yourself, as Mr. Friendly says.

FRIENDLY: And now, Sir John, I give you joy?

SIR JOHN: Of what, pray?

FRIENDLY: That you have recovered your senses.

SIR JOHN: I'd rather recover my money tho', by the mass!

MRS. FRIENDLY: Sir John, as you have lost nothing, but a little money and a bad wife, and this affair has ended so well, I assure you it will give me great satisfaction to relate it in the most particular and circumstantial manner to every body in the world.

SIR JOHN: Prithee, Friendly, put a padlock on your wife's mouth, and then I shall be glad of her company and yours to dinner.

MRS. FRIENDLY: And so I am neither to eat nor speak; I thank you for your invitation, Sir John.

FRIENDLY: We'll attend you, and celebrate Wellford's union and your separation together.

SIR JOHN: Agreed.—And to anticipate all Mrs. Friendly can say of me for the remainder of her life, I will here acknowlege that I have been a sot, a fool, a dupe, a most egregious ass; that my wife was an artful wicked strumpet; that Sharply was an hypocritical rascal; Rose a cozening baggage; poor Emily an injured innocence; the Captain there a generous lover; Friendly a zealous honest fellow; his wife a discerning and prudent matron; and for myself, that, after passing through the fiery trial, I am come out (it is to be hoped) a discreet and sober gentleman.—Now, Madam; have you any thing more to add? I'll lay you fifty pounds, Friendly, she has not another word to say.

WELLFORD: Take up his bett, Friendly, and I'll go your halves.

FRIENDLY: Done, Sir John!

MRS. FRIENDLY: Sir John! I thought after all the money you had squander'd away, and all you were cheated of, and all the debts you have to pay, and all—

FRIENDLY: Well said, my dear; go on—

SIR JOHN: S'death! Friendly, let me off for half my bett.

MRS. FRIENDLY: No, no, Sir John, I have not half done.—

FRIENDLY [*Lays his hand on her mouth.*]: Peace, peace, my dear! let us devote this day to mirth; and that Sir John may not be out of humour at his own lot, let him reflect how many are in the same predicament with himself, without ever finding it out.

SIR JOHN: True, Friendly; but I hope I may at least serve as a warning to my brethren.

> Taught by example better than by rules,
> One dupe expos'd may save an hundred fools.

END OF ACT V

EPILOGUE,

By a Friend.[10]
Spoken by Mrs. Clive.

Ladies—methinks I hear you all complain,
Lord! here's the talking creature come again!
The men seem frighted—for 'tis on record
A prating female will have the last word.
But you're all out; for sure as you're alive,
Not Mrs. Friendly now, I'm Mrs. Clive;
No character from fiction will I borrow,
But if you please, I'll talk again to-morrow.
Then you conclude, from custom long in vogue,
That I come here to speak an Epilogue;
With satyr, humour, spirit, quite refin'd,
Double-entendre too, with wit combin'd,
Not for the ladies—but to please the men;
All this you guess—and now you're out again:
For to be brief, our author bid me say

She tried, but could n't get one to her play.
No Epilogue! why, Ma'am, you'll spoil your treat,
An Epilogue's the cordial after meat;
For when the feast is done, without all question,
They'll want liquors to help them to digestion;
And critics, when they find the banquet light,
Will come next time with better appetite;
So beg your friends to write—for faith 'tis hard,
If 'mongst them all you cannot find one bard.
She took the hint—Will you, good Sir? or you, Sir?
A sister scribbler! sure you can't refuse her!
Some lawyers try'd—not one could make an end on't,
They'd now such work with plaintiff and defendant.
A poet tried, but he alleged for reason,
The Muses were so busy at this season,
In penning libels, politics and satyrs,
They had not leisure for such trifling matters.
What's to be done, she cry'd? can't you endeavour
To say some pretty thing?—I know you're clever.
I promis'd—but unable to succeed,
Beg you'll accept the purpose for the deed;
Tho' after three long hours in play-house coop'd,
I fear you'll say you've all been finely dup'd.

FINIS.

A Journey to Bath

A Comedy

MEN	WOMEN
LORD STEWKLY	LADY FILMOT
SIR JEREMY BULL, Bar^t	LADY BELL AIRCASTLE
SIR JONATHAN BULL, his brother, a	MRS. TRYFORT, a citizen's widow
City K^t	LUCY, her daughter
EDWARD, son to Sir Jonathan	MRS. SURFACE, one who keeps a
CHAMPIGNION	lodging house at Bath
STAPLETON	

Scene—Bath

ACT I

Scene i. The Parade at Bath.
Enter Stapleton at one side, Mrs. Surface at the other meeting him,
stops short.

MRS. SURFACE: Well,—let me dye if at a little distance I knew you!—I declare you trip along as brisk as eighteen, and look as fresh this morning! but my dear Sir where are you going in such haste?

STAPLETON: To look for an other lodging.

MRS. SURFACE: Marry heaven forbid! I'd rather lose every lodger in my house than you.

STAPLETON: Your house! Why your house is like a fair, what between my Lady Filmot's visitors, my Lord Stewkly's hairdressers, and that roystering Westindian and his drunken Negroes, a man can't enjoy an hour's repose.

MRS. SURFACE: I know it my good Sir, I know it, and it grieves me to the very heart—That same Lord Stewkly is no better than he should be (between ourselves); as for my lady Filmot, she is—a fine lady, that's all—I speak ill of nobody behind their backs; and for Mr. Champignion, he is a Fool, poor man; but take no notice that I told you so.

STAPLETON: Then there's that fat woman, that lyes abed one half of the day, and laughs the other half; she and her daughter come thundering to the door at all hours of the night.

MRS. SURFACE: Ha ha ha, Mrs. Tryfort—and yet she is here for her health— Oh these citizens, Mr. Stapleton! Her daughter is going to be married you

161

must know, and the lover and his father, and Uncle are coming into my house to day.

STAPLETON: Then I will go out of your house to night.

MRS. SURFACE: I'd part with my two eyes sooner, you see now I would. No, I'll tell you what I'll do for you; you shall just step another flight of stairs, and then you will have no body over your head but Lady Bell Aircastle.

STAPLETON: What, is that she that's all way sweeping a flimzy train of scowerd silk up and down stairs?

MRS. SURFACE: The very same, ha ha ha, lord help her she is as proud as Lucifer and as poor as Lazarus; lives mostly upon tea, breakfast, dinner, and supper, poor Soul! but she is of a great family—if you will take her own word for it—not over young neither, for all she looks so well; but I wouldn't tell this to everybody.

STAPLETON: Oh I know you are wonderfully tender of reputations, you hate scandal.

MRS. SURFACE: Ay, as I do poison; I do, as I would be done by, Mr. Stapleton. Well now, what pritty nice thing shall I get you for your dinner, for I am going to market.

STAPLETON: Psha—I don't care.

MRS. SURFACE: Oh I know your taste, there is nobody can please you like myself.

STAPLETON: Well, well get you gone, I must make out my walk and then go home to write letters. [*Aside.*] A cajoling baggage.
[*Exit Stapleton.*]

MRS. SURFACE: Good morning to you, good Sir, and a pleasant walk to you, dear Sir—A peevish Cur, but I had rather have him than an empty room. [*Exit Mrs. Surface.*]

Scene ii.
Enter Lady Filmot and Lord Stewkly.

LADY FILMOT: Poh, poh my Lord this Jealousy's all affectation.

LORD STEWKLY: Affectation Madam! Why, don't you think you give me cause for it?

LADY FILMOT: Yes—if you loved me I grant you; but those days are over.

LORD STEWKLY: Upon my word Ma'am, I don't know how it may be on your side; but for my part I assure you very solemnly that my heart is—

LADY FILMOT: As much devoted to you as ever—ha ha ha! You think perhaps that I expect such a declaration from you; but I will spare you the pain of dissimulation, by telling you at once, that I know your heart is as much at ease about me as—

LORD STEWKLY: As what pray Ma'am?

LADY FILMOT: As mine is about your lordship.

LORD STEWKLY: Very well Ma'am, then I suppose our acquaintance is to be at an end.

LADY FILMOT: By no means; why should our being no longer lovers, hinder us from being friends?

LORD STEWKLY: The transition I own is not difficult; but to tell you my mind freely, I believe you never did *really* love me.

LADY FILMOT: I protest I *liked* you vastly; but for *love,* oh lud! a woman, who at sixteen, consented to a match of interest, is not very likely at almost double that age, to be a slave to softer passions.

LORD STEWKLY: That circumstance might have convinced me that your heart was never capable of tenderness: So fine a woman, with your understanding and education, to sacrifice herself in the bloom of youth for money!

LADY FILMOT: Nay, the sacrifice was not voluntary neither: I was only passive on the occasion, and suffered myself to be persuaded by a Mother, to marry a man for whom I did not care a pinch of snuff, because he was heir to a rich old miser. She piqued herself on her dexterity in making the match, and I made a merit of my obedience in accepting it.

LORD STEWKLY: Yes, and the fruits of your meritorious obedience was—

LADY FILMOT: Ruin—I grant you; but that was not my fault: the inexorable old cit turned his son out of doors and declared he would disinherit him. We found ourselves both undone. He indeed would have kindly persuaded me to starve with him; but not being quite fond enough of him for that, I prudently bid him good by, and returned back to my mother. He was unreasonable enough to be offended at this—threw himself into the service of the East India Company, and went abroad in a pet, swearing we should never hear of him more; and thus ended my matrimonial scheme of felicity, which lasted just two months and eleven days.

LORD STEWKLY: A good pleasant history. But one would think Ma'am that such an adventure might deter you from making an interested marriage a second time.

LADY FILMOT: Not in the least—one may make a shift to enjoy life with tolerable tranquility without taking *love* into the bargain; but there is no one comfort to be procured without riches: and your lordship may remember I made that my objection, when on our first acquaintance, you seemed disposed to take me for life.

LORD STEWKLY: Tis true; but yet you hinted at a kinder reason, for you told me that you knew not but that your husband was then living.

LADY FILMOT: Why at that time I really was uncertain about his fate; but there is now no room to doubt of it, as in consequence of his death, you find his niece, Miss Tryfort is her grandfather's heir, for it seems the stubborn old fellow dyed at last without a will.—Come come my lord, take my word for it, we are both now much better qualified to see, and to promote our mutual interests, than when we were foolish enough to be fond of each other.—Your business is to marry a fortune,—so is mine.

LORD STEWKLY: And I think I can guess where *your* shafts are aimed; young Edward Bull is your mark.

LADY FILMOT: The very same, and if you will give me leave to point *your* artillery, I will direct it to—

LORD STEWKLY: Miss Lucy Tryfort, I presume.

LADY FILMOT: Right—and now can you have the face to say you had not resolved on this before?

LORD STEWKLEY: Why no, faith, I'll take example by your frankness, and tell you honestly that I had; but don't you know that the young people are destined for each other?

LADY FILMOT: I know their *parents* intend it; but I hope their stars will dispose of them better. As Lucy's estate would have been my poor dear spouse's, had he lived, I think I have a sort of right in the disposal of it, and would not wish to bestow it better than on your lordship.

LORD STEWKLY: Oh Ma'am, your most obedient. I suppose neither the girl nor her mother suspect in the least who you are?

LADY FILMOT: How should they? I never saw either of them till they came hither. They never heard of me by my present name, and I have a little too much spirit to acknowledge myself the widow of a man whom his purse-proud relations abandoned for marrying. Let them e'en enjoy his fortune, for my stripling will inherit all his father's wealth.

LORD STEWKLY: Oh then you are *sure* of him?

LADY FILMOT: Why—not absolutely, I must totally rout the present sovereign of his heart, before I even let him suspect my design of filling her throne—I have persuaded his Uncle Sir Jeremy, (who by the way admires me prodigiously) to change their former lodgings and come into our house.

LORD STEWKLY: Sir Jonathan and his son, I suppose, follow of course?

LADY FILMOT: Oh to be sure; poor Sir Jonathan you know is to be led by a hair, and looks up to his brother as to an oracle. This you see will give me more frequent opportunities—

LORD STEWKLY: Yes, yes I see, and approve of your design—I suppose Edward breakfasts with me this morning—tho' faith I don't remember where I asked him or not.

LADY FILMOT: For shame my lord! but I'll soon rectify that omission—I fancy 'tis almost the hour. I must just step home and adjust myself a little, and then—but where is't we are to be?

LORD STEWKLY: Oh at Spring gardens—I'll go before you, for I suppose you reserve for your swain the honour of squiring you thither.

LADY FILMOT: Oh certainly.

LORD STEWKLY: Ma'am, I submit.

LADY FILMOT: With a most exemplary patience ha ha ha! Is not this better than being in love now?
[*Exit severally.*]

Scene iii. Stapleton's apartment.
Enter Sir Jonathan followed by two or three servants with trunks.

SIR JONATHAN: There, there, set them down and go get the rest. Lack a day I am so weary! [*He throws himself into an armd chair.*]
[*Enter Stapleton with a pen in his hand.*]
STAPLETON: Why what the plague is all this noise about?
SIR JONATHAN: Sir!
STAPLETON: What's all this lumber here?

SIR JONATHAN: Lumber do you call it? I hope I may bring my baggage into my own lodgings, Sir, without offence to anybody.

STAPLETON: Your own lodgings Sir; why these are my lodgings.

SIR JONATHAN: Hey! introth I believe I am wrong sure enough. Well thats comical! now I think of it my brother Jeremy told me it was up *one* pair of stairs, and I have come up two, ha ha ha. I beg your pardon Sir; sit down, pray don't let me be your hindrance.

STAPLETON: Pray Sir let these things be taken away.

SIR JONATHAN: Presently, when my servants come back; but I protest I am so tired with going to and fro that I must needs rest a while; pray be seated Sir and let us have a little chat, for I don't love ceremony.

STAPLETON: Nor I don't love instrusion Sir.

SIR JONATHAN: No, nor I neither when a man does it designedly; but I like to stumble on an acquaintance by chance; one often gets good friends in that way. May I be so bold Sir as to ask you your name? *My* name's Bull, Sir Jonathan they call me; but a knight batchelor.

STAPLETON [*Aside.*]: This man's simplicity almost tempts me to excuse his impertinence.—Stapleton's my name Sir.

SIR JONATHAN: Ha, Stapleton; married or single, if I may be so free?

STAPLETON: Single, thank my stars.

SIR JONATHAN: One should be thankful for everything to be sure. I buried a very good wife; but I have a son a fine pritty youth as you should see; and I have an elder brother, he's a baronet, a fine man too in his own way.

STAPLETON: Well Sir I am glad of it; but if you please, I'll call my servant to remove your trunks.

SIR JONATHAN: No, no Sir, don't trouble yourself, I am in no hurry; but I wish you knew this brother of mine, you would like him I believe. He has had a fine education. I was only bred to business; but faith it has turned out better than all his learning; for he, poor gentleman, spent what estate there was in the family upon an election, and lost it too; that was the worst of it, for it almost turned his brain.

STAPLETON: Ay, that was bad indeed, to lose his election and his wits too.

SIR JONATHAN: Oh I don't mean that neither, no, no, no God forbid! Wit, he has more wit than I have, for that matter; but it vexd him grievously, for you must know he is a little haughty, being the elder branch of the family as he calls it, and a man of learning: Yet we differ sometimes in opinion; but I durstn't always speak my mind to him, for he has the gift of speech better than I have, and will harangue you so, that he won't leave you a word to say.

STAPLETON: Why you don't seem wanting in fluency of speech yourself Sir Jonathan.

SIR JONATHAN: No, no no, in my own way; but then he was a famous speaker in Parliament once; he is a scholar too, and I have bred my son one. I had him at a grammar school, and he understands Latin almost as well as his uncle. I am going to marry him soon to a young lady that lodges in this house: I don't know whether you know Miss Tryfort?

STAPLETON: Tryfort! I have heard the name. Pray who is she, Sir?

SIR JONATHAN: Why one of those that has had good luck. Her grandfather dyed some time ago and his whole fortune comes to her; for her father's dead, and an uncle she had, that married foolishly and ran away, and so she is the only heir in the family.

STAPLETON: And she is to be married to your son?

SIR JONATHAN: And she is to be married to my son, the affair is settled between—lack-a-day theres my brother Jeremy!

SIR JEREMY [*Calls without.*]: Sr Jonathan! Why where are you?

SIR JONATHAN: Now will he be as angry with me for this little mistake—I am coming, brother. Sir, your humble servant. I shall be proud to be better acquainted with you.

STAPLETON: Sir, I am yours. [*Exit Sir Jonathan.*] Tho I hate to mix with the world I can be entertained with a recital of its follies at a distance. This man seems to be thrown in my way on purpose: I'll cultivate his acquaintance. The communicativeness of his temper will be a means to gratify my curiosity—who's there? [*Enter a Servant.*] Remove these things and set the chamber to rights.
[*Exit Stapleton.*]

Scene iv. A parlour.
Enter Sir Jonathan and Sr Jeremy.

SIR JEREMY: Fy, fy Sir Jonathan, I am ashamed of your blundering thus eternally.

SIR JONATHAN: Well, well brother, don't be angry; there is no great harm done.

SIR JEREMY: Sir Jonathan!

SIR JONATHAN: Brother!

SIR JEREMY: I want some conference with you.

SIR JONATHAN: I am very willing to hear you, brother.

SIR JEREMY: You know I never gave my assent to this junction (for I can't call it an alliance) between my nephew and this girl.

SIR JONATHAN: Gadzooks! brother, why don't we come hither to solemnize this wedding?

SIR JEREMY: No.

SIR JONATHAN: No! Why wasn't it agreed that they should be married the day that Ned was to be one and twenty, and won't that be next Saturday, and would he let me rest till he made me come down hither after Mrs. Tryfort?

SIR JEREMY: I grant you, I grant you all that, Sir Jonathan; yet there are sudden events which sometimes require as sudden a change of measures, and he is a deplorable politician that is not prepared for exigencies.

SIR JONATHAN: I can't for my life see what politicks has to do with my son's marriage.

SIR JEREMY: Ha, ha, I know *you* can't; but I can.

SIR JONATHAN: Why, what fresh objection have you started now?

SIR JEREMY: Ph—uph—no blood, no family, no connections, fy, fy! I'd rather see the boy married to a woman of consequence, tho he didn't get sixpence with her.

SIR JONATHAN: By my faith and so wouldn't I. Put forty thousand pound into one scale, and consequence as you call it into tother, and see which will weigh heaviest?

SIR JEREMY: There's the case! tho' you are of an antient family yourself, yet having had the misfortune to be thrown early into trade it has abased your ideas: now for my part, tho I have somewhat abridged the inheritance of my ancestors in reducing it from twelve hundred, to about two I believe hundred pounds a year,—yet I did it in a cause I am not ashamed of. I am the first eldest son of the family for these seven generations that have been out of the Senate house, I can tell you that.

SIR JONATHAN: Oh brother, you spent a world of money about that same business.

SIR JEREMY: And would spend another world again tomorrow, on the same occasion; and if it should ever be Ned's great happiness to get into Parliament—

SIR JONATHAN: Ned into Parliament. Oh lord, oh lord; lookee brother, with submission, I would not give sixpence, no not sixpence—

SIR JEREMY: I know it, yet tis fit notwithstanding as Edward is the only representative of the family, that the name should be revived with some degree of splendor; but instead of that, you want irretrievably to mix the bloud with the puddle of City.

SIR JONATHAN: Don't abuse the City, brother, I don't know what we should do without it.

SIR JEREMY: I don't, the City may have its use; but don't let us confound all order, all distinction, and fancy trade's people are upon a footing with legislators. I have no object in view for myself (they have thought proper to leave *me* out), but I own it would please me to reflect, that my posterity, even in the collateral line, were to be guardians of the liberty of their country, instead of being doomd to the drudgery of making money.

SIR JONATHAN: Don't abuse money neither, brother, I can assure you it is a very good thing.

SIR JEREMY: It appears so to *you* no doubt, who have been used to buy and sell, and thank the people that you gained by; but I who have been brought up with a Spirit of independence, would sooner be reduced to eat my own shoe leather, than be obliged to e'er a man alive.

SIR JONATHAN: I don't understand such fine-spun notions, not I.

SIR JEREMY: I know you don't, and for that reason have often suspected your legitimacy; for excepting yourself, I never knew any one of the family that had not those notions.

SIR JONATHAN: May be so, brother; have you anything more to say to me, for I have a good deal of business to do.

SIR JEREMY: The old way! When ever *I* was disposed to inform you a little, *you* had always business; haven't I known you, rather than miss your hour of going to Change, refuse to hear me repeat a speech on which perhaps the welfare of the whole nation depended?

SIR JONATHAN [*Hastily.*]: You don't want to speak a speech now brother, do you?

SIR JEREMY: No Sir, not at present; but if you were fit to be trusted with the conduct of your own affairs, I could tell you that there is something now on the tapis that perhaps may be the making of a certain young man.

SIR JONATHAN: What is it brother, I shall be very glad to harken to any thing for the good of my son.

SIR JEREMY: Matters are not yet come to that maturity that I could wish; but I had a mind to sound you, to feel your pulse a little on the occasion, Sir Jonathan; so I shall for the present, only throw out to you at large, that there is a certain person of condition here, that possibly wouldn't be averse to entering into a treaty of marriage with us.

SIR JONATHAN: With *us!* I don't very well take your meaning, brother.

SIR JEREMY: I don't intend you should brother; this is not the juncture for explanations. At a proper time perhaps I may let you a little more behind the curtain; in the meanwhile I have given you a *hint* just to play with, Sir Jonathan; and so now you may go about your *business* as you call it, for I am engaged to breakfast with my lord Stewkly this morning.

SIR JONATHAN: Very well, when you come back I shall be glad of a little further discourse with you, so brother your humble servant.

SIR JEREMY: Good morning to you Sir Jonathan. [*Exit Sir Jonathan.*] A weak man; but he means well. [*Exit Sir Jeremy.*]

Scene v. Spring Gardens.
Enter Lord Stewkly, and Lady Filmot.

LORD STEWKLY: And so you couldn't persuade the stripling?

LADY FILMOT: He coloured, and said he must ask his father's leave.

LORD STEWKLY: I wish my damsel were *capable* of blushing; but she is too ignorant even for that; for when I asked her, she only stared, made me half a dozen curtisies, and then said she was laced so tight, it had given her a pain in the stomach, and asked me if I knew what was good for the cholic ha ha ha.

LADY FILMOT: Oh you must get the mother of your side; she wants of all things to be taken notice of by the *quality,* as she phrases it.—You ought to visit her, tis the vainest poor creature, and the fondest of hard words, which without *mis*calling, she always takes care to misapply.—She perfectly adores me, because I always speak to her, where ever I meet her.

LORD STEWKLY: Lady Bell I think can't prevail on herself to shew her the least civility.

LADY FILMOT: No; and the poor woman does take such pains to get into her good graces! and then Lady Bell draws up her long neck, gives her a supercilious stare, and turning to me, 'shall we walk, Lady Filmot for you see there's *no*body here': and then poor Mrs Tryfort finding herself *nobody,* looks *so* mortified, and follows us *so* close, in order to appear one of our company, that I talk to her out of mere compassion.

LORD STEWKLY: Ha ha ha poor woman!

LADY FILMOT: But how in the name of wonder can you afford to treat such an intolerable crowd as you have collected here this morning?

LORD STEWKLY: To let you into a secret, Champignion pays, tho I have the credit of it. You must know he is *ambitious,* as he calls it, of being galant, immensely rich, ostentatious and never easy but in devising the means to squander.

LADY FILMOT: And I suppose you are kind enough to assist him.

LORD STEWKLY: Oh he has taken me for his pattern; and upon his consulting me what handsome thing he ought to do, I told him I intended giving an entertainment here this morning; but to oblige him, would let him do it in my stead, and as he is a stranger, undertook to ask the company in his name.

LADY FILMOT: That was very kind of you; but won't he discover that you have asked them in your own?

LORD STEWKLY: No, for I told him it would be the height of good breeding not to appear till the company were seated, and to slip away before they rose, to avoid the usual ceremony of bowing and curtsying; so that as he will be fidgeting about all the morning, he will only have the appearance of my deputy.

LADY FILMOT: Very well contrived, I declare.

LORD STEWKLY: Oh I have laid such a train for mirth—you must know he is immoderately vain of his person; and as he wants of all things to captivate some woman of quality, I have told him that Lady Bell Aircastle is in love with him.

LADY FILMOT: Gracious! why she would not condescend to look at him.

LORD STEWKLY: I know it; but I shall give her to understand that he is in love with *her,* which I think may afford us some pleasant scenes. Besides this will lead the profuse coxcomb into a thousand schemes of expensive pleasure, which will serve for entertainment, in our intervals of more serious business.

LADY FILMOT: Ay there you say something—and here comes your fool with all his busy consequence about him.

Scene vi.
Enter Champignion.

LORD STEWKLY: Well, Mr. Champignion, are any of your company come yet?

CHAMPIGNION: A few my lord, but I stepped out of the way to avoid being unpolite you know; tho I deprive myself of the pleasure of gazing at the ladies; there are abundance of your sex, ma'am, are to do me the honour to breakfast with me this morning.

LADY FILMOT: So I hear Sir, and you seem to have prepared a very elegant entertainment for us.

CHAMPIGNION: I have endeavoured to make it as grand, ma'am, as the place would afford; for you know, ma'am, how can we batchelors employ our time better, than in shewing our respect to the ladies ma'am?

LADY FILMOT: Very true, Sir.

CHAMPIGNION: It won't cost me about fifty guineas, and you know, ma'am, that's but a trifle to a single fellow like me, to purchase the favour of the fair sex, especially ladies of quality.

LADY FILMOT: Oh certainly; Lady Bell Aircastle is to do the honours of your table, I think Sir?

CHAMPIGNION: She is of a prodigious great family! Her father was the seventeenth Earl in a direct line; and blood, you know ma'am, entitles people— but apropos, my lord, a word with you.—Your ladyship will excuse me for a minute. [*He takes Lord Stewkly aside.*] I am told she is so monstrously proud that she will not marry any man that can't produce a pedigree (of *gentry* at least) up to the flood, and split me if I can tell who my grandfather was!

LORD STEWKLY: That's a little unlucky; but as you are not known here, you can easily make a pedigree for yourself.

CHAMPIGNION: Ay; but who can I get to vouch for the truth of it, my lord?

LORD STEWKLY: Nay, that indeed I can't tell.

CHAMPIGNION: If I could but find some poor devil (with the appearance of a gentleman tho') who wouldn't scruple to assert an innocent lye, you know my lord, I'd pay him handsomely for his pains.

LORD STEWKLY: Why I fancy such a one may be easily found.

CHAMPIGNION: Egad I have hit it, my lord! that shabby knight that's just come into our house—the poor dog has beggard himself they tell me, yet sets up for something, and knows everybody.

LORD STEWKLY: Who, Sir Jeremy Bull, do you mean?

CHAMPIGNION: Ay, he, my lord, I'll give him a hundred guineas for a handsome lye, provided he'll swear to it.

LORD STEWKLY: Have a care how you make such a proposal to him!

CHAMPIGNION: Nay nay, hang it, my lord, I'll give him two hundred for that matter rather than fail.

LORD STEWKLY: But I tell you, Sir, he is a man that—

CHAMPIGNION: I declare here's Lady Bell just come into the garden. I had best slip aside till she joins you, you know, my lord. [*He skips nimbly a little way from Lord Stewkly.*]

Scene vii.
Enter Lady Bell.

LORD STEWKLY: Good morning to your ladyship.

LADY BELL: Why my lord Stewkly, you have certainly invited the whole corporation of Bath with their wives and children; the place won't contain them, it's quite a mob, don't you think so, lady Filmot?

CHAMPIGNION [*Advancing.*]: A mob, ma'am? here's none but people of quality, and the best gentry, I can assure your ladyship.

LADY BELL [*Aside.*]: Who is this person, my Lord?

LORD STEWKLY: I thought your ladyship knew Mr. Champignion!

LADY BELL: Do you know anything of him, Lady Filmot?

LADY FILMOT: Oh yes ma'am, he is a friend of my lord's.

LADY BELL [*As if observing company at a distance.*]: An absolute Mob I declare, I scarce know any of them.

CHAMPIGNION: I hope your ladyship will excuse my taking the liberty of requesting the honor of—

LORD STEWKLY [*Aside.*]: Hush! you'll spoil all!

CHAMPIGNION: Egad my lord, I must make her know that I am no more company for Mob than her ladyship.

LADY BELL: What does the young man say, my lord?

LORD STEWKLY: That there has been scarce any one asked, ma'am, but people of fashion.

CHAMPIGNION: That was my design, ma'am, or I should not have had the ambition to desire the favour of your ladyship's presiding; but we poor unmarried fellows, you know ma'am, that are so unfortunate as not to have ladies of our own, you know ma'am—

LADY BELL: What does he mean, Lady Filmot?

LADY FILMOT [*Aside to Lord Stewkly.*]: It will all come out—[*Aside to Lady Bell.*] I fancy, ma'am, my lord emploied him to invite some of the company.

LADY BELL: Oh, is it that? and so, Sir, you have asked all your own acquaintance I suppose?

CHAMPIGNION: To be sure Ma'am, and would if there had been more of them; I did not come here to *save* I can assure your ladyship.

LORD STEWKLY [*Aside.*]: Fy! you'll disgrace yourself. Ay ay ma'am, my friend Champignion is as generous as a Prince, and would have me to be so too—Come Sir, will you walk?

CHAMPIGNION: Faith my Lord, I am no niggard when ladies are in the question: we squandering puppies begrudge nothing on our pleasures. I have ordered that no expence be spared, I can tell you ma'am.

LADY BELL: Pray my lord, what has he to do with this entertainment?

CHAMPIGNION: I have the honour of giving it, as I take it ma'am.

LADY BELL: I understood it had been yours, my lord Stewkly?

LORD STEWKLY: (So!) Why to tell you the truth, ma'am, I intended it so; but my friend here is so munificent he has taken it upon himself. I thought I had told your ladyship so.

LADY BELL: Then I hope I shall be excused from presiding; there are some people here possibly that may like such a thing.

CHAMPIGNION [*Aside to Lady Filmot.*]: She is prodigiously proud, and yet for all that—[*He talks apart to Lady Filmot.*]

LORD STEWKLY: A word with you, Lady Bell—I don't know whether you suspect it or not, but the man's in love with you over head and ears, and it is intirely on your account that he has done all this.

LADY BELL: In love with *me!* Why prithee my lord, who *is* the Creter?

LORD STEWKLY: He is worth above a hundred thousand pound.

LADY BELL: Ay; but did he get it by *doing* anything, I suppose he is a trading fellow?

LORD STEWKLY: Why I own he is *but* a private gentleman.

LADY BELL: But are you sure he is *even* a gentleman?

LORD STEWKLY: Of a considerable family at Antigua.

LADY BELL: He he ha I think I'll speak to him; one wouldn't be rude you know even to one's inferior.—Mr. a—I think these gardens are pretty enough.

CHAMPIGNION: Oh quite pretty, ma'am; but nothing to what we have abroad. I have such gardens ma'am, it would delight your ladyship to see them. I have a prodigious taste that way, ma'am.

LORD STEWKLY [*Aside.*]: Mark that.

LADY FILMOT: And then you have such fine fruits, Mr. Champignion!

CHAMPIGNION: Oh lord ma'am, you have nothing like them here; if we had but such fine *ladies* our Island would be a perfect paradise, ma'am.

LORD STEWKLY [*Aside.*]: Do you observe?

LADY BELL: Lord, Mr.—I didn't think you West indians had been so well bred.

CHAMPIGNION: Nobody more so, I assure you, ma'am; we are remarkable for it. I had a good mind to have brought my six fellows to have waited this morning, only my lord told me, some of the fair sex were a little timerous of negroes.

LADY BELL: I don't dislike them for my part.

CHAMPIGNION: If I had known that ma'am, I should have tried to have collected twenty or thirty to have attended your ladyship, ma'am.

LORD STEWKLY: Come ladies, I fancy most of the company are assembled by this time; suppose we were to go to them.

CHAMPIGNION: Will your ladyship favour me with your hand?

LADY BELL: I can find my way, Sir—Come Lady Filmot; my Lord Stewkly, your arm if you please.

LADY FILMOT: I'll follow your ladyship. [*Exit all but Lady Filmot.*]

Scene viii.
Enter Edward, who runs behind a tree making signs to Lady Filmot not to discover him. Enter Lucy running, and looking about. Lady Filmot points to the opposite side and Lucy runs out.

LADY FILMOT: Mr. Edward! Mr. Edward! what you have been at play? [*Edward comes out.*]

EDWARD: Yes ma'am, just to pass away the time till breakfast.

LADY FILMOT: Is that young girl any relation of yours?

EDWARD: Does your ladyship think she favours me?

LADY FILMOT: I dare say she favors you, Sir; but I don't think she resembles you in the least; she doesn't appear to me to be at all handsome, that is she is not at all like you—I mean she is not—in short she is not like you.—But I was going to say, if she were one of your family, I should be glad to introduce her into some of the best company here.

EDWARD: She would be vastly obliged to you, I am sure ma'am.

LADY FILMOT: Ay, but if she is no relation of yours you know—

EDWARD: She is not at present; but one of these days perhaps, who knows?

LADY FILMOT: Oh, I understand you; she's a mistress then?

EDWARD: Ah, you found me out by my colouring; but don't you tell now, Lady Filmot.

LADY FILMOT: Poor girl, I pity her.

EDWARD: Pity her! Lord, ma'am, for what? She likes me as well as I do her.

LADY FILMOT: No doubt ont; and she has no rivals to be sure.

EDWARD: No, upon my credit; we have been in love since we were children no higher than this.

LADY FILMOT: And are likely to continue so! Ah thou little Coquette!

EDWARD: *I* a coquette! Oh heavens, you don't take me for a lady I hope, ma'am.

LADY FILMOT: Oh there are *male* coquets, and you are one or I am mistaken.

EDWARD: Ha ha ha; you are very comical I declare Lady Filmot. Why I protest I don't well know what a coquet is.

LADY FILMOT: No, no, not you, you poor innocent! You don't know how to make yourself agreeable, and to say a thousand things with your eyes.

EDWARD: With my eyes. I say things with my eyes ha ha ha!

END OF ACT I

ACT II

Scene i. Lady Filmot's appartment.
Lady Filmot and Edward. A chess board before them.

LADY FILMOT: This lesson is sufficient for to day; we musn't tire young beginners.

EDWARD: I never can remember that Knight's move; I believe your ladyship thinks me very dull.

LADY FILMOT: I shouldn't judge so by looking at you.—Come we'll have done, I can play no more.

EDWARD: I hope you are not ill Lady Filmot, you look so grave!

LADY FILMOT: I am not very well.

EDWARD: I am vastly sorry, upon my word.

LADY FILMOT: Are you? Why then I wish I were well for your sake.

EDWARD: So do I too, I declare.—How did you like Miss Tryfort's dancing this morning, ma'am?

LADY FILMOT: I didn't mind her.

EDWARD: Oh dear, why didn't you see me dancing with her after Lord Stewkly?

LADY FILMOT: Yes certainly, I saw *you* dance, and observed something moving along with you.

EDWARD: That was she; she is reckond a charming dancer.

LADY FILMOT: She might pass at a City ball.

EDWARD: Why ma'am, don't *you* like her?

LADY FILMOT: If *you* like her, she needn't be solicitous about the opinion of others.

EDWARD: Ay; but *your* approbation ma'am, who are so good a judge—

LADY FILMOT: Agreeable flatterer!

EDWARD: You who are so genteel yourself—

LADY FILMOT: Polished creature!

EDWARD: Now tell me upon your honour which dances best, she or *I?*

LADY FILMOT: What signify *my* thoughts?

EDWARD: I'd give the universe to know them.

LADY FILMOT: Why, then, beyond comparison you are the best, and she is the very awkwardest dancer I ever beheld.

EDWARD: Absolutely? ha ha ha, how she'd be vexed to hear you had said so!

LADY FILMOT: Oh you mustn't tell her, it would mortify the poor thing; for you may suppose that WE *must* understand better what is called grace and elegance than—you'll pardon me; but I really think it a great pity that your lot hasn't thrown you amongst people of fashion.

EDWARD: So it is upon my reputation, and so my Uncle Jeremy always said; I should like it of all things, their ways are so different from ours in the City. I don't know how it is, but they are always in good humour I think.

LADY FILMOT: Oh, ever, ever, tis a characteristic mark of quality never to be out of temper. Why you are of a good family yourself, Mr. Edward.

EDWARD: And I am of a good family myself as you say, ma'am, that's of *one* side.—and then they are so obliging and kind to strangers!

LADY FILMOT: And so sentimental! do you understand sentiments?

EDWARD: Oh yes ma'am, I have drunk sentiments very often; we give them for toasts.

LADY FILMOT: Those are but commonplace things; but some day or other I'll give you a lecture on the subject of sentiments; I am sure you'll like it.

EDWARD: *Any*thing from your *ladyship.*

LADY FILMOT: Really. Why you begin to grow dangerous, Child.

EDWARD: *I* dangerous! I declare, Lady Filmot, you talk strangely! Why you have more danger in your little finger than ten such as me.

LADY FILMOT: Captivating little rogue! hush! here's company.

Scene ii.
Enter Mrs. Tryfort.

MRS. TRYFORT: How does your ladyship do to-day? So Mr. Edward?

LADY FILMOT: Dear Mrs. Tryfort, how came it that you were not at the breakfast this morning?

MRS TRYFORT: It was not for want of being *askd* I assure your ladyship; but I was so ill! ha ha ha! lord it isn't long since I got out of bed.—I declare this is a fatiguing life one leads, and exhilerates one's spirits so much, that I have scarce strength enough to rise in a morning; but then one keeps such good company ha ha that it makes amends for the bad hours.

LADY FILMOT: Ay, as you observe; but I hope you will be able to go to the rooms tonight; Mr. Champignion gives tea.

MRS. TRYFORT: Why if I find myself tolerably well; but I am so low every morning, ha ha ha, I protest I use almost an ounce of salvolatile constantly in my tea—your ladyship I suppose will be there, and Lady Bell, and Lord Stewkly.—To be sure he is one of *the* best bred, most polite, good humourd charming men living! and takes as much pains to teach my Lucy, and make her illiterate,[1] as if he were actually her master.

EDWARD: Pray what is he teaching her, ma'am?

LADY FILMOT: Oh a song I suppose.

MRS. TYRFORT: I left them together practising, and he has such a genteel manner, and keeps time so finely with his head, and says Piano, with such an air! and then takes Lucy by the hand, and is so much the gentleman, lord what difference there is between folks.

EDWARD: Shall we go and hear them Pianoing, Lady Filmot?

LADY FILMOT: No, we won't disturb them now; it will improve Miss; my lord has a very pretty taste in singing.

MRS. TYRFORT: Oh in everything ma'am he is a progeny![2] a perfect progeny, Lady Filmot!—In the first place he is a most prodigious wit, and then he speaks all the languages in the world, and is so full of compliments, and such a charming poet!

LADY FILMOT: He is very accomplished I know.

EDWARD: But how came you to find out all this, Mrs. Tryfort?

MRS. TRYFORT: Why I have had him above an hour with me to day: your ladyship must know he desired leave to come to my toilet, that was polite! it's the way he says in France.

LADY FILMOT: Ay and here too, you know, amongst people of fashion.

EDWARD: I am sure it is not the way in the City, for Lucy would never let me in when she was putting on her cloaths.

MRS. TRYFORT: How *can* you be so vulgar, Mr. Edward! Can't you say dressing? I wish you would learn of my lord.

LADY FILMOT: Oh very soon he'll want no instructions.

MRS. TRYFORT: And my lord dresses so prodigiously, and understands the fashions so well, and has such pritty names for things, and praises everything up to the skies! but *never* flatters: no, *that* he declares he's above.

EDWARD: And you believe him?

LADY FILMOT: No body can doubt my lord's veracity.

MRS. TRYFORT: And Lucy says he dances wonderfully.

EDWARD: Did *Lucy* say so?

MRS. TRYFORT: Miss Tryfort said so, Sir.

LADY FILMOT: There I differ with her a little; I have seen *some* whose dancing pleased me better. [*Lady Filmot looks at Edward and he winks at her.*]

MRS. TRYFORT: Well I know he is a terrestrial[3] man altogether and so free, and comprehensive; he told me all about himself, just as if we had been old acquaintance: and what do you think the comical creature wanted me to do?

LADY FILMOT: What?

MRS. TRYFORT: I declare to put on a little red, ha ha ha! Oh fy my lord, says I, I never did such a thing in all the days of my life. But my dear ma'am says he (stroking my cheek with his hand so agreably) do but *try;* let *me* just touch it for you, only to heighten your bloom a little; you want but that to be the very image of the Marquise de Rouge (who was but eighteen) that I used to visit at Paris. Wasn't that vastly witty and clever?

EDWARD: I hope you won't advise Lucy to paint; but *she* doesn't want it indeed.

LADY FILMOT: No, nor Mrs. Tryfort neither in my opinion.

MRS. TRYFORT: Your ladyship's so obliging to say so. To be sure when I am well I have a pritty good complexion; my lord said it was only my illness that made it not quite so brilliant as my daughter's.

EDWARD: Ha ha ha, My lord's above flattering, you know ma'am.

MRS. TRYFORT: I declare you are so unbred, I wonder her ladyship can bear to talk with you.

LADY FILMOT: Oh I like his plain natural manner of all things.

MRS. TRYFORT: But so vulgar you know ma'am. Dear I wish I could remember the verses my lord made on Lucy.

EDWARD: Verses! did he make verses on her?

MRS. TRYFORT: Just offhand now, I forget what he called them.

EDWARD: Extempore may be.

MRS. TRYFORT: No, none of your nonsensical extemprys; it was some charming French word.

LADY FILMOT: Impromptu.

MRS. TRYFORT: Ay that was the very title of them.

EDWARD: I have a good mind to go and spoil their impromptu.

LADY FILMOT: Indeed you shan't, for I intend you shall gallant me to the pump room.

EDWARD: Well I'll just leave you there, ma'am; but I must run back tho.

MRS. TRYFORT: There's politeness for you!

LADY FILMOT: Nothing but easy freedom.

MRS. TRYFORT: Shall I beg the favour of your ladyship to allow Lucy to practise a little on your harpsichord, just when you are abroad?

LADY FILMOT: Whenever she pleases, ma'am.

MRS. TRYFORT: Your ladyship's immensly good,—I wish I could recollect my lord's verses.—they begin

> When Lucia sings we seek th' inchanting sound
> And bless the notes that do—[4]

lord I forget what comes next—

EDWARD: Ha ha ha! Are those what my lord gave you for his own poetry? Why the song's as old as yourself.

MRS. TRYFORT: Sir, you are a little too pert let me tell you, and so much taciturnity[5] doesn't become a young man.—Your ladyship would be charmd with the verses if I could think of them.

LADY FILMOT: Come ma'am maybe you may recover them as we walk!

MRS. TRYFORT: I'll just step and tell my daughter that she may practise a little here, now your ladyship is going out, and I will wait on you again directly.

[*Exit Mrs. Tryfort.*]

EDWARD: Why Mrs. Tryfort seems to be quite in love with my lord Stewkly, I should be sorry Lucy saw with her mother's eyes.

LADY FILMOT: There's no accounting for people's ridiculous tastes; now to *me,* the artless, unaffected manners of one who has seen less of the world, has ten thousand times the charms of all Lord Stewkly's studied address.

EDWARD: And I am sure your ladyship has ten thousand times more sense than Mrs. Tryfort, with all her airs.

LADY FILMOT: Come then we'll not wait for her; but slip out, and have our own little chat to ourselves. You shall be my cissisbey.[6]

EDWARD: What maam?

LADY FILMOT: I'll tell you as we go along, tis' the prettyest thing in the world.

[*Exit Lady Filmot and Edward.*]

Scene iii.
Enter Mrs. Tryfort, Lucy, and Lord Stewkly.

MRS. TRYFORT: Bless me, her ladyship's gone! I must follow her, or she'll think me monstrously ill bred. Be sure now Miss, mind, and do all that my lord bids you. There child, sit down to the harpsichord; your lordship will excuse me for leaving you so deliberately.

LORD STEWKLY: Oh ma'am, there needs no apology. [*Exit Mrs. Tryfort.*] Come my sweet little pupil: just that single passage over again that charmed me so in the next room.

LUCY: Shan't I play, my lord?

LORD STEWKLY: I had rather hear your voice without the instrument. [*Lucy sings.*] Ravishing upon [**my**] soul! You have the finest ear in Nature, and your voice is absolutely angelic.

LUCY: And my master used always to say I sung out of tune.

LORD STEWKLY: He was a blockhead, and didn't understand his business.

LUCY: And what vexed me more, Mr. Edward used to join with him and say so too.

LORD STEWKLY: And what need you mind what Mr. Edward says?

LUCY: Oh I must mind him because—

LORD STEWKLY: Because what? [*She puts her hands before her face.*] Oh heavens, not a lover I hope! Why sure that raw stripling has not the assurance to pretend to you!

LUCY: He is but young to be sure my lord; but as my mama says, that's a fault that will mend.

LORD STEWKLY: You can't *like* him! That's morally impossible.

LUCY: Why they used to say in town he was a very pritty young man.

LORD STEWKLY: Oh my dear Miss Tryfort, there never was such a mistake, the lad might look well enough behind a counter.

LUCY: He keeps no shop I can assure you, my lord.

LORD STEWKLY: And so you'd be content to sit down for life in Cornhill?

LUCY: Why pray my lord, mayn't one be as happy there as any where else?

LORD STEWKLY: Happy! What! happy in Cornhill! Oh for shame. I must speak to your mama about it.

LUCY: She knows it already, my lord, so you needn't think to make mischief.

LORD STEWKLY [*Aside.*]: So, I find my difficulty will be *here.*—But ma'am, hadn't you rather be my lady, than plain Mrs. Any body?

LUCY: I *should* like to be a lady, that I own; I *may* come to be Lady Mayoress you know my lord.

LORD STEWKLY: Oh paltry! we laugh at those titles at our end of the town: No, no ma'am, a coronet's the thing for you.

LUCY: I would not give a pin for a coronet I assure you, my Lord.

LORD STEWKLY [*Aside.*]: That won't do I see.—No? that's surprising! Shouldn't you like to take place of Lady Filmot, and Lady Bell Aircastle?

LUCY: Yes, that I should vastly; for I don't love either of them; Lady Bell is so proud she'll never speak to one, and Lady Filmot is always whispering with Mr. Edward.

LORD STEWKLY: That you must know she does to teaze me, for she is the arrentest coquet in nature; but I have thought of a way to be even with her, if you would assist me in a little piece of innocent revenge that I have plotted against her.

LUCY: Oh with all my heart, I love mightily to be in plots, I am always plotting when I am at home.

LORD STEWKLY: Well, I'll tell you then; you must know I made some slight addresses to Lady Filmot, and was at first, as you may imagine, very well received: not that I was absolutely in love with her, only I thought her the prettyest woman here, before your arrival, ma'am.

LUCY: Oh my lord, she is a great deal handsomer than I am.

LORD STEWKLY: You are the only person, herself excepted, that thinks so I believe: but, however, fancying herself secure of me, she has a mind to try her power, and giggles with your lover merely to make me uneasy; but I'll let her see I despise her little arts, by making love to another woman before her face.

LUCY: Indeed you'll serve her right.

LORD STEWKLY: Now as you are incontestably the object of every one's admiration here, I have made choice of you for the person, if you will allow me the honour of addressing you.

LUCY: Ay,—but not in Earnest tho', my lord.

LORD STEWKLY: No, no it's to be all in jest; but then you must *seem* to receive me kindly, and that will vex her to the heart.

LUCY: Very well; but then mustn't I tell Edward the truth?

LORD STEWKLY: Not for the world; for he'd tell *her,* and then the Joke would be lost; we shall have time enough to let him into the secret. I only want to pique her pride for a day or two.

LUCY: Well, I own I should like to vex her a little. When shall we begin?

LORD STEWKLY: The very first time we happen to see her. Suppose we were to go now and meet her in her walks—and be sure you smile and look pleased at what I say.

LUCY: Oh never fear, my lord; but remember I am not in Earnest.

LORD STEWKLY: No, by no means—Come then. [*Aside.*] Her love of *mischief,* may probably effect that, to which even her *vanity* couldn't prompt her!

[*Exit Lord Stewkly and Lucy.*]

Scene iv. Changes to the Parade.
Enter Sir Jonathan meeting Stapleton.

SIR JONATHAN: Ha! Mr Stapleton, well met, have you been taking a walk by yourself? That's melancholy like; now I love company and chearfulness, and I'd have you do the same.

STAPLETON: But I love solitude, Sir.

SIR JONATHAN: You are not troubled in mind I hope, Sir. If you have any thing that disturbs you the best way is to tell it; there's great comfort in opening one's mind to a friend.

STAPLETON: But suppose a man has no friend, Sir?

SIR JONATHAN: Nay, faith that would be hard in a Christian country; for my part I am always willing to listen to every body's story; and I am as ready to tell my own.

STAPLETON: I thank you, Sir; but at present I am not in a humour either to hear your story or to tell my own, so good by to you. [*Going.*]

SIR JONATHAN: Harkee, Mr. Stapleton, pray did you meet my son any where?

STAPLETON: Your son Sir, why I don't know him!

SIR JONATHAN: Ha ha ha, how should you, faith; now I think of it I believe you never saw him. He is a pritty slender youth, with his own curld hair.

STAPLETON: And a light colourd frock?

SIR JONATHAN: Ay, ay the same, that's Ned.

STAPLETON: Then I can tell you he is got into very bad hands.

SIR JONATHAN: Bad hands, Sir! How, how, which way?

STAPLETON: A lady's Sir, a *fine* lady's.

SIR JONATHAN: A fine lady, why you don't call that bad hands I hope, Mr. Stapleton? Ned's fit company I can tell you for the finest lady in the land; why he'll make you as handsome a bow, and pen you as pretty a letter, and compose you as moving a love speech too, out of his own head, as e'er a fine beau of them all. No, no, I don't fear Ned's behaviour.

STAPLETON: Nor don't you fear his morals neither?

SIR JONATHAN: Oh, that's another thing, Sir, quite and clear.

STAPLETON: Why then Sir, I tell you as a friend, your son is in danger; I saw him just now enter the Pump room, a fine sprightly female leaning on his arm. Her modish dress, and a certain air of levity which I observed in her countenance, opposed to the plain garb, and modest deportment of the youth, struck me.

SIR JONATHAN: Ay, isn't he a pretty modest youth?

STAPLETON: A mixture of pity and curiosity, excited me to observe them; and as there was no other company in the room (for that's the time I chuse) I took out a paper and pretended to read, to leave them more at liberty.

SIR JONATHAN: Well, Sir?

STAPLETON: Without minding me, she drew him into a corner, and enterd into a conversation—

SIR JONATHAN: Ha ha ha, good, I warrant Ned found enough to say to her.

STAPLETON: Ay; but Sir, she said enough to him to have alarmd a parent, had I been one.

SIR JONATHAN: Ha ha ha, I'll be hang'd if this wasn't Lady Filmot, the pleasantest good humourd woman in the world. She takes great notice of *my* boy and of me too indeed, and of my brother Sir Jeremy—ha ha ha, I can't but laugh at your thinking my son in danger; why she says any thing that comes uppermost, man.

STAPLETON: Well Sir, remember I have warnd you.

SIR JONATHAN: Oh I thank you, Mr. Stapleton; it's kindly done of you, tho you may be a little out in your judgment. That same Lady Filmot is a mighty civil woman, and very jocose too.—Oh here comes my brother, here's Sir Jeremy, will you let me introduce you to him Sir?

STAPLETON: No Sir—fare you well.

[*Exit Stapleton.*]

SIR JONATHAN: Short enough in troth; but he seems melancholy, poor man.

Scene v.
Enter Sir Jeremy.

SIR JEREMY: Who is that you were talking to, Sir Jonathan?

SIR JONATHAN: Who, that gentleman? Why truly I don't know much of him, brother. He is a little crazy I believe, or vapourish; but I take him to be a very good sort of a man. Well but now brother, if you are at leisure, I should be glad to know what you meant by the hint you were pleased to give me this morning?

SIR JEREMY: There is a time for all things, Sir Jonathan; I am not at leisure at present; I am going to see if there are any letters for me to day.
[*Going.*]

SIR JONATHAN: I'll save you the trouble then, for I am just come from the post office, and can tell you there are not.

SIR JEREMY: No! that's pretty extraordinary!

SIR JONATHAN: But Brother, will you do me the favour just to tell me—

SIR JEREMY: Why if I were *just* to tell you as you call it, ten to one if you could comprehend one word of what I should say.

SIR JONATHAN: That will be *your* fault brother, not mine; do you speak plain, and I'll warrant I'll understand you.

SIR JEREMY: I'll be hang'd if you do, tho I shall put the thing as clear as that two and two make four. Well then Sir, you are to know, with regard to the subject of our last Conference that after having maturely deliberated, weighd, considerd, and laid all circumstances together (touching the affair in debate) I apprehend that it is wholly inconsistent, (upon a general view of things) that it is inconsistent I say with our true interest to ratify the proposed treaty; therefore without entering into further preliminaries, in my humble opinion according to the maxims of sound policy, I take it to be the wiser measure to prevent, rather than to remedy; as it is more easy to anticipate than to cure an evil—you apprehend?

SIR JONATHAN: N—ot very clearly, brother.

SIR JEREMY: You don't take my meaning then?

SIR JONATHAN: No, by my troth.

SIR JEREMY: Ho, ho, I thought you were to understand me if I spoke plain.

SIR JONATHAN: But you have *not* spoke plain, brother Jeremy.

SIR JEREMY: I haven't—O mighty well Sir, mighty fine! I honour you extremely.

SIR JONATHAN: I don't understand mysteries for my part, nor I can't abide concealments.

Scene vi.
Enter Champignion.

SIR JEREMY: Silence, Sir Jonathan.

CHAMPIGNION: What's your argument, gentlemen, for I love dearly to be in secrets?

SIR JONATHAN: Then my brother Jeremy's your man, Sir, for he makes a secret of everything.

SIR JEREMY: Or rather Sir Jonathan's your man, Sir, for he makes a secret of nothing.

CHAMPIGNION: Prithee gentleman, let's have the secret between you?

SIR JONATHAN: Why my brother Jeremy here—

SIR JEREMY: So, you will shoot your bolt in spite of me!

SIR JONATHAN: Well, tell it yourself then.

CHAMPIGNION: Let me beseech you, Sir Jeremy, I am inclined to think beforehand that I shall be of your side of the question. [*Aside.*] I'll coax him a little.

SIR JEREMY: There *may* be something in that—you may inform the gentleman.

SIR JONATHAN: By my troth, I don't know well what to inform him of, for I don't know myself what you'd be at; but you talkd something to me this morning about marrying my son to a great lady—

CHAMPIGNION: Oh if that be the case you are quite right, Sir Jeremy.

SIR JEREMY: You are of that opinion, Sir?

CHAMPIGNION: I am clear in the thing: and I assure you the young gentleman is beginning to be taken great notice of by the ladies; if I were you, Sir Jonathan, I would'nt let him look lower than a viscount's daughter at least. We handsome rogues can set just what price we please on our persons.

SIR JONATHAN: Ned is a handsome youth to be sure; but I don't want to sell him, Mr. Champignion.

CHAMPIGNION: Oh fy, fy, Sir Jonathan, hang it, no, I don't mean a money bargain.

SIR JEREMY: Ay; but Sir Jonathan understands no other.

CHAMPIGNION: Oh filthy! I have no notion of that; here your son has his pockets full of money, and is a very pretty figure. This, (if I don't flatter myself) is just my own case. What do we want then but the distinction of ingrafting our families upon nobility? I declare I would rather have my wife calld my lady, than be married to a cherubim.

SIR JONATHAN: Oh heaven forgive you, Mr. Champignion!

SIR JEREMY: And Sir Jonathan would rather add a few dirty thousands to his son's heap, than enrich his grand children's veins with the first blood in the realm.

SIR JONATHAN: And so I would, Sir Jeremy, for I never knew good come of those matches. When a plain man marries a lady of quality, he is master of nothing that belongs to him; it is my lady such a one's *house,* my lady such a one's *liveries,* and my lady such a one's *children;* and e'gad he's nobody but my lady such a one's husband himself.

CHAMPIGNION: Now, that would be *my* pride Sir, to have people say, there's Mr. Champignion—what of such a place? No, he that married my lady— no matter who; but perhaps I may have the honour of giving my name to a certain lady of quality before it be long.

SIR JEREMY: Oh we can guess who—Lady Bell!

CHAMPIGNION: I name no names, Sir Jeremy; but with regard to the fair sex I am the luckiest dog in the universe.

SIR JONATHAN: Lady Bell! Why if it be Lady Bell Aircastle they say she is not worth a souse.

CHAMPIGNION: The very reason, why I would chuse her ladyship, Sir.

SIR JONATHAN: And I suppose that's the very reason why her ladyship chuses you, Sir, ha ha ha.

CHAMPIGNION: Ha ha ha, I declare, that only wants the circumstance of being true, to be a pretty good thing; but the lady has *Eyes,* Sir Jonathan, and without vanity I take it my *money* is not my only recommendation.

SIR JEREMY: But it is his criterion of merit, Mr. Champignion; he thinks there can be no good quality without it.

CHAMPIGNION: The rascallyest thing in nature; I declare I am never so happy as when I'm a throwing it away. I have been looking out these two or three days for some honest gentleman that may have occasion for a small sum that I may give it to him, for you must know I pique myself upon doing generous things.

SIR JEREMY: I fancy Sir there may be such honest gentlemen found in the world.

CHAMPIGNION [*Aside.*]: Oh he takes my meaning I see; I'll make him the offer.—I have a hundred guineas loose in my pocket at this present which are at your service, Sir Jeremy; I came on purpose to look for you.

SIR JEREMY: At my service, Sir! for what?

CHAMPIGNION [*Apart to Sir Jeremy.*]: I tell you that another time; you may do me a good turn; but mum! [*Speaking aloud.*] Oh dear Sir, I have only a mind to oblige you with a trifle.

SIR JONATHAN [*Aside to Champignion.*]: Gadso Sir, you'll make him angry.

SIR JEREMY: Oblige me with a trifle!

CHAMPIGNION [*Aside.*]: I'll double it if you'll swallow an oath—not a word more—

SIR JEREMY [*Advances to him laying his hand upon his sword.*]: Look in my face, Sir! And tell me if you see anything there that could encourage you to presume—

CHAMPIGNION: No faith Sir, it was not your face that encouraged me; but—
but to tell you the truth—

SIR JEREMY: My Garb perhaps! I am not an embroiderd puppy; but Sir I
despise dress, and Sir you are an illiberal coxcomb, and I am inclined to
think are sprung from the dregs of the people!

SIR JONATHAN: There—there! I told you so; Oh he has a very high spirit.

CHAMPIGNION: I declare, Sir Jonathan, that I am very glad there are no
ladies present to hear him treat me so very ungenteely, and hang me if I
know what it's for either.—May I perish if here isn't Lady Bell herself! For
heaven's sake gentlemen, don't be familiar with me before her, for she
can't endure any thing but a beau.

Scene vii.
Enter Lady Bell.

CHAMPIGNION: Oh ma'am isn't your ladyship tired with walking? But I
protest your ladyship's presence is as necessary as the Sun's, to give light
and warmth to everything.

LADY BELL: Ha ha ha, well enough imagined; but I really am fatigued, and
am now going home. Lord, who are those ordinary people that you were
talking to?

CHAMPIGNION [*Half-aside.*]: Only tradesmen of mine, ma'am, to whom I
have been giving orders.

SIR JEREMY [*Advancing.*]: Whom do you call tradesmen, Coxcomb?

SIR JONATHAN: Ay whom do you call tradesmen, Mr. Coxcomb, as my
brother Jeremy says? Why *I* am not a *trades*man, much less this gentleman, who is a baronet by birth, and a man of learning too.

LADY BELL: What is the meaning of all this?

CHAMPIGNION: Oh ma'am, they are a couple of very uncivilized persons, I
assure your ladyship. Will you allow me to wait on your ladyship home,
ma'am?

SIR JEREMY: Ay you do well to put yourself under a lady's protection, or I
should teach you how to treat men of lineage.

LADY BELL: Lineage! I must enquire into this, if he be really a man of
lineage!

SIR JONATHAN: Of as antient a one as any in England I can assure your
ladyship, tho' I say it that am but his brother.

SIR JEREMY: *That* I should think beneath me to mention, if this plantation fop
here, this vender of molossus[7] hadn't dared to offer me a bribe, for what
ends he best can tell.

LADY BELL: Oh insufferable, and have I been acquainted with a fellow that
deals in sugar! Sir, I desire you will never presume to approach me again!

CHAMPIGNION: Oh heavens ma'am, your ladyship can't be so hard hearted
sure! I declare I was only offering him a little of my bounty, for every body
knows I have the spirit of an Emperor, and the poor gentleman I really
apprehended was one that had met with misfortunes.

SIR JEREMY: I have met with disappointments I grant, such perhaps as don't
happen every day.

CHAMPIGNION: Faith Sir, I only heard you had spent a good Estate, and that happens every day in the year as I take it.

LADY BELL: You are not the only person of condition, Sir, that has suffered in that particular; but thank my stars, it is not in the power of fortune to rob us of our illustrious birth.

SIR JEREMY: Madam, you seem to have a just estimate of things; but for this paltry fellow here, who has been emploied to offer me money—

LADY BELL: Why he must be ignorance itself, Sir Jeremy!

SIR JEREMY: I question if he be so ignorant as he appears, Madam. If I ben't mistaken a certain person that shall be nameless is at the bottom of this; but I'll let them all see that my integrity is as unshaken as when—I won't name the Æra—This fellow may be a spy too, for what I know.

LADY BELL: M^r, I shall dispense with your attendance; this gentleman will wait on me home.

SIR JEREMY: With all my heart, Madam, for to tell you the truth I don't much admire that young man's looks.

LADY BELL: Nor I neither, I assure you, Sir Jeremy.

[*He gives his hand to Lady Bell, who casting a disdainful look at Champignion, she and Sir Jeremy strut out together.*]

CHAMPIGNION: Do you understand the meaning of all this, Sir Jonathan? for perish me if I do!

SIR JONATHAN: Egad they are both too high flown for me or you either, so you had best leave them to one another.

CHAMPIGNION: Let me dye if I am not the most unlucky dog in the universe; I must go and look for my lord Stewkly, that he may make up this breach between her Ladyship and me. I wish you and your antient blood were at the Antipodes, as I hope for mercy, Sir.

[*Exit Champignion.*]

SIR JONATHAN: Heaven forbid, Mr Champignion, what would my poor boy do for me then? I must go and see what's become of him tho; I believe he is lost.

[*Exit Sir Jonathan.*]

END OF ACT II

ACT III

Scene i. Parade.
Enter Lady Filmot and Edward.

EDWARD: But wasn't your ladyship surpriz'd to see with what attention she seemd to listen to my lord?

LADY FILMOT: Nay, she absolutely flirted with him! but I wouldn't have you be alarmd, there *may* be nothing in it, at least I hope so for your sake.

EDWARD: You are very good, Madam, to say so; perhaps I have taken the thing more seriously than I ought to have done.

LADY FILMOT: I dare say you have.—and yet we women are very fantastical; and *dress* often does more than person, especially with young people, who haven't been used to the beau monde. If you were to appear as gay as Lord Stewkly, the difference between you would then be so apparent!

EDWARD: I'd give the world to make the experiment, and go to the rooms to night dressed as fine as him.

LADY FILMOT: Oh you little tyrant, what a thought is that! and yet I like it so well, that I am resolved you shall put it in execution.

EDWARD: Lord ma'am, which way! My father never lets me wear any thing but these nasty plain cloaths.

LADY FILMOT: That's nothing—Champignion's wardrobe shall supply us, as it might half the town. A trifling alteration will make a suit of his cloaths fit you. I'll borrow one which he has never worn just for the Joke's sake, and my frizeur⁸ shall dress your hair in the very height of the mode.

EDWARD: Oh my dear Lady Filmot, that will be charming; but I'll let nobody know a word of my design.

LADY FILMOT: Not a syllable, till you flash upon them all at once, and for that reason you shall dress in my appartment; you know you are my Cicisbey, and those little liberties are always allowable.

EDWARD: That's true. I protest, I had like to have forgot that I was your Cicisbey.—What's this that I am to do? let me con it over now that I may remember it. In the first place, I may come into your room in a morning before you are up, in the next—

LADY FILMOT: Hold, hold, not that *yet,* you are only to be admitted to my toilet for the first week.

EDWARD: Oh, ay, that's true; I may come in when you are dressing. I am to put essence into your handkerchief, reach you your combs, your pins, and yʳ powder as you want them, and if your woman should not be in the way, I am to tye your necklace string and adjust your Tucker.

LADY FILMOT: Very right, and by way of reward I am to—

EDWARD: Oh I remember, you are to let me stick a patch on just where I think it will become you best.

LADY FILMOT: Good.

EDWARD: I am never to be from your elbow all day if you command me. I am to help you to tea, coffee, and fruit before any other lady in the company, and give it you on my knee.

LADY FILMOT: I shall dispense with that part of the ceremony, except when we are alone. Well what next?

EDWARD: I am to read to you when you don't chuse to see company at home, and to carry your knotting bag in my pocket when you go to make a morning visit. I am to attend you to all publick places and home again, and to see you up to your chamber door.—Is there anything else?

LADY FILMOT: Those are the most material articles, the rest are but trifles, such as never paying attention to any lady in my presence—

EDWARD: What, not to Lucy?

LADY FILMOT: No, not even to *her* without my leave; but I shan't be strict.

Never to approve of any thing that I have not first commended. To be always ready to smile when I seem pleased, and to look melancholy if I should happen to frown.—That's all I think.

EDWARD: I declare it's mighty pretty.

LADY FILMOT: Oh amazingly, and I dare say you'll acquit yourself very well.

EDWARD: And when I am *dressed,* I fancy your ladyship won't dislike me.

LADY FILMOT: Insinuating creature! I shall be almost afraid to trust myself with you.—But come, you shall go home with me, and I'll transform you into a beau in a trice.

EDWARD: I think I shall be even with Miss Lucy for her airs.

LADY FILMOT: Isn't that she, and her mother, just turned the corner? We'll not let them see us.

[*She takes him by the arm and exit.*]

Scene ii.
Enter Mrs. Tryfort and Lucy.

MRS. TRYFORT: You see what it is, child, to circulate with people of quality; when would you have heard such language in the City?

LUCY: But indeed, mama, it's only a Joke, just a little plot between my lord Stewkly and me; he is not in earnest.

MRS. TRYFORT: But I can tell you he *is* in earnest, Miss, and to let you into a secret, ever since the agitation⁹ of your fortune, I resolved that you should marry a lord.

LUCY: A lord, Madam! and what's to become of poor Mr. Edward?

MRS. TRYFORT: Don't tell me of Mr. Edward, a little insignificant mechanic. I hope we may look over his head now, for if you must know the truth, I left London on purpose that you might abdicate him.

LUCY: But madam you know he has your promise, and indeed I like him better than I do Lord Stewkly.

MRS. TRYFORT: I declare you are so inarticulate in your notions, that I believe you are a changling. You haven't a grain of your mother's spirit! Ha ha ha, I vow I wish his lordship had chosen *me* instead of you; and perhaps if I had encouraged the thing—but no matter—oh here's Mrs. Surface, I'll ask her judgment on the affair.

Scene iii.
Enter Mrs. Surface.

MRS. SURFACE: What walking still, ladies? Oh I have news to tell you; we are to have a masquerade tomorrow night: I have been at a ware house to enquire after some habits.

MRS. TRYFORT: And can they be had here? I'll certainly go to it.

MRS. SURFACE: Ay that they can. Some fine gay sparks had such a design about a month ago, and engaged a shop keeper here in town to bring down a great parcel of dresses; but they dropd the frolic, and the cloaths were never used, so the man has them still.

MRS. TRYFORT: Oh I'll infallibly go, and so shall you too, Miss Lucy. I suppose this is my Lord Stewkly's thought, he is so ingenious and full of his artifices.

MRS. SURFACE: Ay, that he is, as e'er a man in England.

MRS. TRYFORT: Mind that, Lucy.

MRS. SURFACE: Between ourselves he has more art than honesty; but I wouldn't say that to every body.

LUCY: Mind that, mama!

MRS. TRYFORT: What do you mean by every body, Mrs. Surface? Why isn't he a prodigious fine gentleman?

MRS. SURFACE [*Aside.*]: Oh sits the wind there.—Fine! nay for that matter there isn't a *finer* gentleman in Europe. Ay, ay, no body can deny that. I warrant you can distinguish a *fine* gentleman with half an eye.

MRS. TRYFORT: What do you think now, Miss Lucy?

LUCY: Nothing Madam; but that I still prefer Edward to him.

MRS. SURFACE: Why then by my truly that's a *pretty* young man, so modest, so bashful!—

MRS. TRYFORT: Lord Mrs. Surface, where's your taste? I thought you were a woman of more speculation.[10]

MRS. SURFACE: Oh he's but a sorry stripling to be sure, my dear Ma'am; but then considering you know—

MRS. TRYFORT: But my lord Stewkly is so embelished,[11] Mrs. Surface! No body can be embelished that has not been abroad you must know. Oh if you were to hear him describe contagious[12] countries as I have done, it would astonish you. He is a perfect map of geography.

LUCY: I dare say Edward understands geography as well as *he* does.

MRS. SURFACE: I'll lay my life a sensible lad, and well-disposed. If I were as young and as handsome as some body he shouldn't be long without a wife.

MRS. TRYFORT: Oh monstrous! I declare, Mrs. Surface, you are enough to give one the vapours.

MRS. SURFACE: But I don't compare him to my Lord Stewkly tho; no no, no, hold you there, they are not to be named in a day, no not in the same day.

LUCY: I wish Sir Jonathan were to hear you, Mrs. Surface.

MRS. SURFACE: My sweet creature, you won't tell him I hope. You know I am as fond of Mr. Edward as if he were my own child, I don't know his fellow!

MRS. TRYFORT: But Mrs. Surface!

MRS. SURFACE: My lord Stewkly to be sure is the very perfection of a man—

LUCY: But Mrs. Surface!

MRS. SURFACE [*Aside.*]: Lord what shall I say between these two fools.— Well my beauty, what were you going to say?

LUCY: Why only that you may praise one man without undervaluing another.

MRS. SURFACE: Now blessings on your pretty constant heart! Mr. Edward must be the man then.

MRS. TRYFORT: Was there ever anything so satyrical? Silly chit that might be a Countess if she had the grace to deserve it.

LUCY: But Madam, I don't desire it.

MRS. TRYFORT: There's for you, Mrs. Surface, a foolish metamorphosis!

MRS. SURFACE: A countess! I'll lay all the money in my purse, you'll be a Countess yet; I saw it in your cup when you drank coffee with me t'other day.

MRS. TRYFORT: Do you observe that, Miss?

MRS. SURFACE [*Aside to Lucy.*]: I dreamt last night you were married to Mr. Edward, and my dreams always come to pass!—But good Madam, hadn't you better step home and take something comfortable? I'm afraid you'll be sick I declare. A glass of Jelly, or a little chicken broth, I have both ready made.

MRS. TRYFORT: I don't care if I do, Mrs. Surface.—Come child.—I wish you could persuade this low minded girl to be a countess.

MRS. SURFACE: Leave it to me, I'll warrant you.

[*Exit Mrs. Tryfort.*]

LUCY: Dear Mrs. Surface, I beg you will try to reason my Mama out of this notion about Lord Stewkly; indeed he has no thoughts of me.

MRS. SURFACE [Aside.]: Oh ho, is that the case.—Give yourself no trouble about it; Mr. Edward's the man, mark what I say to you.

[*Exit Mrs. Surface and Lucy.*]

Scene iv.
Enter Lord Stewkly and Champignion.

CHAMPIGNION: A barbarous old dog to talk of plantations before her lady-ship. And my looks too, to find fault with them, when all the world allows no body ever lookd better!

LORD STEWKLY: It was horribly unlucky, that's certain; and *I* shall be in disgrace too, for having introduced you, for I know as fond as she is of you, it will be hard to reconcile her to the thoughts of a man who has ever defiled his hands with trade.

CHAMPIGNION: Gad's mercy my lord, what shall I do? if I could purchase nobility for fifty thousand pounds I would let out every drop of blood in my veins, so I could fill them again with your lordship's; poison me if I would not.

LORD STEWKLY: Why, *blood* you know, my dear friend, is not to be pur-chased; but a title may, and I have been casting about how to assist you a little in that way.

CHAMPIGNION: Have you? My dear dear lord, you will make me the hap-piest dog in Nature; for what signifies person and fortune, if a man's discarded by the fair sex for want of a title, you know my lord?

LORD STEWKLY: True; but yet I am afraid at present we can't well procure more than Knighthood for you.

CHAMPIGNION: Well, well hang it my lord, Sir Christopher's better than nothing, you know, just to make a beginning with.

LORD STEWKLY: Why if that will content you, I think I have interest enough to recommend you to a red ribbon; *that* you know will be an additional honour!

CHAMPIGNION: Oh my lord! the thing of the Universe that I sigh for; for then you know every body *sees* that a man's somebody. Besides, it sets off the figure so charmingly!

LORD STEWKLY: Oh, nothing more becoming—the fees tho on these occasions are pretty high.

CHAMPIGNION: Your lordship can't recommend the thing more to me than by saying so; *I* who can make ducks and drakes with doubloons!

LORD STEWKLY: Nay it's no very great matter, five or six hundred pound I believe.

CHAMPIGNION: Oh paltry, my lord, I was in hopes it had been five or six thousand. I detest everything that is cheap,—besides I always give double the worth of a thing.

LORD STEWKLY: Well, I believe I have influence enough to get this done for you, if it is not already disposed of.—That indeed—

CHAMPIGNION: Oh heavens, my lord, send an express off directly, and if you will be so good as to negotiate the affair for me I shall be everlastingly obliged to your lordship.

LORD STEWKLY: There is no time to be lost, as you observe. I'll write about it immediately. If we are not too late, I am sure of it; and in that case the fees of office may be necessary.

CHAMPIGNION: Here's my pocket book for you, my dear lord; you will find that paltry sum in it, for I never carry less about me; and if your lordship will but inform Lady Bell of the honour which is intended me, I think I may face her boldly.

LORD STEWKLY: Doubtless; but take no notice of it to any one else, till the thing is done. I suppose Lady Bell will be at the Masquerade to morrow night?

CHAMPIGNION: Deuce take me if I have the courage to invite her ladyship as yet; but now I think I'll venture.

LORE STEWKLY: By all means; but come, I had best go and dispatch my letters, so I'll bid you good by.

CHAMPIGNION: Your lordship's most devoted; you will do me the honour to remember I give a little supper to night after the ball!

LORD STEWKLY: I shall attend you, Sir—thou art the very prince of Planters!

CHAMPIGNION: I am no *Miser,* as your lordship shall find.

[*Exit severally.*]

Scene v. Changes to Mrs. Surface's parlour.
Stapleton and Mrs. Surface.

STAPLETON: This parlour of yours is the very Mart of Scandal. I always know when you pull me in here, that you have some scurrilous anecdote to communicate, and ten to one a *lye* into the bargain.

MRS. SURFACE: Did you ever know me tell you an untruth? Me! No, not for all I am worth, I would not tell you an untruth, Mr. Stapleton.

STAPLETON: The only circumstance that makes me doubt, is, that the *girl* you say is not as fond of the match as the mother is.

MRS. SURFACE: Poor foolish thing, she fancies herself in love with that raw cub, young Bull. Not but he'd be a better match; for my Lord isn't worth a groat; but that's between ourselves.

STAPLETON: And why didn't you hint that to Mrs. Tryfort?

MRS. SURFACE: My dear Sir, it's no business of mine! What is it to me, you know? They are none of them good for anything. And as for Sir Jonathan, he is such a troublesome, inquisitive, meddling old blockhead that—Bless us!

Scene vi.
Enter Sir Jonathan.

MRS. SURFACE: Talk of—you know who, they say and he'll appear! Oh Sir Jonathan, I was just speaking of you; if you had come in but a little sooner, you would have heard—

STAPLETON: *Such* enconiums on you, Sir Jonathan! as would have made you blush; our landlady here has been saying *such* things!

MRS. SURFACE: That's my foolish way; I can't for the life of me help praising people when I take a fancy to them, both to their faces and behind their backs, 'tis all one to *me*.

SIR JONATHAN: Ay, ay, there's nothing like being plain and downright, Mrs. Surface, always speak as you think.

MRS. SURFACE: In troth, I am a little too blunt sometimes, for I told Mr. Edward this morning that he didn't hold up his head, and I gave him a chuck under the chin, just this way; I hope I don't make too free with *you*, good Sir— [*Curtsying to Sir Jonathan.*]

SIR JONATHAN: No, no, no, you are heartily welcome, Mrs. Surface.

MRS. SURFACE: And the pretty Soul, smiled in my face, and said thank you Mrs. Surface. Oh you are happy to be father to such a son.

STAPLETON: But I am told that Mrs. Tryfort wants to marry her daughter to this Lord Stewkly; do you know anything of that, Sir Jonathan?

SIR JONATHAN: Whu-ph! As soon as she'd marry her to the great Mogul! No, no Mr. Stapleton, don't believe a word of it.

STAPLETON: Mrs. Surface is my Author.

MRS. SURFACE: Lord Sir, how should *I* know? [*Aside to Stapleton.*] Why would you bring *me* in? I only gave you the hint as a friend.

STAPLETON: But you ought in justice to tell Sir Jonathan what you know.

SIR JONATHAN: An *honest* woman! I'll be sworn she would; but there's nothing in it, nothing in it, Mrs. Surface, depend upon it.—That's just like my friend Stapleton here, who fancy'd Lady Filmot had designs upon *my* son, ha ha ha, do you remember, Mr. Stapleton?

STAPLETON: I do, Sir Jonathan, and you will find both the one, and the other true.

SIR JONATHAN: You are a very good man, I believe, Mr. Stapleton; but I wouldn't be suspicious for all the money in the Bank. A man has no comfort that doubts this, and believes that, and fears t'other: now I never suspect any body; but take the world as it comes.

STAPLETON: And were you never deceivd, Sir Jonathan?

SIR JONATHAN: Not that I remember; I always dealt with honest people, and believe every man and woman so till I find them otherwise.

STAPLETON: Well Sir, repentance is often the fruits of credulity. I wish you mayn't find it so.—Fare you well.

MRS. SURFACE: Don't you drink coffee with us, Mr. Stapleton?

STAPLETON: No—I drink it by myself.

[*Exit Stapleton.*]

MRS. SURFACE: A whimsical captious fellow as ever came into a house! I wish I was well rid of him.

Scene vii.
Enter Sir Jeremy.

SIR JEREMY: But Mrs. Surface, I thought our coffee had been ready.

SIR JONATHAN: And so did I too, that was what I came in for.

MRS. SURFACE: I'll go and order it in the next parlour directly, good Sir Jeremy.

[*Exit Mrs. Surface.*]

SIR JONATHAN: Why then I'll go and take another turn on the Parade till it's ready—Will you walk, Brother?

SIR JEREMY: No, Sir Jonathan, I have had walking enough.

[*Exit Sir Jonathan.*]

Scene viii.
Enter Lady Filmot.

LADY FILMOT: Oh Sir Jeremy, I have been looking for you; I have a request to make.

SIR JEREMY: Your ladyship may always command me.

LADY FILMOT: You must know I have been endeavouring to make your nephew look a little more like one of us: I have left him to dress in my apartment, but as I intend to surprise Sir Jonathan and the ladies, I want you to make some excuse for his not attending them to the rooms, as I purpose taking him with *me.*

SIR JEREMY: With all my heart Madam; and I should be very glad your ladyship would take him intirely under your tuition, for Sir Jonathan will absolutely undo the young man.

LADY FILMOT: I protest I am afraid so too, Sir Jeremy, for the youth is amazingly confined in his notions. I am surprized, Sir, that you, who to the advantages of great parts, have joined those of a learned education—

SIR JEREMY: Oh your humble servant, madam.

LADY FILMOT: That you, I say, have not had influence enough to get him out of the hands of *poor* Sir Jonathan, in order to train him your way.

SIR JEREMY: Why, I have endeavoured at it, madam; but *poor* Sir Jonathan, as you very justly and emphatically call him, has the misfortune to think his *own* head as wise as other people's.

LADY FILMOT: Lud, what an incredible difference there is between you and your brother! *He* a plodding, simple, plain creature; humble to a fault, ignorant of everything but traffic, and fond of nothing but wealth.—

SIR JEREMY: A very just description, Madam.

LADY FILMOT: *You,* on the other hand, active, and enterprizing, profoundly versed in *men* as well as books; and from a consciousness of the dignity of your character, joyned to a noble spirit of freedom, shew a manly pride in everything you do, and a thorough contempt for riches.

SIR JEREMY: Your ladyship has a very discerning Eye!

LADY FILMOT: I have been told, Sir Jeremy, that you were a most incomparable speaker in Parliament.

SIR JEREMY: Why—I was generally pretty well heard, Madam—tho I fancy there were some who now and then wished me silent.

LADY FILMOT: I don't in the least doubt it, Sir Jeremy.

SIR JEREMY: I have said such things! Oh Lady Filmot, there *was* a time! if you were but to have heard me when my indignation was rouzed! but that's all over with me—

LADY FILMOT: Lord, it must have been amazingly fine! so animated! so patriotic!

SIR JEREMY: Oh Madam, I could thunder like Jupiter in those days; but— heaven knows what they are doing now! I was willing to have lent them my assistance; but let that matter rest.—

LADY FILMOT: Dear, what a loss it is to your country that you are not in Parliament!

SIR JEREMY: Oh Madam—I *hope* not. To be sure, every man is not blessed with equal talents; yet I flatter myself we have some pretty good men— very decent I dare say,—I should hope that *my* loss is not *considerably* felt.

LADY FILMOT: Ah, Sir Jeremy, I very much fear it is.

SIR JEREMY: Your ladyship's regard to the good of the common-weal may make you apprehensive; tho, without vanity I *was* considered as somebody in my day.

LADY FILMOT: If you have any of your speeches written, Sir Jeremy, I should take it as an infinite favour, if you would lend one or two of them to me.

SIR JEREMY: Why Madam, I did make a few that I believe I can recite from memory—pretty strong they were—ticklers i'faith!

LADY FILMOT: And you'll repeat them to me some day?

SIR JEREMY: Your ladyship has a taste for Orations, I presume?

LADY FILMOT: Oh I doat on an Oration!

SIR JEREMY: You don't like flimzy flowery stuff, do you?

LADY FILMOT: Oh by no means.

SIR JEREMY: You like nerve?

LADY FILMOT: Of all things.

SIR JEREMY: I *think* I shall please you.

LADY FILMOT: You are always manly, I dare say.

SIR JEREMY: I was no chicken, Lady Filmot.

LADY FILMOT: Bold sentiments delivered in bold words, I'll answer for it.

SIR JEREMY: Yes—I fancy I can please you—I have one speech that I think is a chef d'oeuvre, a two-edged sword i'faith. Away I flashed, down with them by dozens egad like ninepins.—none of your water gruel Oratory for me.—What do you think my Crest is?

LADY FILMOT: I don't know, a Lyon perhaps.

SIR JEREMY: An Oak, and my motto is—you understand Latin?

LADY FILMOT: No, Sir Jeremy.

SIR JEREMY: That's a pity; I'll tell you in English then, Sooner break than bend—a whim of my own, it wasn't the family device.

LADY FILMOT: Sooner break than bend! vastly expressive I declare.

SIR JEREMY: Sooner break than bend, Iron and Steel, Iron and Steel—

LADY FILMOT: What a charming preceptor you would make to your Nephew!—

SIR JEREMY: Oh lord Madam, why that fool his father has no more ambition than a Dervice[13] of four-score. I own my utmost wish is to see the boy in Parliament.—That's the sphere of action, Lady Filmot. My sun is set; but I should rejoyce to see a little star of my family twinkle there.

LADY FILMOT: Certainly, Sir Jeremy.—My lord Stewkly has a borough in his gift, and the present representative is extremely old; but I don't know how it is, my lord has such a strange partiality to his kindred, that he will give it to none but a relation; he has often told me, if I were a man I should have it.

SIR JEREMY: Ha ha, your ladyship is akin to him then, I presume?

LADY FILMOT: Very nearly.

SIR JEREMY: Why then Madam, tho' your ladyship can't accept of it in propria persona, you may *give* him a relation who may, you know?

LADY FILMOT: Oh lord, Sir Jeremy, do you think I'd marry again?

SIR JEREMY: Why not, Madam?

LADY FILMOT: Oh dear! Well we won't talk of that now.—I fancy by this time your nephew is dressed. Suppose you were to come up stairs with me to see him, and who knows but you may oblige me with one of your speeches!

SIR JEREMY: I can refuse your ladyship nothing. But first I'll go and make apology for my nephew's not attending his father, and some other idle company here that perhaps expect he should go with them.—I'll wait on your ladyship again immediately.

[*Exit Sir Jeremy.*]

LADY FILMOT: So, this same borough has made Sir Jeremy my fast friend and ally; I dare say he will beg my acceptance both of his nephew's person and fortune.—If he should, I think I shan't refuse the poor thing.

[*Exit Lady Filmot.*]

Scene ix. The Rooms.
Different parties at cards. One table filled with Children at lottery Tickets.
Mrs. Tryfort has just done playing with Lord Stewkly and Champignion.
Lady Bell looking on.

LORD STEWKLY: Do you *always* play with such good success, Ma'am? I never saw anything like it!

MRS. TRYFORT: Ha ha ha, I am generally prodigious lucky indeed, my lord; but this evening I contribute[14] it intirely to your lordship's skill.

LORD STEWKLY: Oh dear Ma'am, you play infinitely better than I do.

MRS. TRYFORT: I am sorry, Mr. Champignion, I am to carry away so many of your guineas, ha ha ha—does your ladyship *never* play?

LADY BELL: Never, in such mixed companies.

MRS. TRYFORT: I believe you are to give me thirty, Sir.

CHAMPIGNION: Lord Ma'am, I am quite ashamed of paying you such a *trifle;* when I play with ladies I always deprecate good fortune; for you must know, Ma'am, tis death to me to win of them.

LORD STEWKLY: In that case, Mr. Champignion, I should think myself rather unfortunate to have you for a partner: what do *you* think, Lady Bell?

LADY BELL: I think, my lord, that in those sort of places, one is often forced to take up with strange sort of creters for partners: I wish people of fashion would make it a rule never to play with any below themselves.

MRS. TRYFORT: Perhaps, Madam, that might oblige them to play lower than they would chuse, ha ha ha.

LADY BELL: And one is so shock'd by ill breeding some times, my lord, that I shall forswear coming for my part.

CHAMPIGNION: Then, Madam, your ladyship will make an absolute desert of the rooms, for I am sure *I'll* never come.

LADY BELL: And *you* are all the world, you know, Mr.—[*Aside to Lord Stewkly.*] The man however has some manners.

CHAMPIGNION [*Aside to Lord Stewkly.*]: I am glad her ladyship vouchsafes to speak to me again.

LORD STEWKLY [*Aside to Champignion.*]: Oh, I told her the honour you were to receive.

Scene x.
Enter Lucy.

MRS. TRYFORT: Lord child, where have you been?

LUCY: I was only getting a dish of tea, Mama. Have you done playing?

LADY BELL: Heavens above! What Company! My lord, shall we saunter about a little?

LORD STEWKLY: My dear lady Bell, how can you be so severe? Why you'll break this poor fellow's heart if you discard him.

LADY BELL: Oh ridiculous, you can't imagine how unfeeling the common people are!

LORD STEWKLY: Upon my life tho, he hasn't been himself since you forbid him your presence.

LADY BELL: You may tell him I don't forbid him to follow me.
[*She goes to the other end of the room. Lord Stewkly whispers to Champignion and he follows her.*]

LORD STEWKLY: Why Miss Tryfort, you look so enchantingly, that both the ladies and the men will consider you as a common enemy tonight.

LUCY: I am sure, my lord, I don't want to inchant anybody; I have no desire of being taken for a witch.

LORD STEWKLY: A lady may possess natural magic, Madam, without a crime; besides 'tis evident that the charms you deal in are celestial!

LUCY: I don't understand you, my Lord.

MRS. TRYFORT: My Lord, she has so little alacrity, that your lordship's fine language is thrown away upon her. Your lordship must speak, in the vulgar tongue, for her to comprehend you.—I think I'll go and see what the company are doing in the next room.—Miss, you needn't come, it looks so odd to have such a great girl dangling after one.

[*Exit Mrs. Tryfort.*]

LORD STEWKLY: My dear Ma'am, you are not afraid I hope of trusting yourself a little while with me?

LUCY: I am not afraid, my lord; but I don't know that we have anything to talk of.

LORD STEWKLY: If I had your permission I could soon find a very agreeable subject.

LUCY: I had rather sit and look at the company, my lord.

[*They sit.*]

Scene xi.
Enter Lady Filmot and Edward dressed like a beau, Sir Jeremy following.

LADY FILMOT: I knew we should be full early; but you were so impatient, Mr. Edward! and I'll swear, Sir Jeremy, you had me fast by the ear that I could have listend till tomorrow morning!

SIR JEREMY: Ha ha, persons of your ladyship's taste—but my *best* speech I have reserved for the last: it was made on occasion of a bill that was brought in—

[*Lady Filmot and Sir Jeremy talk in dumb shew.*]

LUCY: Good stars! why sure, that can't be Mr. Edward that is with Lady Filmot? As I live and breathe it is he—look, my lord!

LORD STEWKLY: Mercy on us, what a figure she has made of the boy! Ha ha ha, that's good, faith.

LUCY: I *will* go and ask the meaning of it.

LORD STEWKLY: My dear creature, what are you about? Would you go to be laugh'd at by Lady Filmot? You see the thing's done on purpose.

LUCY: I thought he had some design in his head by his keeping so much out of my sight today.

LORD STEWKLY: Lady Filmot's designs with regard to *me,* you find are now apparent; but I beg you'll help me to disappoint them.—Remember our plot as soon as she observes us.

LUCY: Yes, yes, I see well enough what she would be at; but I wonder Edward would be so silly as to joyn her in her contrivance without telling me of it!

LORD STEWKLY: For the same reason I suppose that you have not told him of ours.

[*They talk in dumb shew.*]

LADY FILMOT: Oh I long to hear it! What fire, what enthusiasm you must have exerted!

SIR JEREMY: The Subject, you see, demanded my whole force.

LADY FILMOT [*Aside to Edward.*]: Bless me, that can't be Miss Tryfort sure in such easy familiar chat with my lord Stewkly!

SIR JEREMY: And faith when once I was up, *out* it pourd like a torrent.

LADY FILMOT: A very inundation I dare say, Sir Jeremy. [*Aside to Edward.*]
  Why the girl's coquetting I declare!
SIR JEREMY: And then hear him, hear him, hear him, was the word!
LADY FILMOT: Ay Sir Jeremy, hear him. [*Aside to Edward.*] Why this is
  astonishing Mr. Edward, do you observe?
EDWARD: I'll go and interrupt them, upon my reputation!
LADY FILMOT: By no means Sir, no interruptions.
SIR JEREMY: Interruptions! If any man dared to interrupt *me* he was soon
  called to order.
LADY FILMOT: No doubt of it, Sir Jeremy—. [*To Edward.*] Don't you know
  that it is one article of your duty not to speak to any lady without my
  leave?
EDWARD: Ay; but you know, Ma'am, you said you would not be strict.
LADY FILMOT: At present I will; for I see my lord Stewkly wants to nettle
  me; you know what I told you today?
EDWARD: Oh that's true, upon my credit I had forgot. How Lucy and I shall
  laugh whan we come to explain!
LADY FILMOT: Oh it will be an inexhaustible source of mirth when you two
  are at your fireside next winter, so comfortably with your City neighbours.
SIR JEREMY: What does your ladyship say of the City, for I was in a sort of a
  revery?
LADY FILMOT: I was saying, Sir Jeremy, how happy your Nephew and Miss
  Tryfort will be when they are married.
SIR JEREMY: Between ourselves, Madam, I hope that will never be.
LADY FILMOT: You don't like the match then, Sir Jeremy?
SIR JEREMY: Oh shameful, degrading to the last degree. If I had your lady-
  ship at Bull-hall, I could shew you a line of Ancestry, that would convince
  you we are not a people of yesterday.
EDWARD: Pray Uncle, how came it, you never shewd them to me?
SIR JEREMY: Why the land and the Mansion house has slippd thro' our
  fingers, boy; but thank heaven the family pictures are still extant.
LADY FILMOT: That's a great consolation, Sir Jeremy!
SIR JEREMY: Why so it is, Madam; this stripling is not a mushroom, I can tell
  you, Lady Filmot.
LADY FILMOT: I knew it well, Sir.
SIR JEREMY: Edward!
EDWARD: Uncle!
SIR JEREMY: Do you think you have courage enough to make love to this
  lady here?
EDWARD: Who *me,* uncle! Why my lady Filmot would laugh at me if I
  should.
SIR JEREMY: Try, my child; if I were at your age I should hardly be deterred
  thro' the fear of a fine woman's laughing at me.
LADY FILMOT: Oh Sir, my respect for Sir Jeremy, as well as my good opinion
  of you, will secure you against that.
SIR JEREMY: Lookee there! Harkee Edward, if you have any of my blood in
  your veins [*He whispers him.*] I leave you to give you the opportunity.
  [*Sir Jeremy retires to the other end of the room. Seems to enter into*

conversation with Lady Bell who is sitting with Champignion; but keeps his eye on his nephew and Lady Filmot.]

LADY FILMOT: What does Sir Jeremy say?

EDWARD: That he will go away, Madam, to give me the opportunity.

LADY FILMOT: Oh he has a mind to divert himself; suppose we were to humour him now and pretend to carry on a little courtship, just for his entertainment—he is observing us, you see.

EDWARD: If I were capable, Ma'am, of saying such handsome things as your ladyship deserves—

LADY FILMOT: Everything you say, Sir, receives such a grace from your manner!—

EDWARD: I must be very dull, *indeed,* Ma'am, if your ladyship didn't inspire me; you are the Iphigenia in the fable.

LADY FILMOT: Oh that thou didst but resemble Cimon[15] in the *real* as well as the assumed passion!

EDWARD [*Aside.*]: Ha, I vow I believe she likes me in down right earnest.— If I were sure of being as successful, Ma'am!

LADY FILMOT [*Aside.*]: How solemn the young rogue looks! I declare I think he is half serious.—I should not else desire the resemblance. [*Edward muses.*] You are wrapt, Mr. Edward! What are you thinking of? I shall be jealous.

EDWARD: Then your ladyship must be jealous of yourself; for I assure you I was thinking of you.

LADY FILMOT [*Aside.*]: Oh, he improves apace! Lucy, thy throne begins to totter!—Oh, you must think of *me* when I am absent.

EDWARD: Does your ladyship ever think of *me* when I am absent?

LADY FILMOT: Come and sit down with me younder, and I will tell you.
[*They retire a little and sit down.*]

Scene xii.
Enter Sir Jonathan looking curiously about at all the Company.

SIR JONATHAN: Where can this boy of mine be?

Scene xiii.
As he is peeping about, Mrs. Tryfort enters and meets him.

SIR JONATHAN: Ha Mrs. Tryfort! I am glad I have met you. A man's in a wilderness here! Do you know where Ned is? In some corner with Miss Lucy, I'll lay my life!

MRS. TRYFORT: I know nothing of him, Sir Jonathan; do you think Miss Tryfort doesn't understand punctuality better than to go into corners with young fellows?
[*She goes and joyns Lord Stewkly and Lucy.*]

SIR JONATHAN: Heighty toity! What's the meaning of this? Oh, yonder's Lady Filmot, I'll go and ask her.
[*He goes to her and Edward.*]

LADY FILMOT: What, Sir Jonathan! Then you have ventured amongst us, I see.

SIR JONATHAN: To look for a stray son of mine an't please your ladyship, that's all.

LADY FILMOT: And can't you find him, Sir Jonathan?

SIR JONATHAN: No in troth, I enquired for him of Mrs. Tryfort just now, and I thought she answerd me a little short or so.

LADY FILMOT: May be this gentleman can inform you.

SIR JONATHAN: Can he? Pray, Sir, do you know—mercy upon me! Why sure—pray Sir—this can't be Ned?—Yes faith, it is too—and I not to know him! Not to know my own son! ha ha ha, a good joke, faith.

LADY FILMOT: Ha ha ha, Well Sir Jonathan, how do you like him?

SIR JONATHAN: Like him! in troth I think he is not to be *dis*liked (You sly young varlet to play me such a trick), but how come you by all these trappings, Ned?

LADY FILMOT: 'Tis only my livery, Sir Jonathan.

SIR JONATHAN: Your livery, Madam?

EDWARD: Oh yes Sir, I am her ladyship's Cicesbey.

SIR JONATHAN: Her ladyship's what, Edward?

EDWARD: Her Cicesbey, Sir.

SIR JONATHAN: Pray Madam, what may that be?

LADY FILMOT: 'Tis only a title that a lady bestows on a galant young man, who for a time devotes himself to her service.

SIR JONATHAN: Ha, I never heard of the title before. Does your uncle know that you are a Cicesbey? He is very fond of those out o' the way conceits.

LADY FILMOT: Oh, Sir Jeremy is quite delighted with it.

SIR JONATHAN: Ay, I knew it would please him; but what does Lucy say to it?

LADY FILMOT: Why really Sir Jonathan, she has been so taken up with Lord Stewkly that she doesn't seem to take the least notice of anything else.

SIR JONATHAN: What I suppose his lordship is *her* Cicesby? I have a mind to go and join them; perhaps Mrs. Tryfort may be in a better humour now.
[*Sir Jonathan goes up to them. Lady Bell and Champignion advance; Sir Jeremy joyns Lady Filmot and Edward.*]

LADY BELL: It's true; and then the honours you are to receive may be a step to nobility. Pray what were those services that you did the Government abroad?

CHAMPIGNION: Services, Ma'am?

LADY BELL: Ay, my lord Stewkly told me it was upon that account you were to have the compliment paid you.

CHAMPIGNION [*Aside.*]: Gadzooks what shall I say? he should have prepared me for this.—Oh dear Ma'am; trifles, not worth entertaining your ladyship with; but we lucky fellows often have our services overpaid especially when the ladies do us the favour to smile on us.

LADY BELL [*Aside.*]: Modest enough and not ungenteel.—Well, I won't press you.

CHAMPIGNION [*Aside.*]; Egad, I am glad of it!

LADY BELL [*To lady Filmot.*]: A'n't you tired of being so long in one place, Lady Filmot? Suppose we were to go and look at them dancing in the next room.

LADY FILMOT [*Aside.*]: Pish, how unreasonable!—I'll wait on your ladyship. Come Mr. Edward, I command you to attend me; you are not weary of your service already, I hope?

EDWARD: If your ladyship's command are always so obliging, you will not hear me complain.

LADY BELL [*Aside to Champignion.*]: I'll swear he is not ill bred!

CHAMPIGNION: Oh Ma'am, there's nothing like the conversation of the fair sex, for polishing a man.

LADY BELL: Provided they are of quality!

CHAMPIGNION: I never give that apellation to any other, Ma'am.

LADY BELL: I declare your notions are rather above the vulgar.

CHAMPIGNION: Lord Ma'am, I detest the Vulgar.

LADY BELL: U—gh, so do I! Come Sir.

[*Exit Lady Bell and Champignion, Lady Filmot, Edward and Sir Jeremy.*]

SIR JONATHAN: Why you are not to mind those things, Miss Lucy; he is her Cicesbey, I tell you; ha ha ha tis the pleasantest frolic!

LUCY: With all my heart Sir Jonathan.

MRS. TRYFORT: I dare say Miss's mind is in a state of the utmost agility[16] about it.

SIR JONATHAN: 'Tis but a joke, you know; you will have him again with you presently.

MRS. TRYFORT: Dear Sir, you needn't incommode yourself; we don't in the least want his Company.

SIR JONATHAN: Come, come, I know you are angry with Ned; but I'll go and bring him to you; the quarels of lovers, you know—ha ha ha.

[*Exit Sir Jonathan.*]

LORD STEWKLY: If I were you now, I wouldn't gratify the boy's vanity, nor Lady Filmot's ill nature, by letting them see they had made you uneasy; poor Sir Jonathan's awkward zeal will be for making up the quarel as he calls it, in the face of the company.

MRS. TRYFORT: I'll disappoint him then, my lord, for Miss and I will quit the rooms directly, to let him see we don't want to come to any embarrassment.

LORD STEWKLY: Oh the very thing, Ma'am; you have hit on the nicest expedient!

[*Re-enter Sir Jonathan.*]

SIR JONATHAN: Ned will be with you in a minute; I gave him a whisper, and he said he would steal out to you presently.

LORD STEWKLY: *Steal* out, Sir Jonathan! Why of whom is he afraid?

LUCY: Of Lady Filmot, I suppose.

SIR JONATHAN: True, that's true, in troth I had forgot how the thing was.

MRS. TRYFORT: Come Miss; my lord, will you be so kind as to put her into her chair—give my lord your hand, Lucy—Your servant, Sir Jonathan.

[*Exit Mrs. and Miss Tryfort and Lord Stewkly.*]

SIR JONATHAN: Your servant, Sir Jonathan! and your servant, Mrs. *Tryfort* if you go to that! By my faith, I think these quality notions have turned the woman's brain. I'll talk with my lady Filmot about it, and my brother Jeremy, they'll advise me between them; for I don't know what to make of all this for my part.

[*Exit Sir Jonathan as returning again to ye company in ye other room.*]

Scene xiv.
Re-enter Lord Stewkly. Lady Filmot enters as from the other room, meets,
and stops him.

LORD STEWKLY: What, have you quitted your Adonis?

LADY FILMOT: I have engaged him in the dance merely to detain him, and slippd out on purpose [**to**] intercept you; for I would have him think that you are gone home with Lucy, which Sir Jonathan this minute whisperd me you were.

LORD STEWKLY: And so I should; but that they are engaged to sup abroad.

LADY FILMOT: I know it, and for that reason concluded you would return.— Matters are now in the finest train you can imagine. You would have been amazed if you had heard him talk; he began to say pritty things. I assure you, his new cloaths inspired him.

LORD STEWKLY: Why as lightly as you treat it, there is more in that than you imagine. I have seen many a young fellow who in a plain coat and a bob wig, wouldn't open his mouth amongst ladies, when dressd in a birth-day suit, become the very bel esprit of the company.

LADY FILMOT: I know it, and it was upon that experience I founded the success of my hopes. I wanted to give my stripling courage to speak his mind to me.

LORD STEWKLY: I wonder you weren't afraid of creating to yourself rivals, for the lad really lookd handsome.

LADY FILMOT: Oh my lord, you are a mere novice; my first view was to make my Narcissus fall in love with himself and no transition more natural from that, than to fall in love with the woman, who *next* to himself he supposed his greatest admirer.

LORD STEWKLY: You ladies are better versed in those mysteries than we are; but I believe you are right.

LADY FILMOT: Infallibly—for raise but a man's vanity, and who will he think so worthy of him as the first discoverer of his extraordinary merit?

LORD STEWKLY: Ha ha ha, what a fool you have made of the poor boy.

LADY FILMOT: You mistake, I have only made a *Coxcomb* of him; *any* woman (provided she has influence) can make a *fool* of any *man* (as far I mean as it regards herself), but to make a coxcomb pro bono publico, requires parts, and that I think I have effected.—Do you know that we are to meet at Lyncoln Spa tomorrow morning? I proposed the assignation; he bowed, and said he wouldn't fail, for the tender creature really begins to pity me.

LORD STEWKLY: Ha ha ha! How you could bring him to do that with so utter an insensibility on your side astonishes me!

LADY FILMOT: Lud, my lord, one would imagine you had stepd into the world but yesterday; why that's the very thing! Take it for granted, a woman never plays the coquet well with a man she really loves. *I* acknowledge myself one, intended so by Nature; who the better to enable me to act my part, never incommoded me with those troublesome companions calld *tender feelings:* women who *have* those sometimes affect our character; but it never sits easy on them.

LORD STEWKLY: Well—from this meeting of yours, do I hope to make a total separation between the lovers. Lucy is already piqued and not so averse to me as she was. Her mother doats on me. I am to breakfast with her tomorrow, and if I can contrive to get them both to your place of rendesvous where they may have an opportunity of seeing you, I think the business will be done effectually.

LADY FILMOT: It was the very thing I meant to have proposed to you, as it will forward both of our schemes together. Sir Jeremy is already my fast friend, and Sir Jonathan, you know, is everybody's friend—so, get you away, my lord, for I wouldn't have any of the family see you here.

LORD STEWKLY: Well, I'll go somewhere and kill an hour at picquet; so wishing your ladyship success I leave you to return to your love.

LADY FILMOT: Adieu, cruel indifferent!

[*Exit severally.*]

END OF ACT III

[Here the manuscript ends.]

Appendix

Two Rejected Prologues by James Boswell

The introduction, above, provides an account of the circumstances of the composition and rejection of the two prologues James Boswell wrote for *The Discovery* in January of 1763. Anyone who reads the verses here, in this Appendix, will easily see that the Sheridans were unhappily correct in their assessment of the young Boswell's achievement. The first attempt (I.), an indifferent piece of some thirty-two lines, Frances rightly (and somewhat charitably) characterized as too general to be appropriate. The second effort (II.) is sixteen lines longer, and though it is much better it lacks the depth and sustained cleverness that the playwright's husband—who called it "light"— required. Frances' own prologue, which Boswell found dull, is obviously little more than a revision of the longer of her young friend's two pieces; it borrows its main ideas directly from Boswell and shamelessly steals one of his couplets (lines 13–14) almost verbatim, adding only a certain polish and shapeliness to the whole. It is surprising that Boswell did not anywhere comment on these plagiarisms, incensed and hurt as he was by the sharp tones of Thomas Sheridan's repudiation of his verses.

Neither of these two prologues by Boswell has ever before been printed.

I.

What various shifts have Prologue makers found
To consecrate this little spot of ground
What magic circles have contriv'd to draw
To keep the wondering multitude in awe.
In buskin'd strut with sublimated wit
Have rous'd th' attention of th' important Pit
Or tripping lightly in the gentle Socks,
Tickled with gay conceit each sparkling Box
Or to our jovial rattling freinds above
Thrown the bluff humour they so dearly love.
What servile fawning has been pactic'd here
Hoping to gain a favourable ear
Hoping you could not cruely refuse
Your kind comparison to a trembling muse
For shame for shame a freeborn muse for shame
To cringe for favour which she dare not claim.
We have prepar'd no similes so fine

No metaphors to raise the lofty line
We have no flash to dazle all your eyes
No tropes to strike no figures to surprise.
And in these happy days when Albion's throne
The worth of learning does not blush to own
Genius which long cold neglected lay
Feels the warm influence of the country ray
No more mean artifice we hope to see
Our gracious Monarch bids us all be free.
   We would not now discover all we know
Nor on the signpost would our monsters show
Some scenes of human life shall be pourtray'd
Checquer'd (as fate decrees) with light & shade
We would not for a false indulgence sue
But wish your bosoms may pronounce 'em true.

II.

   A female Author once again appears
With all the usual hopes & usual fears;
With all the flutterings on that dreadfull day
That tries the fate of a beloved Play.
   But e'er the Court to tryal does proceed,
I as our Author's Council duely fee'd,
Beg leave her just Petition to declare
And to you gentle folks this message bear.
   From the tremendous Pit she does appeal,
These boistrous Tyrants in our Commonweal;
Who have rebell'd 'gainst those they should obey
And rul'd the house with arbitrary sway.
She pleads great Magna Charta on her side
That British Subjects by their Peers be tried.
Ladies on you tonight she rests her cause
From you she fears contempt, and hopes applause.
For you her darling comedy has writ,
And, freind to Virtue dar'd to aim at wit.
Too oft the Stage with jest profane has rung
And Syren vice [*sic*] in tunefull numbers sung;
Too oft Obscenity with harlot air,
Has here insulted every modest fair:
Our Author swears she can't her sex despise
Nor Ladies by your shame would wish to rise;
She conscious boasts that her unsullied lays
On Vestal cheeks the crimson would not raise.
   This World presents, tho' Mortals know not why,
A varied prospect to th' observing eye;
Look as we may attentively around,
Unclouded bliss is rarely to be found.
Nor is dark evil's necessary pain
Permitted long to hold it's direfull reign.
'Tis hard the bounds of Comedy to trace;
'Tis hard to walk exact, yet move with grace.
With some the scene has too pathetic grown,
And Sorrow's voice has swelled the pompous tone.

While others thinking Mirth would best succeed,
Have been *immensely* comical indeed:
As at the * Booth where sounds the fork & spoon
Euterpe chaste has turn'd a low Buffoon.
  Our Author has not ransack'd classic lore,
Nor turned the Books profound of Science o'er:
By nature's aid she strives a Mean to keep
Free from the tragic stride, or farcic creep.
  Some scenes of human life shall be pourtray'd
Checquered (as fate decrees) with light & shade.
We would not for a false indulgence sue,
But wish your feelings may pronounce 'em true.

*Bartholomew Fair [Boswell's note].

Notes

Introduction

1. Alicia Le Fanu, *Memoirs of the Life and Writings of Mrs. Frances Sheridan, Mother of the late Right Hon. Richard Brinsley Sheridan, and author of "Sidney Biddulph," "Nourjahad," and "The Discovery." With Remarks upon a late life of the Right Hon. R. B. Sheridan; also Criticisms and Selections from the Works of Mrs. Sheridan; and Biographical Anecdotes of her Family and Contemporaries* (London: G. and W. Whittaker, 1824). Hereafter cited as *Memoirs of Mrs. Frances Sheridan.*

2. Manchester, Eng.: privately printed, 1924.

3. This juvenile work was not published until 1791, some twenty-five years after Frances' death.

4. *Boswell's London Journal 1762–1763,* ed. Frederick A. Pottle (New York: McGraw-Hill, 1950), pp. 54–55. Hereafter cited as *London Journal.*

5. *Thomas Sheridan of Smock-Alley* (Princeton, N.J.: Princeton University Press, 1967). See pp. 40–45 for a full account of the *Cato* controversy, which was started by the notorious Theophilus Cibber, whom Sheridan had hired to play for the summer season of 1743. The occasion itself was trifling, arising as it did from confusion over a performance of Addison's play; but Cibber turned it into a vitrolic paper war whose major offensives and counteroffensives are collected in *Cibber and Sheridan.*

6. "To Quilca" (1725), *The Poems of Jonathan Swift,* ed. Harold Williams, 2nd ed. (Oxford: Clarendon Press, 1958), 3:1035.

7. Alice Le Fanu, *Memoirs of Mrs. Frances Sheridan,* pp. 35–38.

8. Samuel Whyte, *Miscellanea Nova,* ed. Edward Athenry-Whyte (Dublin: Printed by G. A. Procter for the Editor, 1810), pp. 116–17. Hereafter cited as *Miscellanea Nova.*

9. *Thomas Sheridan of Smock-Alley,* pp. 208ff.

10. One complaint arose from Thomas' decision to send his wife's brother Walter to stay at Quilca for a week to avoid some alleged lawsuit. Unfortunately, Walter not only stayed for three months, but so contaminated the house with his "running Sores or Ulcers" that beds, linens, and furniture to the value of £60 had to be destroyed when he finally left.

11. See Sheldon, *Thomas Sheridan of Smock-Alley,* p. 212n.

12. *Thomas Sheridan of Smock-Alley,* p. 216.

13. *The Letters of Samuel Johnson,* ed. R. W. Chapman (Oxford: Clarendon Press, 1952), 1:135.

14. *The Correspondence of Samuel Richardson,* ed. Anna L. Barbauld (London: Richard Phillips, 1804), 4:143.

15. *Thomas Sheridan of Smock-Alley,* p. 222.

16. This is according to a letter from Frances to Richardson dated November 20, 1756 (Richardson, *Correspondence,* 4:145–50).

17. Richardson, *Correspondence,* 4:154.

18. Richardson, *Correspondence,* 4:163.

19. Whyte, *Miscellanea Nova,* p. 96.

20. *Boswell's Life of Johnson,* ed. G. B. Hill and L. F. Powell (Oxford: Clarendon Press,

1979), 1:390. Johnson was by no means alone in his admiration of *Sidney Bidulph*, which was very popular in England and, in several French translations and adaptations, on the Continent as well. For a brief but reliable account of the reception of this and Mrs. Sheridan's other nondramatic works see Norma H. Russell, "Some Uncollected Authors XXXVIII: Frances Sheridan, 1724–1766," *The Book Collector* 13 (1964): 196–205.

21. Whyte, *Miscellanea Nova*, pp.110–11.

22. *London Journal*, p. 113.

23. *London Journal*, p. 150.

24. Boswell does not say as much in the January 18 journal entry, where he describes the whole episode (pp. 150–52). But it is curious that he altogether drops the matter thereafter, referring to his disappointment again (February 3) only as an excuse for refusing to damn the play on its opening night—he did not wish to appear vengeful.

25. Both of the Boswell prologues are transcribed in the Appendix.

26. Boswell, *London Journal*, p. 178.

27. *Recollections of the Life of John O'Keeffe* (London: Henry Colburn, 1826; reprinted New York: Benjamin Blom, 1965), 1:86.

28. Alicia Le Fanu, *Memoirs of Mrs. Frances Sheridan*, pp. 235–36; and see Whyte, *Miscellanea Nova*, pp. 117–118. The actress referred to may be the lively Kitty Clive, but she cannot be certainly identified.

29. William Hopkins, the Drury Lane prompter, wrote of the first performance that the play was "well Acted, but the subject seem'd to displease." See *The London Stage 1660–1800. Part 4: 1747–1776*, ed. George Winchester Stone, Jr. (Carbondale: Southern Illinois University Press, 1962), p. 1025. Richard Bevis, in *The Laughing Tradition: Stage Comedy in Garrick's Day* (Athens: University of Georgia Press, 1980), finds *The Dupe* overly sentimental, and attributes its failure to this quality. It is "close to melodrama," he says, "in the affectation of its language and the flatness of its characterization" (p. 53). Bevis is largely right about the language of the play, or at least large portions of it, but he is otherwise too severe in his judgments against Mrs. Sheridan's performance.

30. The letter in which Millar enclosed the bank note makes it abundantly clear that he was motivated in part by kindness. See Whyte, *Miscellanea Nova*, p. 118. A comparison of the London edition (1764) of the play with the Licenser's copy of the manuscript in the Huntington Library (presumably this is the text from which the acting script was adapted) reveals that relatively few lines were omitted or changed when *The Dupe* was printed. It is thus difficult to account for its more favorable reception in the closet than on the stage. Some cuts had apparently been made for the second and third performances in the theater. There is no way of knowing what these were, and in any case they seem to have done little to please the audience (see Stone, *The London Stage 1660–1800. Part 4: 1747–1776*, pp. 1025–26). Perhaps Andrew Millar simply liked the play as written, and saw no point in tampering with it as the actors had done with such small success.

31. *The Private Correspondence of David Garrick*, ed. James Boaden (London: Henry Colburn and Richard Bentley, 1831), 1:16–18.

32. Garrick here alludes to lines from Act III, Scene i of *The Rehearsal* (1671), by George Villiers. In Villiers' burlesque, Bayes (a parodic portrait of John Dryden) is the foolish author of the play being rehearsed to the accompaniment of his effusive self-congratulatory remarks, and Smith is one of his bemused listeners. In her letter to Mrs. Victor, above, Frances speaks wryly of her refusal to imitate Bayes by immoderate praise of her own composition.

33. *The Letters of David Garrick*, ed. David M. Little and George M. Kahrl (Cambridge, Mass.: Harvard University Press, 1963), 2:478–79.

34. *Sheridan's Plays: Now Printed as He Wrote Them. And his Mother's Unpublished Comedy, A Journey to Bath* (London: David Nutt, 1902).

35. Nothing has survived of this tragedy, if indeed more than a few lines of it were ever written.

36. Whyte, *Miscellanea Nova,* pp. 34–35.

37. *Memoirs of Mrs. Frances Sheridan,* pp. 32–33.

38. Whyte, *Miscellanea Nova,* p. 37.

39. See *Memoirs of Mrs. Frances Sheridan,* pp. 304–11, for Alicia Le Fanu's full account of her grandmother's last illness and death.

40. The entries in Stone, *The London Stage 1660–1800. Part 4: 1747–1776,* and Charles Beecher Hogan, *The London Stage 1660–1800. Part 5: 1776–1800,* provide full information on the eighteenth-century performances of *The Discovery.* For a succinct account of all the earliest production history of the play, together with other information concerning its reception, see Sheldon, *Thomas Sheridan of Smock-Alley,* pp. 265–68, 281.

41. See Stone, *The London Stage 1660–1800. Part 4: 1747–1776,* pp. 1025–26.

42. Thomas Sheridan gives it this name in his letter to Samuel Whyte of August 1, 1766 (*Miscellanea Nova,* p. 34).

43. BM. Add. Ms. 25,975.

44. See *The New Cambridge Bibliography of English Literature,* ed. George Watson (Cambridge: At the University Press, 1971), 2: 859.

45. The *National Union Catalogue* lists, under Frances Sheridan's name (but without further identification or location), a seventy-page *Journey to Bath* published in London in 1890. We have found no extant copy of this transcription of the manuscript; apparently its existence was unknown to Rae, whose title page refers to Mrs. Sheridan's work as an "unpublished comedy."

The Discovery

1. The prologue was spoken by Garrick. A quick comparison with the second of the unacceptable prologues written by James Boswell (see Appendix) will reveal how closely Mrs. Sheridan came to outright plagiarism. The theme of her lines is Boswell's theme, and the couplet (lines 17–18) with which she concludes her fourth stanza is borrowed almost directly from him.

2. This is the cast of the original production, which opened at Drury Lane Theatre on February 3, 1763.

3. These doggerel lines seem to be Lord Medway's own. Damon, the shepherd singer of Virgil's Eighth "Eclogue," is the poetic name for a rustic swain. James Thomson, in *The Seasons* ("Summer," 1727), made him the central figure in the episode of Damon and Musidora, a love story.

4. A conventional pastoral image of the weeping young maiden. Again, Lord Medway himself seems to be the poet.

5. The opening lines of a popular seventeenth-century lyric of unknown authorship.

6. A continuation of the lyric begun by Sir Harry three speeches earlier.

7. "battledore and shittlecock": the paddle and feathered cork (shittlecock or shuttlecock) used in playing a popular game, the forerunner of modern badminton; also, a name given to the game itself *(Oxford English Dictionary;* hereafter *OED).*

8. "Lady Snap": apparently, a generic name for a pert, snap-tongued woman.

9. "Jack-a-dandy": a pert or conceited fellow; also, a name of contempt for a fop *(OED).*

10. "taws": fancy marbles, often variegated in color, used by a player to shoot in a game of marbles *(OED).*

11. These lines appear to be of Sir Anthony's own composition. "Flavia" was a familiar type-name for a blonde (from Latin *flavus*). Pope's Flavia, in the *Moral Essays* ("Epistle to a Lady," lines 87–100), is a female wit—irreverent, raffish and pleasure-loving, foolish.

12. "willow garland": a conventional symbol of grief, particularly for the loss of a lover or mate *(OED).*

13. "whiffling": aimlessly and lightly drifting in and out, all about, as if blown by the wind *(OED)*.

14. Here, Lord Medway multiplies ironies upon Sir Anthony's head. In eighteenth-century numerology, the number nine was associated with man's intellectual, incorporeal nature. Paradoxically, it was also associated with melancholy and misfortune, and with ideas of fruition and fulfillment—as in the nine-month gestation period preceding human birth.

15. "Scipio": Scipio Africanus Major, Publius Cornelius (c. 235–c. 183 B.C.), the great Roman conqueror of Spain and of Hannibal. He is reputed to have denied temptation when a beautiful young girl fell into his hands following his victory at Carthago Nova; he returned the girl to her family and sent presents to her intended bridegroom. Sir Anthony places himself in very good company.

16. Lord Medway misquotes from Dr. Thomas Fuller's popular and respected book of aphorisms and wise sayings, *Gnomologia* (1732): "Nothing is good or bad, but by comparison."

17. "Knight of the inflexible countenance": a wry comparison of Sir Anthony to Don Quixote, the "Knight of the Woeful Countenance."

18. *"capuchin"*: a hooded cloak, so called after the garment worn by Capuchin monks.

19. "Park": probably Hyde Park, London, a fashionable public place for walking.

20. "Armida": a sorceress of the period of the first Crusade who (according to Tasso's *Jerusalem Delivered,* 1576–93) assisted in the defense of Jerusalem by luring the Christian soldiers to an enchanted garden.

21. "the cat in the fable": an allusion to one of Aesop's fables, which tells of a young man who falls in love with his cat, persuades Venus and Jupiter to turn her into a beautiful maiden, and then marries her. On the wedding night, Venus and Jupiter let loose a mouse in the room; the bride pounces upon it, and is transformed back into a cat.

22. According to a handwritten note in the Huntington Library copy of the second London edition of *The Discovery,* the Epilogue was spoken by Mrs. Hannah Pritchard.

The Dupe

1. The Prologue was spoken by William Havard (Stone, *The London Stage 1660–1800. Part 4: 1747–1776,* p. 1025).

2. This is the cast of the original production, which opened at Drury Lane Theatre on December 10, 1763.

3. "froptious": fretful, peevish; a variant of *froppish (OED)*.

4. These appear to be lines of Sharply's own invention.

5. "cross": i.e., a coin *(OED)*.

6. "magdalen-house": an allusion to Magdalen Hospital, a London home for the reformation of prostitutes.

7. "willow": familiar symbol of grief for the loss of a lover *(OED)*.

8. "bastinado": to punish, in Eastern fashion, by beating the soles of the feet with a stick *(OED)*.

9. "stock": lifeless, motionless, devoid of sensation, as a trunk of a tree; hence a senseless or stupid person *(OED)*.

10. We have been unable to identify this "friend."

A Journey to Bath

1. "illiterate": i.e., literate. Mrs. Tryfort's abuses of the English language anticipate those committed by Richard Brinsley Sheridan's greatest comic character, Mrs. Malaprop *(The Rivals)*.

2. "progeny": i.e., prodigy.

3. "terrestrial": i.e., terpsichoreal.

4. These appear to be lines from a familiar song in the manner of Robert Herrick or Richard Lovelace, but we have been unable to identify them.

5. "taciturnity": an unintentional reversal of meaning by Mrs. Tryfort.

6. "cissibey" (or cisisbey; cicesbey): *Cicisbeo,* a fashionable Italian term for the acknowledged gallant of a married woman *(OED).*

7. "molossus": a variant of *molasses.*

8. "frizeur": one who curls the hair; a hairdresser.

9. "agitation": i.e., acquisition.

10. "speculation": i.e., perspicacity.

11. "embelished": i.e., accomplished.

12. "contagious": i.e., contiguous.

13. "Dervice": a variant of *dervish,* the name given to a Moslem friar who has taken vows of austerity and poverty *(OED).*

14. "contribute": i.e., attribute.

15. "Cimon" and "Iphigenia": the inspired lovers of one of Boccaccio's tales in the *Decameron* (V, i). Cimon (or Cimone, Cymon) is a type of the naturally passionate man, and he is ennobled by love for the ravishingly beautiful Iphigenia (or Efigenia). Dryden had retold this story in his *Fables, Ancient and Modern* (1699).

16. "agility": i.e., agitation.